ISBN No 0 9520762 – 3 –3

Published in Great Britain by:

W G CLARKE *(Military Books)*
199 Bulford Road
Durrington
Wiltshire
SP4 8HB

Printed in Great Britain by:

St Ives (Roche) Ltd
Victoria Business Park
Roche
St. Austell
Cornwall
PL26 8LX

CONTENTS

"SOLDIERS OF THE SIXTIES"

INTRODUCTION

The 1960s has gained something of a cult following in recent years. Music from the period is often heard on the radio and much has been copied and re-released. There have also been many exhibitions and television programmes celebrating a period that has come to symbolize to many the dawn of a social and liberal revolution – not only in Britain, but also throughout the western world. Certainly no decade of the twentieth century (save those of the two world wars) brought such a marked change in social attitudes to British society as did the period known by everyone who lived through it, and historians the world over, as the "Swinging Sixties". "JFK", "Ban the Bomb", the Beatles and "Flower Power" are expressions, groups and movements synonymous with the era that saw, for the first time "Youth Culture" dominate the mood, styles and tastes of every generation in the land.

For Britain and her army the roots of this remarkable phenomenon can be found at the end of the previous decade when the newly elected Conservative government confirmed their plan to end the "call up" - National Service, at the end of 1960. This single act released a whole generation of young men from the onerous (to some) commitment of two years military service at a time in their lives when they were just about to establish their identity as an adult. Thus, energies that were once channelled into "squarebashing" and "spit and polish" now conjured with a revolution in popular tastes and styles that were to be emulated by people from virtually every nation on Earth.

The new regular recruits of the early 1960s were, like many of the conscripts they served alongside and eventually replaced the last of the "War babies" and the last children of Empire. They too, were keen to embrace the new social culture as was evident by the hairstyles and clothes of those who joined the new Regular Army.

Though "Teddyboy" drape suits and crepe-soled shoes were still common at the beginning of 1960, and the popular music of the period continued to include such '50s "Rock and Roll giants as Elvis Presley and the Everly Brothers: change was in the air. Early in the decade came new styles and tastes that were more continental than trans-atlantic. "Drainpipe" trousers gave way to rather more slick and stylish Italian style suits with sharp-toed "Winklepicker" shoes. "Homegrown" stars such as Cliff Richard and Shadows, Adam Faith and Helen Shapiro began to displace the American performers. And for the first time the youth of the nation had its own proper TV "Pop" shows with "Oh Boy", "Ready Steady Go" and later "Top of the Pops".

It was against this background of radical social and cultural change that the Army had to recruit its new Regulars. At the beginning it was not so difficult for most prospective recruits would have had a parent or relative that served during the War or as a National Serviceman at home or abroad - some of whom would have played a part in one of the many colonial conflicts that took place during Britain's retreat from Empire. This generation therefore were well used to seeing the military at relatively close quarters, and tales (embellished or otherwise) of military life would have been almost part of their daily diet. Few would have felt they were stepping into the unknown when setting off on a military career. Most of those, like myself, who joined at the very beginning of the decade, were attracted by the promise of travel, a reasonable wage, and above all a "career" in the new professional army.

Despite the advertisements, the Army of 1960 was still very similar in structure, style, equipment and culture to that of 1945 – as can be seen in the stories published in this book. National Service with its very transient young population had served in many respects to keep it that way. With the new Regulars however, came new uniforms, new equipment and a new style of management. Perhaps most important of all, there came a new enthusiasm and attitude from the soldiers themselves, that reflected a generation that was growing up in an era that looked more to the future than the past, and with a belief in more liberal attitudes to both life and social relationships. This new attitude, the changes that took place and how they impacted upon the military and its culture, are what Soldier magazine captured with its stories, features, photographs and readers letters each month.

There were of course other factors – both economic and political - which shaped British society in the early 1960s. For this was the decade that began with virtually full employment, a growth rate in the economy of about 5% and inflation stood at about 2%. As Prime Minister Harold Macmillan had boasted at the end of the 1950s, Britain really "never had it so good." Things would be very much different by the end of the decade. Changes in any society inevitably impact upon the armed forces they sustain, and the " Swinging Sixties" certainly made their mark upon the British Army.

In early 1963 the last National Serviceman returned to "Civvy Street". The Army had at last become the all-regular, professional force the recruiting posters boasted. More changes were now taking place that would gradually transform the Army and its image from one of conscripts and Battledress, to that of professional regular soldiers. A smart new service dress – No 2 Dress- for parades and "walking out" came into service in 1960 along with a purpose-designed Combat Dress for exercise and operations. The latter was a great step forward for the British Army, which had for too long relied upon uniforms that doubled as both combat dress and parade dress.

By the middle of the decade the social pressures and excitement of Britain's Youth dominated society had begun to have a dramatic affect upon recruiting. To counter this a new recruiting campaign was launched with the slogan: join the Regular Army and be a "Soldier of the Sixties". In addition the age of entry for adults was lowered to 17. The popular revolution in tastes and styles in Britain was now in full swing. British groups such as the Beatles and the Rolling Stones were at the top of Hit parades everywhere, and London's Carnaby Street had become the centre of young people's clothing fashions.

This revolution in Youth culture extended even to the means of broadcasting. Several pirate Radio stations - in the form of offshore Radio ships such Radio London and Radio Caroline were set up to provide "round the clock " music and advertisements. The country was buzzing with youthful enthusiasm and optimism keen to bring about change and make its own mark on the world. Inevitably the young soldiers of the period tried as far as possible to emulate their civilian counterparts in this stylish revolution. Certainly so far as music was concerned, many a military Band produced its own Pop group and there were even service sponsored talent shows at Home and abroad for aspiring service groups.

This emphasis on youth and modernism was never more evident than in the results of the General Election of 1964, when the country returned a Labour government led by the youngest leader since the end of the previous century. Harold Wilson was elected with a mandate to "modernise" Britain and its Institutions. Unfortunately for the Armed Forces this included cuts in defence spending and the proposal to complete a speedy withdrawal from the remnants of Empire "East of Suez".

Whilst the political policies to change the Armed Forces were being put into effect the British Army was as usual heavily involved in a variety of anti-terrorist operations throughout the world. The majority was instigated by political groups intent on gaining power after British rule had ceased. In the case of the Borneo and Brunei campaign, British troops were involved in a very unpleasant jungle operation to ward off the hostile attempts of neighbouring Indonesia, whose leader was intent upon crushing the new confederation of Malaysia.

Many of these conflicts had been going on for some time. They were in many ways the principal tasks that the new Regulars of the sixties had inherited from the conscripts before them. They were in effect policing the final withdrawal from Empire. It proved to be as bloody and complicated a business for the Regulars as it had been for the National Servicemen.

By the middle of 1967 the implementation of much of the government's Defence Review was well under way, though there were still many more regimental amalgamations to be completed and yet more barracks to be modernised or demolished. By far the worst job to be finished however, was the hasty withdrawal from Aden, which was scheduled to be complete by the end of the year. As departures go, the withdrawal of the British Army from the Aden peninsula was a hasty, violent and action-packed affair. Indeed, the sight of the last commander of the British forces departing by Helicopter as the warring factions below him shot it out for control of the port of Aden, was perhaps one of the low points in Britain's retreat from Empire.

As 1968 dawned many of the troops from the Middle and Far East were returning to new billets in the United Kingdom. Others already at home were heavily involved during the early part of the year assisting the civil authorities to control a nation-wide outbreak of Foot & Mouth disease. Britain meanwhile, was in the grip of the latest "flower power" and "psychedelic" pop culture. The "Swinging Sixties" had not lost any of its early impulsion. Other notable aspects of 1968 included the fact that it was the first year since the end of the Second World War that no British soldiers had been killed on active service. Apart from one minor deployment of troops to Mauritius to quell civil disturbances there prior to the granting of Independence, the Army was in not engaged on active operations anywhere. It was not to last.

In the meantime however, the apparent lack of overseas postings, the redundancy programme as well as the proposed regimental amalgamations and disbandments that resulted from the Defence review all conspired to produce a negative effect on recruiting. The situation became so bad that the government re-introduced the 3-year engagement, last used during the National Service years.

As the decade drew to an end therefore, the British Army continued with its programme of yet more reorganisation, reductions and regimental amalgamations. Some units were lucky and managed to escape the turbulence unscathed and depart for operations overseas. Others were not so fortunate. During the autumn of 1969 British troops were deployed on the streets of Northern Ireland to assist the civil authorities in controlling a worsening catalogue of violence and civil disobedience. As demonstrations and riot turned to outright terrorist activity by a self–styled "Irish Republican Army"; more troops were rushed to the Province to control the situation.

Ominously perhaps matters in Northern Ireland did not improve. What appeared at the start to be a matter of re-enforcing civil authority began to turn into a full-scale anti-terrorist operation. And as the last year of the decade closed several thousand British troops found themselves separating the warring factions in Northern Ireland and preparing for what appeared to be a long stay.

Despite all the upheavals and turbulence of the period, the individual officer and soldier serving in the sixties had seen their quality of life improve. This was especially true of pay, which, as a result of the introduction of the "Military Salary" in 1969 at least put it on a footing comparable to those in the civilian workforce. The iniquities of the various allowances contained in the old system were swept away with the new pay review. Especially the business of ration allowance being taken off married men when they went on exercises or operations. The Army finished the decade smaller in size than it had been at the start and with almost half the overseas garrisons – some of which carried a degree of notoriety or affection for the "old sweats". Though smaller, it was much better equipped, better motivated and better trained. Moreover, it was a more flexible army that could now concentrate on its principal role of representing Britain as part of NATO in the defence of Europe from the Warsaw Pact countries.

So there it is. A military resume of the 1960s as seen through the eyes of the "Soldier", the British Army's own magazine. It was a decade like no other – before or since. Above all perhaps it was a decade of change - both socially and militarily. The end of Conscription, the end of Empire, and for many the end of much of the old social "Order". The changes brought joy for some and grief for others. The British soldier as usual, experienced both emotions – not always in equal measure, as he fought and often died, maintaining some semblance of law and order in the myriad of "Bushfire" wars that marked the end of Britain's Empire.

In compiling this book I have chosen extracts that I believe would give the reader a good "feel" for the mood of the period and how both it and the magazine changed over the years. I hope they also give a clear view of how the Army went about its business during this remarkable decade.
I have tried to include every aspect of military life; from the military campaigns and training exercises to the barrack room, sports field and married quarter. Also included are stories and photographs of soldiers and their families at work and play, at Home and abroad at one of the many overseas stations that existed at the time. The book is, I hope, a fitting record – if not a tribute, to those who served as " Soldiers of the Sixties".

Acknowledgements

Many people have assisted me with the compilation of this book and I am very grateful to them all for their time and patience. I would however, like to make special mention of the following organizations and personalities without whom nothing would have been possible:
The Royal Artillery Institution for providing the necessary funds to ensure publication. The Editor in Chief and Staff of Soldier magazine. In particular, the Editor in Chief himself, Mr Chris Horrocks, the Librarian, Mr Gerard Sutton and Miss Kath Adams the design artist, who produced the superb cover for the book.

Indeed, the book would not have been possible at all if it were not for the professionalism and fortitude of the journalists and photographers of Soldier magazine during the 1960s, who produced the extracts I have used in its compilation. I am extremely grateful to them for their excellent work and to Soldier magazine for allowing me to publish them again. I am also grateful to all those command PR departments whose reports and photographs are also included. Sadly, most no longer exist.

Finally, I received a great deal of encouragement and support from countless numbers of people who served at the time and, on learning of the project, offered many useful suggestions on its compilation. I would like to express my thanks to them all for their support.

W G Clarke
Upavon
1st September 1999

1960

Beginnings and Ends – The best is yet to come

As the young men of the period danced to the music of Cliff Richard and the Shadows, most were celebrating the fact that this would be the last year any of them would be called up to complete their National Service. For Conscription was one of the casualties of the Defence Review of 1957, as Britain sought to streamline its Forces and reduce Defence expenditure. The subsequent regimental amalgamations and disbandments that arose from the review continued throughout the year, though it would be some time before they were all completed.

As part of this modernisation programme, many of the worst of the old Victorian barracks and married quarters in Aldershot and many other Garrison towns were undergoing demolition. Other improvements to service life included the introduction of a new "walking out" uniform - No2 Dress - to replace the ageing, uncomfortable and very outdated Battledress.

There was also much new equipment, including a new heavy machine gun - the General Purpose Machine Gun - for the Infantry, as well as the "Thunderbird" Heavy Anti-Aircraft Missile for the Royal Artillery and a new Tank gun for the Centurion Tank. Overseas there were also changes. The British Army Currency vouchers - affectionately known to every serviceman as "BAFS" - were finally phased out in Germany (except for Berlin) and Air Trooping took over from the cross-channel troopships that plied between the Hook of Holland and Harwich.

Operationally, this was the year that saw the official end of the twelve year long Malayan Emergency as well as the end of the EOKA campaign in Cyprus, which had claimed the lives of many servicemen and their families. The end of this first year of the decade therefore marked the beginning of a new era for a British Army marching into the future as a modern, well equipped force that would soon be an all-regular army for the first time since the 1930s.

TWELVE YEARS OF

A patrol of the Suffolk Regiment warily crosses a log bridge, weapons at the ready in case of ambush. The Suffolks accounted for nearly 200 bandits.

THE emergency in Malaya—long since dubbed "the forgotten war"—will be declared officially at an end on the last day of this month.

But the British Commonwealth troops—from Britain, Australia, New Zealand, Fiji, East Africa, Nepal and Malaya —who, for the past 12 years have been waging a grim, "cat-and-mouse" war with Communist terrorists in the jungles, swamps and rubber plantations, will not give up the fight.

They will continue to seek out and destroy the remnants of the once 13,000-strong force of guerillas who have taken refuge in the jungles on the Thailand border.

The ending of the emergency, however, will mark the final phase in a bitter struggle in which British troops, fighting under difficult and unaccustomed conditions, have played an outstandingly gallant and effective part.

More than 80,000 officers and men from 63 Commonwealth units (including 50,000 from 38 British Army Infantry regiments) have taken part in the campaign and more than 500 have been killed and nearly 1000 wounded. But, up to last month, the troops and the Federation's Police Force had killed 7000 terrorists, wounded nearly 3000 and captured nearly 3000 more.

The Malayan campaign, which disproved the theory that the Infantry had had its day, also proved yet again how adaptable and inventive the British soldier is.

Operating in small, mobile gangs from secret hide-outs in the steaming jungles, the terrorists could strike swiftly and hard and then disappear without trace. But it was not long before the troops who were rushed to Malaya in June, 1948, found ways of bringing them to battle and learned the hard way how to live in the jungle and outwit the bandit in his own backyard. The King's Own Scottish Borderers, for instance, went into battle floating silently down a river in rubber car tyres; the Queen's Royal Regiment paddled to a terrorist camp in dug-out canoes; the men of another unit cycled 20 miles to surprise and capture a bandit in his lair; and the Devons went into action by train, concealed under tarpaulins in steel wagons. One Gunner officer even took a bow and arrow on patrol.

Later, 22nd Special Air Service Regiment, which holds the record for the longest spell in the jungle—122 days—discovered a way to parachute safely into trees. Gunners manned searchlights to direct night bombers on to their targets and, when the inhabitants of outlying villages were terrorised into helping the bandits, the Army placed them in settlements and gave them cooked rations so that no food could be passed to the enemy.

FOR MORE THAN A DECADE BRITISH COMMONWEALTH TROOPS HAVE BEEN FIGHTING A DESPERATE

JUNGLE BASHING

hastily despatched to Malaya from Britain in June, 1948, carried out a dual role in their armoured cars and on foot and accounted for 66 terrorists.

Between them, the Grenadier, Coldstream and Scots Guards captured more than 250 terrorists. The men of No. 3 Company, RASC, have now covered more than 10,000,000 miles delivering supplies to the troops.

As the campaign grew in ferocity more troops were sent to Malaya from Britain, Australia, New Zealand, Fiji and East Africa and the local Malay Regiment expanded from two to seven battalions and the Federation Regiment. Eight battalions of the Brigade of Gurkhas have been in constant action since 1948 and claim 1616 dead terrorists.

Of the 38 British Army Infantry regiments who have fought in Malaya none achieved greater success than the 1st Battalion, The Suffolk Regiment, which had 199 bandit casualties to its credit. One Suffolk patrol killed two terrorists within 24 hours of the murder by them of three civilians. Other patrols accounted for two guerilla leaders who had a price of £1500 on their heads. In their two-and-a-half years in Malaya,

Left: With his flame-thrower, the Infantryman sears the forest edge in the vicinity of a suspected terrorist camp. The Malayan campaign was an Infantryman's war learned the hard way.

Above: Gunners of 2nd Field Regiment, Royal Artillery, pound the terrorists in their jungle hiding places. The gun is a 5.5-inch medium gun which fires a 100 lb shell. Below: Speed is essential once terrorists have been spotted. Here, Australian troops scramble aboard a helicopter to be rushed into action

The guerillas were not the only enemy the troops had to face. The jungles and swamps had first to be overcome before the bandit lairs could be reached and wild animals were a constant source of danger. More than one patrol had the unnerving experience of being attacked by an angry tigress.

Among the first troops in action were the Gunners of 26 Field Regiment, Royal Artillery, who were stationed in Malaya when the emergency broke out. Operating as Infantry for nearly three years, they killed more than 100 terrorists and destroyed 127 camps. The 4th Queen's Own Hussars, who, with 2nd Guards Brigade and No. 3 Company, Royal Army Service Corps, were

AND CLEVER ENEMY IN MALAYA'S JUNGLES AND SWAMPS. BUT THE END IS NOW IN SIGHT.

By 1957, the troops, now often taken into action by helicopter, had systematically cleared thousands of square miles of jungle in Southern Malaya and the terrorists were on the run. They fought bitterly and often bravely but, denied help from civilians and harried night and day by Infantry patrols, artillery searching fire and Royal Air Force bombers, they retreated northwards. By 1959, only some 500 hard-core terrorists were active.

The troops who have scored such outstanding successes in this gruelling campaign will be the first to give credit to the skill of the Iban trackers from Borneo who, time and again, have led patrols to bandit hide-outs by signs which have been invisible to the troops. Since 1953 nearly 4000 of these little brown men with eyes that miss nothing have served in Malaya. They are still carrying out their important work as members of the 400-strong Sarawak Rangers whose commanding officer, Lieutenant-Colonel G. Baird, is the only British officer entitled to wear the shoulder title "Sarawak."

As the fighting draws to a close the British troops in Malaya can be proud, too, of the prosperity and better conditions they have brought to the country. Thousands of miles of roads, opening up hitherto impenetrable jungle and swamp, have been built by the Sappers. Signalmen have erected hundreds of miles of telephone cable and saved at least two villages from economic extinction. And the military medical authorities have drastically reduced casualties caused by the once dreaded scrub-typhus and leptospirosis.

After the fighting is over British troops will not leave Malaya. They will remain, as part of the British Commonwealth Strategic Reserve, ready to go into action should trouble break out again in the Far East.

THEY WERE THERE

The following major Commonwealth units have served in Malaya since June, 1948:

ROYAL ARTILLERY: 2, 25, 26 and 48 Field Regiments; 1 Singapore Regt. RA: 105 Fd Bty, Royal Australian Artillery.

ROYAL ARMOURED CORPS: King's Dragoon Guards; 4, 11, 13/18 and 15/19 Hussars; 12 Lancers.

INFANTRY: Grenadier, Coldstream and Scots Guards; Queen's, R. Lincolns, Devons, Suffolks, Somerset Light Infantry, W. Yorks, E. Yorks, Green Howards, R. Scots Fus, Cheshires, R. Welch Fus, South Wales Borderers, KOSB, Cameronians, R. Innisk. Fus, Worcestershires, R. Hampshires, Foresters, Loyals, R. West Kent, KOYLI, Wilts, Manchester, Seaforth, Gordons, 22 SAS, Rifle Brigade, Parachute Regt, Gurkha Rifles (8 battalions), King's African Rifles, N. Rhodesia Regt, Rhodesian African Rifles, Fiji Inf. Regt, Royal Australian Regt, New Zealand Regt and Singapore Inf Regt.

Right: Men of the Special Air Service Regiment took the war on to the bandit's doorstep when they found a way of parachuting into trees. Here, a patrol, dropped into the jungle by aircraft, cheerfully wades across a river.

Below: The 1st Devons go into action by rail. The goods train carried them to a spot opposite a bandit lair in secondary jungle while bombers and fighters attacked overhead. The attack surprised and routed a strong gang.

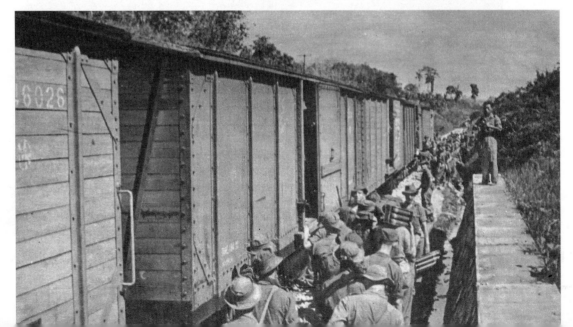

Vol. 15, No. 11   **SOLDIER**   JANUARY 1960

THE BRITISH ARMY MAGAZINE

Libya, 4 piastres;   Cyprus, 40 mils,   Malaya, 30 cents;   Hong-Kong, 60 cents;   East Africa, 75 cents;   West Africa, 9d.

Surrounded by glaciers and frozen snow, Sergeant M. McKenzie and Corporal T. Woods stand on the rim of the crater at Gilman's Point, 18,600 feet up.

KILIMANJARO, THE WORLD'S LARGEST SINGLE MOUNTAIN, HAS BEEN CONQUERED BY 26 SAPPERS WHO CLIMBED TO THE SUMMIT AT DAWN—AND IT WAS ALL PART OF THEIR NORMAL TRAINING!

SAPPERS TAME KILIMANJARO

AS the sun rose over Mount Kilimanjaro, 26 exhausted Sappers, straining for breath in the rarefied air, painfully dragged themselves over the frozen rocks to the rim of the summit crater at Gilman's Point and gazed in wonder at the enormous glaciers and fantastic ice formations around them.

It was a moment they will remember all their lives and one which has gone down in the history of Army mountaineering as a brilliant achievement by untrained climbers.

Kilimanjaro, highest mountain in Africa and the largest single mountain in the world—it rises from a plateau to 19,565 feet—has often been climbed before, with the help of porters and oxygen. But the Sappers who conquered it—men of No. 3 Troop, 34 Independent Field Squadron, Royal Engineers—used neither. None had climbed a mountain before and they had nothing in the way of special equipment to help them, save *anoraks* to keep out the biting winds, six Bergen rucksacks and four climbing ropes.

A Centurion tank of the 5th Royal Inniskilling Dragoon Guards crunches its way up the beach after landing in Eckenforde Bay.

THE BATTLE OF

AS the first red glow of dawn rose over the Baltic Sea, six landing craft, their bow doors open and ramps down, nosed into a beach on the east coast of Schleswig-Holstein.

From the ships, following up the first wave of assault troops, poured British Infantrymen, Gunners, Sappers and 50-ton *Centurion* tanks. Overhead roared jet fighter-bombers and out to sea German destroyers "shelled" enemy strongpoints.

Twenty-four hours earlier more than a thousand paratroopers and their equipment

When a trailer gets stuck there's only one answer: push it out, as these British assault troops found out when they landed on the beaches.

had darkened the skies as they dropped north of the Kiel Canal.

These were the spearheads of the aggressor troops in *Holdfast,* the biggest land, sea and air exercise ever mounted by forces of the North Atlantic Treaty Organisation.

The amphibious and parachute landings were made by Orangeland, a four-brigade group "enemy" of British and Canadian troops attacking northwards in Schleswig-Holstein towards the Kiel Canal. Defending Blueland, and fighting side-by-side for the first time, were German and Danish soldiers.

Under the command of General Sir Horatius Murray, Commander-in-Chief, Allied Forces, Northern Europe, more than 45,000 troops and 12,000 vehicles took part in this three-day exercise to test NATO defences in the Jutland Peninsula.

Holdfast began with a thrust northwards by 4th Canadian Infantry Brigade Group, supported by 11th Infantry Brigade Group and 4th Guards Brigade Group, towards the Hamburg-Lübeck Autobahn—a canal for the purposes of the exercise.

Many of the bridges over the "canal" had been blown and the remainder were heavily defended by a German Panzer-Grenadier division. Bringing up helicopter-borne troops, Orange Force seized one of the bridges and by the end of D-Day had forced the "canal" at seven points.

At dawn, men of 16 Independent Parachute Brigade had dropped behind enemy lines to hamper Danish and German reinforcements moving southwards to defend the Kiel Canal.

The first paratroopers—450 men of the 3rd Battalion, The Parachute Regiment — dropped in the mist, watched by German farmworkers roused by the deepthroated roar of *Beverley* and *Hastings* aircraft of the Royal Air Force's Transport Command.

A DUKW-load of men from the 2nd Battalion, Grenadier Guards, rumbles ashore, ready for battle with German and Danish troops.

While the commander searches for targets, a Canadian recoilless anti-tank crew stands by ready for instant action. ▶

The exercise supply system, which operated for ten days, proved a triumph of organisation. Four thousand tons of food and153 tons of other supplies were delivered to British forces by the Royal Army Service Corps. More than 384,000 gallons of fuel were used, enough to take a Centurion tank eight times around the world. About 1500 miles of roads were sign posted by the Corps of Royal Military Police.

The paratroopers were followed by 44 air-dropped platforms—the largest number ever landed in one exercise — carrying light vehicles, heavy weapons, ammunition and food.

A hundred miles further north, in central Jutland, the 1sf Battalion, The Buffs (Royal East Kent Regiment), representing an air-landed brigade, went into battle against the 10th Danish Division while parachutists of 22 Special Air Service Regiment sabotaged Blueland communications.

The Danes had mobilised for the exercise, but their Army, police and Home Guard were unable to prevent the saboteurs from accomplishing their missions and even removing top secret documents from a Danish brigade headquarters!

Territorials of 21 Special Air Service Regiment also fought in Orange Force, while men of the sister 23rd Regiment undertook secret missions for Blueland.

The seaborne battalion group of the 2nd Grenadier Guards, which included elements of 33 Parachute Light Regiment, Royal Artillery, equipped with the 105-mm. pack howitzer, and

JUTLAND - 1960

of the 5th Royal Inniskilling Dragoon Guards in *Centurions*, sailed under cover of darkness in four German landing ships and two tank landing craft of 76 Squadron, Royal Army Service Corps.

As light assault craft and DUKWs carried the first wave of Grenadier Guardmen towards the beach, jet fighter-bombers screamed overhead and shells from German destroyers and rockets launched from smaller craft plastered the enemy defences. From the beachhead the seaborne troops quickly pushed inland and within 36 hours had linked up with 16

Independent Parachute Brigade.

The main assault northwards met heavy opposition and both aggressors and defenders made a number of mock nuclear strikes, in which *Corporal* and *Honest John* missiles were "fired."

Just before the battle ended British armour was within two miles of the Kiel Canal which was first reached by men of the 1st Battalion, The King's Own Yorkshire Light Infantry, rushed forward in helicopters.

The attackers had reached the canal—but NATO's defence of Jutland had held firm.—*From a report by Sergeant Brian Dexter, Military Observer.*

◀ *Only minutes after dropping from the air on Schleswig-Holstein, paratroopers of the 3rd Battalion, The Parachute Regiment, crash into action with their Mobat anti-tank gun.*

"Party, party pu—. Wait for it!"

They catch them young in the Royal Artillery Junior Leaders Regiment. And then they train them to become not only fully-fledged soldiers but outstanding leaders as well

THE SCHOOL FOR GUNNERS

The gamecock crest on the gates of the barracks, once occupied by the Royal Navy, is happily appropriate.

Right: Although the young Gunners spend only a part of their time on military training they get plenty of practice on their 25-pounders. Here they are introduced to the mysteries of gun-laying at night.

A KEEN wind snatches at the young Gunners taking theodolite readings and whistles past other groups as they dash into mock action on their 25-pounder guns.

It soughs through the vast hangars where more Gunners march up and down on squad drill and rocks the straw-stuffed sack as the bayonets plunge into it.

It's a keen wind, but these Gunners, just as keen, thoroughly enjoy the outdoor life. They're young and fit, proud to be serving in the Royal Artillery Junior Leaders Regiment and eager to become fully-fledged Gunners in a man's Army.

Their Regiment, housed in the former Royal Naval Air Station at Bramcote, near Nuneaton in Warwickshire, is a miniature Royal Military Academy where the Army takes a boy and makes a man out of him.

Gamecock Barracks—a title handed on by the Admiralty and happily appropriate to the role of the Regiment—provide splendid facilities for these future warrant and non-commissioned officers who spend a third of their routine in schooling, military training, sport and physical education.

The Junior Leaders Regiment aims to produce soldiers and leaders, able to hold their own morally, mentally and physically in a modern world and prove themselves loyal servants of the Crown.

Boys join the Regiment at any age between 15½ and 17¼ years and enlist for six or nine years with the Colours. They muster for man's service at 17½ and leave the Regiment at the end of that term for further training as wireless operators, drivers, radar operators or gun numbers at a training regiment.

Unless they have passed two subjects in the General Certificate of Education—many lads come from grammar schools—or Certificate "A" of the Army Cadet Force, recruits must pass a simple enlistment test. For the first six weeks at Gamecock Barracks they serve in the Recruit Troop, gradually earning the privileges of being allowed to salute and to wear a cap badge, and then join one of the 12 troops, all named after famous Gunners, which make up the Regiment's three batteries— 39 (Roberts), 77 (Wardrop) and 44 (Campbell) Battery.

The Regiment is organised as a military college and the boys are squaded on academic attainment. The entry standard varies considerably but within the last year or two has so improved that the junior certificate—a "must"— is now being taken much earlier. This is followed by intermediate and senior certificates, equivalent to the Army's 2nd and 1st Class Certificates and, in the top classes, by the General Certificate of Education.

A staff of officers and senior non-commissioned officers of the Royal Army Educational Corps, most of them trained teachers, give the boys a good general education to fit them for both military and civilian life.

Reveille at 6.30 a.m. starts a normal day's routine in which the boys first parade and drill in their own troops. Then the whole Regiment assembles in one of the hangars for morning prayers.

Mornings are spent in classrooms, gymnasiums and in practical military training, including gunnery, weapon training, march-

A COMMANDO VC, Lieutenant-Colonel P. A. Porteous, Royal Artillery, is to take over command of the Junior Leaders Regiment in September from Lieutenant-Colonel D. R. M. Owen DSO.

Colonel Porteous won the Victoria Cross during the Dieppe raid on 19 August, 1942, when a captain in 4 Commando under Lieutenant-Colonel Lord Lovat. He was acting as liaison officer between two parties of the Commando in their attack on a coastal defence battery.

Two officers fell as the Commandos went in with the bayonet across 250 yards of open ground. Captain Porteous, already wounded in the hand, closed with his assailant and killed him with his own bayonet, and then led the race to the wire surrounding the battery. He broke in with his men close beside him, grenading, bayoneting and shooting their way through to the guns where he fell unconscious from a further wound in his thigh.

Colonel Porteous was commissioned into the Royal Artillery in 1937. He served in 6 Anti-Aircraft Regiment in France, for four years in 4 Commando and subsequently in 1st and 6th Airborne Divisions.

Left: Survey apprentices like these two lads taking a bearing, are also trained at Nuneaton. They go direct to units when they have completed their course.

Right: You've got to look determined when it's bayonet practice. A keen type with the right ideas shows how it's done.

Below: A gun detachment at drill with a 25-pounder. Gun drill is one of the highlights of the boys' training.

ing and rifle drill. On every afternoon except one the boys are out on the playing fields. Then, as at any other boarding school, it's back to work, with prep, military history or hobbies. Every boy has the choice of some 20 hobbies —from chess and metalwork to ballroom dancing, vehicle maintenance and even campanology. Roller-skating is a current favourite but outdoor hobbies like canoeing and cycling are always popular. The cyclists maintain their club's 98 machines. The canoeists build their own craft and have paddled canoes through France (on an adventure holiday) and in the Devizes-Westminster race which the Regiment won last year.

Like all schoolboys the young Gunners enjoy making something to take home on holiday—perhaps a coffee table from the woodwork class or a model plane, musical box or cuckoo clock from the modelling room. Others prefer a more utilitarian (and lucrative) hobby like boot and shoe repairing for the permanent staff and fellow boys—and even for girl friends.

A NEW LOOK

THE soldier in Britain's new stream-lined, all-Regular Army (lowest-paid private £4 7s 6d a week and all found) will not only be better armed and equipped than ever before.

He will also be the best-dressed soldier in the world..

On parade and when walking out he will look like an officer in a smart new Service Dress and on training and in action he will wear the latest thing in combat suits.

The battledress, which has served the Army well, if unglamorously, for more than 20 years, is to be abolished in the Regular Army,

although it will continue to be worn by men of the Territorial Army.

The new Service Dress—chosen from five which have been on trial for more than a year to test the reactions of the men who will wear it and the civilian population—is an officer-type jacket and trousers made of khaki barathea. The jacket has pleated breast pockets, flap side pockets, shoulder straps, a cloth belt and gilt buttons which will not need polishing. With this uniform, which will also be worn for ceremonial, the soldier will wear a khaki shirt and tie, the present No. 1 peaked hat and black boots.

This is how the troops will look in their new Service Dress. It is in khaki bara-thea and will be worn with the No. 1 peaked hat.

Right: Back view of a sol-dier in the new combat suit and web equipment. The Regular of the future may also get new boots.

THE REGULAR SOLDIER IS TO HAVE THREE NEW SUITS: TWO OFFICER-TYPE SERVICE DRESS UNIFORMS FOR PARADE AND WALKING OUT AND A COMBAT OUTFIT FOR FIGHTING. THE ARMY'S WOMEN WILL GET A NEW LOOK, TOO

This Korean-type, fur-lined parka will be worn in very cold climates. Note the hood, sloping pockets and codpiece.

SOLDIER TO SOLDIER

THERE have been few more important moves on the military chessboard since the end of World War Two than the recent decision (reported elsewhere in this issue) to set up under the North Atlantic Treaty Organisation a multi-nation "fire brigade."

This hard-hitting strike force will act as a danger signal to any potential aggressor and be visible proof of Allied solidarity in an emergency.

It will be far from symbolic. Armed and equipped to deal with any contingency, it will be ready to rush to trouble spots at a few hours' notice to snuff out incidents which could lead to world-wide conflagration. Its very existence will make an enemy think twice before embarking on dangerous military enterprises.

The British troops who are selected to serve in the strike force alongside the men

from other NATO nations will have a proud and vital task to perform.

THE Press, the public and the Army have all been enthusiastic in their praise of the new Service Dress and combat suit which the troops of the all-Regular Army are to have.

And rightly so. It is high time that the best fighting man in the world was also the best dressed.

But little has been said about the battle-dress which, in the not-too-distant future, will disappear from the Regular Army to make way for the combat suit.

Admittedly, the battledress, with its all-too-often bulky blouse and trousers that rarely fit and are almost never the same shade of khaki, is not glamorous. But it has served its purpose well for more than 20 years in every kind of climate and country.

IS ON THE WAY

Every Regular will eventually receive two new Service Dress uniforms. The first will be issued in 1961 and the second after all troops have received the first. "Blues" will remain, for the present, the dress uniform of officers, non-commissioned officers and bandsmen.

All other ranks in the new all-Regular Army may also get a civilian-style, belted raincoat made of fawn wool gaberdine, which has been on troop trials for more than a year, and a suitcase to go with a new-style kit bag.

The new combat suit consists of a water-resistant, windproof smock of cotton-sateen and a pair of trousers of the same material. It is an improved version of the combat uniform worn by British troops in Korea. The smock, which is fitted with a detachable hood, has a "poacher's" pocket at the rear and its breast pockets slope inwards to allow easy access.

In very cold weather troops will wear a fur-lined parka and be issued with a special pullover and long woollen pants.

New web equipment, designed to spread the load more evenly and keep the front of the soldier's body clear of encumbrances, has also been undergoing troop trials. It includes a pack which is larger than the present one and which can be jettisoned in seconds to leave the soldier fully-equipped for battle. New boots with moulded rubber soles and plastic insoles and a new foam-rubber liner for the steel helmet are also being tested.

Troop trials have been taking place with a belted raincoat of wool-gaberdine, similar to that shown at right. It may replace the groundsheet.

This is the attractive new Service Dress, in Lovat green, for the WRAC.

THE CLASSICAL LINE FOR THE WRAC

OTHER ranks in the Women's Royal Army Corps and Queen Alexandra's Royal Army Nursing Corps have not been overlooked in the plan to give the Army a new look.

They will be issued with a "figure-hugging" Service Dress coat and skirt to replace battledress, and high-heeled shoes.

Both uniforms are cut on the same classical lines—the WRAC Service Dress in Lovat green worsted and the QARANC uniform in grey worsted. The jacket, which has no belt or breast pockets, will have shoulder straps piped in dark green for the WRAC and in scarlet for the QARANC. With both uniforms go nylon stockings and black court shoes, a white poplin shirt and a tie (bottle-green for the WRAC and grey for the QARANC).

• •

It is the uniform in which World War Two was won.

Whatever its faults, the battledress is comfortable, hard wearing and has no buttons and badges to keep clean. There may be many who will lament its passing.

★

"FOR the first time since the end of World War Two no British troops are in action anywhere in the world."

So recently wrote a leading London newspaper which ought to have known better.

Many readers probably believed it, but soldiers chasing the last of the fanatical terrorists in Malaya, patrolling the Yemen border and hunting rebels in the mountains and deserts of the Oman are not amused.

Ignorance of the Army's activities in the Oman is perhaps not surprising because little news comes out of that country where, for eight years, British troops and the Trucial Oman Scouts have been waging a bitter, hit-and-run little war with dissident tribesmen and rabble-rousers from across the border in Saudi Arabia.

But the news is there to be had if only the Press would take the trouble to seek it instead of giving so much space to the unsavoury sexual adventures of film stars.

★

EACH year, when the Army Estimates are debated in the House of Commons, Members of Parliament are prone to make some profound, and generally sensible, statements about the Army.

This year was no exception, as for instance when Brigadier Sir Otho Prior-Palmer, formerly Commander of 7th Armoured Brigade, told the House: "There are far too few bands in the Army and they do not play often enough in public. I am convinced that they have a tremendous emotional effect. In my own regiment, a great friend of mine once walked over to the orderly room to hand in his resignation. On the way, he met the regimental band coming round the corner. Thereupon, he tore up his resignation papers and threw them in the waste-paper basket."

And Colonel George Wigg, the only Member of Parliament with a Long Service and Good Conduct medal, had a point when he suggested that the present pay system was "anachronistic nonsense."

He was more or less mollified when told that the Army is soon to install an electronic calculating machine, costing several hundred thousand pounds, which would make "either a mass of errors which would put everyone in credit to the tune of millions or would avoid the nine months' delay that troops had suffered in the past."

In the shadow of a Thunderbird guided missile, the last of the 3.7s trundle across the parade ground into retirement.

FAREWELL TO A FAMOUS GUN

At the home of the Royal Artillery the Gunners said goodbye to the guns that had fired their last round. And with them went the last Regular regiment to man them.

FIVE HUNDRED Gunners stood rigidly at the salute and the strains of "Auld Lang Syne" echoed round the barracks as the Regular Army's last surviving 3.7-inch anti-aircraft guns went into honourable retirement.

It was a doubly sad and moving moment. On the Front Parade at the Royal Artillery Barracks, Woolwich, the Gunners were saying goodbye to a famous gun and to a famous regiment, for behind the ten gleaming guns as they were driven off in pairs, marched the men of the last unit to man them— 57 Heavy Anti-Aircraft Regiment, Royal Artillery, for whom this was the last parade before disbandment.

As the Regiment, accompanied by fellow units of 7 Army Group, Royal Artillery (Anti-Aircraft), came on parade, the ten 3.7s were drawn up in immaculate line abreast. Nearby stood two *Thunderbird* guided missiles, their warheads thrust aggressively to the sky, marking the new era in the history of anti-aircraft weapons and the revolution that brought about the eclipse of the conventional guns.

The Director, Royal Artillery, takes the salute as the men of 57 Heavy Anti-Aircraft Regiment march past.

RAEC Masters Them All

Captain John Dominy, the RAEC skipper, soars above his opponents as he fights for possession in a line-out. He missed only one of the Corps' first 20 games.

THREE years without a single defeat. That is the proud record of the Royal Army Educational Corps' rugby team which has not been beaten since October, 1956.

In the past three years the team has won ten and drawn three of its 13 matches against other corps and the Royal Military College of Science—a feat unequalled by any other corps team in the recent history of Army rugby. It is doubtful if any other rugby team in Britain has remained undefeated for so long.

The Corps' achievement is all the more remarkable since the team was formed only in 1953 by a small group of enthusiasts, including Major R. Dock, a Cumberland and Westmorland cap, as secretary, and Captain A. B. Edwards, the Welsh international, as skipper.

The opening game heralded great things to come with a 6-5 win over the Royal Army Service Corps, but the next five matches brought the team only one solitary success. So the Corps was scoured for players and under the leadership of Captain Edwards and later Captain John Dominy, the present captain, today's powerful side was fashioned.

As SOLDIER went to press the RAEC fifteen set the seal on its record by thrashing the Royal Military College of Science by 19 points to nil.

SOLDIER recently watched the RAEC take sweet revenge for its last defeat in October, 1956, by beating the Royal Army Ordnance Corps at Blackdown by 23 points (a goal, three tries and three penalty goals) to six (two penalty goals).

The winners, who had two Army caps in the side—Second-Lieutenant Stanley Purdy at wing forward and Sergeant Keith Bennett at stand-off half—took advantage of their opponents' mistakes and were brilliantly led by Captain Dominy. Outstanding were Second-Lieutenant Ken Dalziel, a forward, and Sergeant Arthur Leitch, left wing. Dalziel, who was playing his first game for the Corps, kicked three penalty goals and made one excellent conversion. Leitch, a former Scottish schoolboy long-jump champion, showed a remarkable turn of speed that often left the opposition standing.

The RAEC team is now looking forward to its big match of the season—against the Royal Army Service Corps—and hopes to complete a hat-trick of wins. In each of the past two seasons the RAEC has robbed the RASC of its hitherto unbeaten record.

JOHN STEELE

No doubt about the outcome of this forwards' tussle as the RAEC collapse in a heap under the sheer weight of numbers.

Members of the Royal Army Educational Corps have won many distinctions in the rugby world in the past 12 years. Captain A. B. Edwards played for Wales and Sergeant D. M. Scott for Scotland. These two, with Captain B. J. Hazel, a Scottish trialist, and Warrant Officer J. D. Clancy, have played for Combined Services.

The present skipper, Captain Dominy, and Major W. E. Townsend have both captained Aldershot Services. Many Corps players have gained county honours and since 1947 have won 38 Army caps.

The Corps has had three representatives on the Army Rugby Selection Committee—Lieutenant-Colonel D. J. Reidy, Major Townsend and Captain Edwards—and Major-General S. Moore-Coulson, Director of Army Education, is chairman of the Army Rugby Referees' Society and vice-president of the Army Rugby Union.

Vol. 15, No. 12 **SOLDIER** FEBRUARY 1960

THE BRITISH ARMY MAGAZINE

Libya, 4 piastres;　Cyprus, 40 mils;　Malaya, 30 cents;　Hong-Kong, 60 cents;　East Africa, 75 cents;　West Africa, 9d.

Symbolising the end of an era, a wall of an Aldershot barracks that for a hundred years echoed the ring of Army boots and bore the orders and the pin-ups of soldiers of four wars, crashes in a dull rumble of crumbling bricks.

A FACE-LIFT FOR ALDERSHOT

FOR MORE THAN A CENTURY, MILLIONS OF BRITISH SOLDIERS HAVE PASSED THROUGH "THE CAMP" AT ALDERSHOT, MARCHING OFF IN GREAT HEART TO CRIMEAN, SOUTH AFRICAN AND WORLD WARS AND RETURNING IN TRIUMPH TO THOSE SAME UNCHANGED GAUNT AND BLEAK BARRACKS. NOW IN A SINGLE £11 MILLION SWEEP, MILITARY ALDERSHOT WILL BE REBORN IN ITS SECOND CENTURY IN UP-TO-THE-MINUTE BARRACKS AND QUARTERS WORTHY OF THE NEW REGULAR ARMY'S TRADITIONAL HOME

ALDERSHOT, traditional home of the British Army for over a century, is to become the Army's first "new town." Within the next eight years, the uncomfortable and hideous old barrack blocks and the squalid married quarters, known and unloved by millions of soldiers, will all have disappeared.

In their place will rise spacious new barracks, embodying every amenity, large estates of modern houses and maisonettes and of revolutionary patio-type houses which may set a pattern for both military and civilian homes of the future.

"Everything in Aldershot is terribly out of date," says the General Officer Commanding Aldershot District, Major-General R. A. Bramwell Davis DSO, who for five years has nursed the re-building plans through innumerable committees and conferences.

Now the General can see the first results in the 200-odd married quarters already rising Phoenix-like on the site of the old Waterloo East Barracks and in the £50,000 sergeants' mess, the first of seven, which he recently opened at Lille Barracks.

The Army is to spend £17½ million on new building and modernisation in Aldershot District, and over £11 million of this will be spent in Aldershot itself.

Appropriately, the first on-

A FACE-LIFT FOR ALDERSHOT CONTINUED

A model of a group of patio-type houses of future Aldershot.

slaught on military Aldershot has been made in Wellington Lines where some of the oldest barracks stand next to the town of 40,000 people which has grown up on the Army's doorstep.

Waterloo East Barracks, built in 1855 and the old home of field artillery, have already been demolished, giving way to the first married quarters of the new Waterloo estate.

Talavera and Waterloo West Barracks, now coming down, will become the site of a further 298 maisonettes and patio-type houses and two children's schools, primary and secondary. At a later stage, Badajos and Salamanca Barracks which, with Talavera, were the first permanent

barracks in Aldershot, will almost certainly be demolished, followed by two of the old cavalry barracks, Willems (West Cavalry) and Warburg (East Cavalry).

Beaumont, known as South Cavalry Barracks until the three barracks were renamed just before World War Two, have been used by Territorial Army and other auxiliary units and may not be entirely demolished.

Although not the oldest, Cavalry Barracks are probably the best-known quarters in Aldershot and housed the 1st Cavalry Brigade for 80 years.

The first 222 houses of the Wellington estate, costing £450,000, are due to be completed in June, 1961. Eighty-nine of

£50,000,000 IN SIX YEARS

WITHIN the next six years the Army is to spend over £50 million on new barracks alone in the United Kingdom. Over a hundred modern barrack blocks have already been built.

Rebuilding is in an advanced stage at Colchester and Woolwich, while Catterick, largely a World War One camp, is to undergo a face-lift costing over £5 million.

London's Chelsea Barracks are to be rebuilt at a cost of £2,200,000, followed by Knightsbridge and Wellington Barracks.

With the reconstruction of barracks well under way, the War Office has now been able to authorise the rebuilding, starting next year, of the Guards' Chapel in Wellington Barracks which was destroyed by a flying bomb during morning service in June, 1944.

The Army also plans to rebuild the Women's Royal Army Corps Depot at Queen Elizabeth Camp, Stoughton, Guildford, by replacing the existing hutted accommodation with permanent buildings.

AND NOW "THE PATIO" HOUSE

A REVOLUTIONARY new type of other ranks' married quarters–centrally-heated "patio" houses built in groups and each facing inwards on to its own private walled and paved courtyard, lawn and shrubbery–will be erected in Aldershot if the War Office Works Directorate's ideas are approved.

The plan is to build 170 "patio" homes on the present sites of Talavera and Waterloo West Barracks. Three-bedroomed types will be L-shaped, with part of the accommodation, including the living room, in an adjoining "bungalow." Two-bedroomed types will be of two storeys only. Each group will have built-in garages.

On the same sites will be built 128 maisonettes in four storey blocks. The "patio" type house will offer a convenient compromise between maisonette and traditional house for the family that wishes to enjoy the privacy of a small garden without too much work in maintaining it. It is an innovation in civilian as well as Army housing and some "patio" houses of a different design from those planned at Aldershot, will be built by the Army at Catterick Camp and may also be incorporated in some of London's future housing estates.

them will have three bedrooms and the remainder two; some will be semi-detached and others built in terraces stepped to avoid the straight-line appearance of the barrack blocks they displace.

These new homes will have every modern amenity—built-in wardrobes, portable electric fires on bedroom walls, plastic-tiled

ground floor, modern bathroom, immersion heater, electrical ring circuit with ample plugs, and a kitchen with cooker and wash boiler and with space for a refrigerator.

Each house will have its own garden and the estate includes spaces for children's playgrounds and a garage for every two houses.

THE OLD . . .

For years this was the unmarried soldier's home in Aldershot—a cheerless, draughty barrack room where warmth and comfort were to be found only by huddling, Cinderella-like, round a dirty and often petulant stove.

AND THE NEW

Tomorrow's soldier may live in a "bed-sitter" for four, with this fold-away bed, fitted wardrobes, modern bed light and even an electric razor socket. Note (left) the twin washbasins and mirror cabinets above them.

"GOODNIGHT

Dockside cranes, twinkling lights on quay and station and the lighthouse beam recede as the SS Vienna *leaves the Hook on her final voyage.*

The old troopships are disappearing one by one. Latest victim of the growth of air trooping is the *Vienna*, retired from service after carrying a million and a half Servicemen and their families between Harwich and the Hook of Holland

Pictures by SOLDIER Cameraman PETER O'BRIEN

GENTLY, patiently, the SS *Vienna* eased away from the Hook of Holland quayside and headed down the channel towards the open sea and home. It was as if the 31-year-old ship sought to slide shamefacedly away on her final trooping voyage across the North Sea.

But, as the quayside cranes, silhouetted against the night sky, began to recede, the *Vienna* seemed to shake off this mood of self-effacement and regain her pride. The pennants dressing her forward and spelling out a simple "goodbye" to the Hook, lost their limpness and fluttered jauntily in the breeze.

As she drew abreast the *Duke of York*, at her berth, three blasts of the *Vienna's* siren shattered the still night. Back came three answering blasts in final salute; across the water floated a faint voice—"All the best to you"—and the indistinct notes of a faraway bugle.

It was a poignant moment; the death rites of a gallant old trooper which in her lifetime had carried a million-and-a-half Servicemen and their familes between Harwich and the Hook of Holland.

With the lights of the Dutch coast a distant twinkle, the

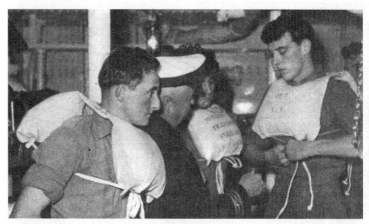

Above: Once aboard and settled in, it's time for life-belt drill. Here, Troop Officer W. B. Causer checks to ensure the tapes are properly tied.

Left: Vienna, *her foremast dressed in farewell, lies alongside at the Hook of Holland. The first train has arrived and its soldier-passengers move towards the embarkation hall.*

VIENNA!"

Vienna paid her last respects to the Hook, hooting her thanks to the pilot cutter and all the Dutch pilots who had taken her safely in and out of the river over the years.

Most of her Army and Royal Air Force passengers had turned in for the night before the *Vienna* cast off and only a few—those who had previously sailed in her —shared the sentimentality of the crew's farewell to Dutch workers gathered on the quay.

But it was a leave-taking tinged by more than sentimental acknowledgement of a happy ship and a true *entente cordiale*. The withdrawal of the *Vienna*, heralding the advent of air trooping to Germany, foreshadowed, too, the possible eventual dismissal of her sister troopers, *Empire Wansbeck* and *Empire Parkeston*, and the demise of the transit camps at Hook and Harwich.

As the *Vienna* throbbed through the night, her crew relived the excitements of her career as they went about their tasks for the last time or joined parties quietly celebrating in the sleeping ship.

Troop Officer W. B. Causer recalled the highlight of his seven years aboard when 17 military prisoners broke through a bulkhead door and found temporary solace in a wine store. Captain R. Good, for four years the *Vienna's* commander and a sailor for 45 years, remembered a night three years ago when the *Vienna*, sighting a fire at sea, sent out an SOS which, misinterpreted by the Press as coming from her, caused a flutter in hundreds of British homes.

There was, too, that better-forgotten incident when, leaving Harwich in fog, the veteran trooper collided with the Suffolk ferry.

For all it was a wrench from a real home; for the few who could claim to have sailed on her

"Finished with engines"—and Greaser A. Halls (left) and Fourth Engineer T. Stewart, watched by Chief Engineer A. D. Williams, turn the valves.

Below: Troop Officer Causer chats with his counterpart, Major E. W. Young, Royal Pioneer Corps, who was for a year the Vienna's *Ship's Commandant.*

UNAUTHORISED PERSONS ARE NOT ALLOWED ON BOARD TRESPASSERS WILL BE PROSECUTED

UNDER the new air-trooping plan, which was inaugurated in October, some 7000 Servicemen and their families will fly in Hermes aircraft between Britain and west BAOR each month.

Silver City Airways are to operate about 50 flights a month in each direction, taking off and landing at Manston, in Kent, and Dusseldorf and Wildenrath, in Germany.

The remainder of Rhine Army will continue to travel by troopship, on twice-weekly sailings in the *Empire Wansbeck* and *Empire Parkeston* between Harwich and the Hook of Holland.

THE 4326-ton Vienna, the largest cross-Channel vessel at the time of her building in 1929 at Clydebank, began life as a passenger ferry for the old London and North Eastern Railway, plying between Harwich and the Hook of Holland.

Taken over by the Ministry of Transport in December, 1939 she carried soldiers to and from France and Holland until Dunkirk. She was subsequently employed on miscellaneous duties with the Royal Navy and as a motor torpedo boat depot ship, returning to trooping in September 1941.

Six years later *Vienna* was refitted as a permanent troopship with a passenger capacity of 1048 and run by British Railways for the Ministry.

maiden and final voyages— Second Steward V. West, Purser L. J. Fletcher and Donkeyman C. H. Baker—it was a parting from an old friend.

For the Ship's Commandant, Major E. W. Young, of the Royal Pioneer Corps, and Ship's Regimental Sergeant-Major G. A. Bell, of The Royal Highland Fusiliers, the *Vienna* represented a brief but happy phase—and they at least were assured of another ship.

So passed the night. Now the *Vienna*, her foremast dressed again with bunting, lay alongside at Harwich, enjoying for the last time the bustle and joy of a home disembarkation as she disgorged her complement of Servicemen and families to the waiting trains.

Later, stripped of her stores, she drew out to her mooring, her future undetermined, but her past a glorious record of faithful service.

PETER N. WOOD

Pensively, Captain R. Good eyes the quayside as he brings Vienna *in to her Harwich berth for the last time.*

Right: Disembarking soldiers hand in pillow slips to RSM Bell, ex-Drum-Major of The Royal Scots Fusiliers.

Vol. 16, No. 3   # SOLDIER   MAY 1960

T H E   B R I T I S H ✕ **A R M Y   M A G A Z I N E**

Libya, 4 piastres;   Cyprus, 40 mils,   Malaya, 30 cents;   Hong-Kong, 60 cents;   East Africa, 75 cents;   West Africa, 9d.

BRITISH TROOPS WILL PLAY THEIR PART IN A NEW, THREE-NATION STRIKE FORCE — ARMED WITH CONVENTIONAL AND NUCLEAR WEAPONS— WHICH CAN MOVE TO THE RIGHT PLACE AT THE RIGHT TIME. THEY WILL SERVE SIDE BY SIDE WITH AMERICAN AND FRENCH CONTINGENTS

A British Infantryman stands guard with the new FN General Purpose machine-gun.

Below: A French Infantryman in action with his country's new machine-pistol.

A FLARE-UP FORCE FOR NATO

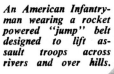

An American Infantryman wearing a rocket powered "jump" belt designed to lift assault troops across rivers and over hills.

BRITISH soldiers at present stationed in Germany will soon be making history.

By the end of the year they will become part of a fully integrated, 3000-strong, three-nation task force—the first of its kind in peace or war—and will serve alongside American and French troops as the North Atlantic Treaty Organisation's highly mobile, hard-hitting "fire brigade."

The new task force, which will be equipped with both conventional and tactical nuclear weapons, will have its own fleet of transport aircraft and naval forces always standing by to rush its men and weapons to trouble spots anywhere in the world at a moment's notice.

Announcing this revolutionary plan—one of the biggest practical steps forward in military co-operation between the armies of the NATO countries since the alliance was formed eleven years ago—the Supreme Allied Commander, Europe, General Lauris Norstad, said that 1000 men from each of the three countries would form the task force in its early stages. They would come from units already serving under NATO command and would continue to carry out their normal tasks but would be withdrawn periodically for training together in their new role. The new force would have its own commander and staff,

and weapons and supplies would be earmarked for it.

"It will be a small force but it could have a very direct military significance," he added. "It could move to the right place at the right time and would give an allied complexion to problems in any area."

SOLDIER understands that the task force may later be increased to 5000 men by the addition of German and Italian troops and possibly develop into a "division" of seven or eight NATO nations.

The commander of the new force has not yet been decided but, says General Norstad, "I hope that it is not an American."

TWO BECOME ONE

Guns dipped in salute, tanks of the two regiments drive past General Sir Harold Pyman to symbolise amalgamation.

A SPECTACULAR drive-past by 50 Centurion tanks on a barrack square in Germany provided a fitting climax to the recent amalgamation parade of the 3rd and 6th Royal Tank regiments.

After the regiments, which now become the Third Royal Tank Regiment, had been inspected by Lieutenant-General Sir Harold Pyman, Deputy Chief of the Imperial General Staff and Colonel Commandant of the Royal Tank Regiment, the Centurions took up station and drove through each other's ranks in double column, dipping their guns in salute as they passed.

They circled and, to symbolise their merger, came together. To the tune of "Auld Lang Syne" the old regimental flags were lowered and a six-gun salute was fired. Then, led by the first commanding officer of the new Regiment, Lieutenant-Colonel P. A. L. Vaux, the tanks drove past General Pyman with guns dipped.

Appropriately, there has always been a close association between the 3rd and 6th Royal Tank Regiments which served in France, North Africa, Greece, Iraq, Syria, Egypt, Abyssinia and Italy in World War Two.

The 3rd was one of the first two battalions of tanks to go into action in World War One.

MILITARY
MISCELLANY

RHINE ARMY GETS A NEW BOSS

General Sir James Cassels. He was 12 years a subaltern.

A SOLDIER who in less than five years rose from the rank of captain to major-general in World War Two takes over this month as Rhine Army's new Commander-in-Chief.

He is General Sir James Cassels DSO who, at 52, is the British Army's youngest general. He also becomes commander of Northern Army Group.

General Cassels, who is six feet two inches tall and rejoices in the nickname of "Gentleman Jim," joined the Army in 1926 and was commissioned into the Seaforth Highlanders, of which Regiment he is now Colonel. He was a captain at the outbreak of World War Two (having been a subaltern for 12 years) and in 1945 became Commander of the famous 51st Highland Division. In 1946 he commanded 6th Air-borne Brigade in Palestine and in 1948 became Director of Land/Air Warfare at the War Office.

After a spell as Director of emergency operations in Malaya, General Cassels commanded 1st British Commonwealth Division in Korea between 1951-2 and last year was appointed General Officer Commanding Eastern Command.

General van Fleet, the United States Commander in Korea, once said of General Cassels: "He is a gentleman—and he is also a scrapper."

NEW CLUBS FOR THE TROOPS

Striped door canopies and travel posters decorate the intimate bar in one of Bicester's new clubs for the Army's junior ranks.

SOLDIERS stationed in the Bicester area will whole-heartedly endorse NAAFI's recent claim that junior ranks "have never had it so good."

They now have two new Junior Ranks clubs, built at a cost of £83,000, to cater for the needs of two battalions of the Royal Army Ordnance Corps, a 200-strong company of the Women's Royal Army Corps and several smaller military units.

Both clubs—"The Cannons" for 16 Battalion, RAOC, and "St. Davids" for 17 Battalion, RAOC—have a restaurant, tavern and games rooms divided by partitions that slide back to provide a ballroom for 600 people. Corporals have their own restaurant and lounge and each club has a television room.

Each will cater for more than 1000 troops who have formed their own committee to organise and control social activities.

A similar club, built at a cost of £54,000, has been opened at Palace Barracks, Holywood, Northern Ireland.

● The Army's first launderette, where Service wives can use four washing machines and a spin drier, has been opened by NAAFI at Catterick.

Vol. 16, No. 10 **SOLDIER** DECEMBER 1960

T H E   B R I T I S H   ARMY   M A G A Z I N E

Libya, 4 piastres;   *Cyprus, 40 mils;*   *Malaya, 30 cents;*   *Hong Kong, 60 cents;*   *East Africa, 75 cents;*   *West Africa, 9d.*

GOD REST YE MERRY...

CHRISTMAS again—and SOLDIER's muse,
Greets you all with clerihuse
(Odd little jingles with a mis-spelt rhyme
Only permissible at Christmas-thyme.)

FRÖHLICHE Weihnachten! Joyeux Noël!
Greetings to all and good wishes as woël–
On picket, on guard, or confined to a coël
Drilling in depots or firing a shoël,
Ski-ing in Norway or climbing Snaefoël,
Or spending a leave in a seaside hotoël.

TO soldiers East of Suez with those bare brown knees
(And Caribbean Hampshires) we say, "'Allo, plees."
To Sappers in Gibraltar, tunnelling the Rock,
To passengers in transit, from Dover to Bangkock,
To ACF and CCF and APTC, too,
Who celebrate a hundred years—a happy Yoole to yoo.

SALUTE to the troopships now
withdrawn,
Liaison groups (some carrierbawn),
United Nations bent on peace,
The War Department's stout poleace,
And SIB men seeking clues . . .
Ahoy, you water transport crues
In LCTs Mks IV and VIII
(Oh, why must one abbreviVIII?)

HERE'S to rear Guards at the Palace
Spared at last the shocks and stares
Of tourists come from Wapping Stares,
From Pennsylvania, Maine or Dalace.

SOLDATEN on leave mit der Bundeswehr
(Thehr's less "bull" thehr, they all declehr)—
To model soldiers, combat suits—
To trumpets, brass, complete with muits—
To Army Air Corps flying the *Beaver*—
To units catching the karting feaver—
To recruiting tours in Sunny Devon—
A farewell to the 3.Sevon—
To No. 3 Dress (keep well pressed!)—
To Monty's car (passed 10-year tessed)—
To Cleveland fixed wheel bucket trencher—
The Army life's a great advencher.

GREETINGS to the conquerors of Annapurna II,
Of Kilimanjaro, Kenya and Mount Kinabalu;
To the military contingent at the Madison Tat II;
To *Malkara*, *Wombat*, *Vigilant* and the new *Blue Water*, tu.

LET'S sing a glee
For an LADee,
For all at see,
For "A" and "Gee,"
For those who skee—
And you and mee.

TO soldiers in Aden we send our best wishes;
Cheers to the last troops to serve in Maurishes;
Wassail to Sappers in Dharan Basaar;
Joy to Somalis who train at Buraar;
Regards to Pioneers, come of age this year;
Noël, Field-Marshal Festing, and congratulations, sear!
And a greeting—Bhalo hos— to King Mahendra's men,
Those splendid little Gurkhas, on show here once agen.

AND here's a toast
To guest and hoast,
To Chatham's ghoast,
To MO-doast,
To Christmas poast,
And the furthermoast . . .

FOR whatever your regiment, unit or corps,
And whether you're stationed in Singaporps,
In Kowloon or Kameroons or Kuala Lumpur,
In Kolchester, Katterick—or whether on tur
In Cyprus or Muscat or far-off Nepal:
The merriest of Christmases!
God bless you al!

P.N.W.

14(I)DU

14th (Independent)
DISINFESTATION UNIT
MBULURUKI
362 MILES →

. FRANK FINCH .

1961

The new Regulars

The modernisation and reorganisation of the Army continued apace during 1961. Yet more new equipment entered service as many old favourites - such as the 3.7inch HAA gun, which saw service during the Second World War - were finally consigned to the scrap heap. Much of the new equipment along with weaponry still on trial was brought together on Salisbury Plain during the summer months in the biggest firepower display - "Ex Noisy Nora" - seen on the British mainland for some time.

Great emphasis was also given during the year to recruiting for the new Regular Army. As well as a myriad of military Tattoos and displays that took place annually around the country - which always attracted great interest and support from the public, as well as a great many recruits, there had also been introduced a "Bounty" scheme of £200 to each man who recruited another to the ranks of his regiment or the Army. In addition, many regiments conducted their own recruiting drives throughout their home recruiting area.

Overseas, there was still plenty of action for both the new Regulars as well as those National Servicemen who still had time to serve. Early in the year British troops were called upon to quell rioting during a state of emergency in the Cameroons. There was also trouble with dissident tribesmen in the Radfan area of the Aden Protectorate. And toward the end of the year a whole Brigade had to be deployed to the Middle East kingdom of Kuwait after threats of invasion from neighbouring Iraq. Though thwarted on this occasion, Iraq, as we are all now aware, would try again.

Finally as the year ended, international tension in Berlin reached its highest level for sometime, when the East German authorities introduced new restrictive measures to prevent the movement of people between East and Western sectors of the city. The infamous Berlin wall had arrived.

QUICKLY

Brigadier Derek Horsford DSO and bar, who commanded the field force. He has been a Rifleman, a Gunner, and an Infantryman.

Above: Seconds after landing Royal Marine Commandos at Farwanja airfield, helicopters return to their parent ship, the carrier HMS *Bulwark*, to ferry in more troops and equipment. Six hundred Commandos were landed in the first few hours.

Right: As a *Centurion* tank goes forward, two Marine Commandos direct helicopters on to a landing strip near the frontier town of Houtlah. The Marines sailed to Kuwait in a carrier which had been cruising off India.

INTO KUWAIT

Only hours after receiving the call for help, men of 24 Infantry Brigade and Royal Marines landed in troubled Kuwait. It was a triumph of organisation and training and the first operation of its kind. There was no fighting but the troops won a notable victory by keeping the peace

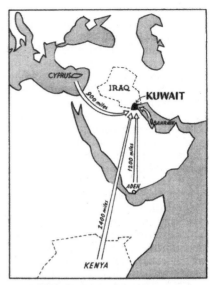

KUWAIT (two-thirds the size of Wales and one of the richest oil-producing countries in the world) became independent only two weeks before Iraq threatened invasion and the Sheikh appealed to Britain for help.

Britain, which has been closely linked with Kuwait since 1899, when the territory accepted British protection, last year received nearly 40 per cent of all its oil supplies from Kuwait. Oil production is in the hands of the Kuwait Oil Company, jointly owned by British Petroleum and Gulf Oil Corporation of America.

Stripped to the waist, men of 2nd Battalion, The Parachute Regiment, who flew from Cyprus, dig themselves into the desert near the Iraqi border. At the time the temperature was 130 degrees in the shade.

WHEN British troops poured into Kuwait, the fabulously rich oil sheikhdom in the Persian Gulf, they were making military history.

For the first time Britain's Strategic Reserve—the "fire brigade" force which has the task of nipping trouble in the bud—was being tested in action and in a bloodless operation, carried out with remarkable speed and efficiency, it brilliantly achieved the object for which it was set up.

Not a shot was fired in anger. The mere presence of the troops was sufficient to prevent the threatened Iraqi invasion of Kuwait.

Never before have British troops moved so rapidly or done their job more effectively. Only hours after Sheikh Abdullah al-Salim, the ruler of Kuwait, had appealed for Britain's help, more than 600 Royal Marine Commandos were being flown ashore by helicopters from the Royal Navy Commando carrier HMS *Bulwark* which, three days before, had been cruising off Karachi, 1000 miles away. At the same time, the 3rd Dragoon Guards, with 14 *Centurion* tanks,

rushed from Bahrain by tank landing ship, went ashore at the port of Shuwaith, digging in around the Farwanja airport.

Though the landing was unopposed it was difficult and uncomfortable, for as the troops came ashore a red-hot wind from the desert brought a blinding sandstorm in its wake.

Meanwhile other units from 24 Infantry Brigade in Kenya, 2400 miles away, and in Bahrain, Aden and Cyprus, were on the way by air and the next day more than 3000

Left: The 11th Hussars prepare their *Saracens* for action before moving off to the Iraqi border. Above: Sappers of 34 Independent Field Squadron cool off at a rest camp. Note Arab headdress.

troops, with weapons, vehicles and equipment, had been landed.

Movement to the Iraqi border was equally rapid. By evening on the second day forward troops were astride the 1000-yard Moutla Ridge, the only route for Iraqi tanks, overlooking the frontier.

In this desolate countryside of jagged rocks, shale and sand, turned into a furnace by the searing sun, the men dug themselves in and waited while armoured cars probed ahead. With that extraordinary facility the British soldier has of making himself at home in any part of the world, the troops soon settled down in spite of the overpowering heat, seeking shelter in bivouacs and slit trenches and, in one case, in a Bedouin sheep pen. Their biggest problem was shortage of water which was soon remedied when helicopters plied backwards and forwards with ice-cold drinks.

On the third day more troops and equipment arrived by air from Cyprus and Kenya and made their way to the front through a swirling, stinging sand storm while in the rear areas stores and weapons were ferried ashore.

Five days after the first troops had landed more than 7000 men were in position, holding an 80-mile defence line near the border, in case of attack.

The attack never came, for in a remarkably short time the build-up had been completed and an assault on Kuwait would have been doomed to failure. The danger was over and, step by step, the "fire brigade" force was withdrawn and re-deployed, ready to return at an hour's notice if trouble broke out again.

The biggest enemy turned out to be the weather. Scores of men (though, significantly, not those who had been acclimatised in Bahrain and Aden) were prostrated by the overpowering heat, and violent sand storms tore at the troops as, handkerchiefs tied round their mouths, they prepared their positions.

The Army was quick to help alleviate the arduous conditions and within four days of the landing had set up rest centres on the coast and in Kuwait city for men suffering from heat exhaustion. NAAFI was soon on the job, too, shipping thousands of bottles of beer, soft drinks and half a million cigarettes to the men sweating it out in the desert.

As a demonstration of speed and strength the landings in Kuwait were impressive and many valuable lessons were learned, not the least being the need for more transport aircraft and helicopters so that the Army's "fire brigade" force can move even more quickly to a trouble spot.

A picture to bring back memories of North Africa in World War Two. *Centurion* tanks take up position on the Moutla Ridge to guard the invasion route into Kuwait.   Picture: *Daily Express*.

Above: Men of 42 Commando camouflage their vehicles in a forward area.   In a country devoid of features and vegetation, hiding weapons and vehicles was a problem that called for ingenuity.

Below: The job completed. An observer could see there was something, but he would not know what was beneath the scrim.   Some of the scrub in the middle distance concealed foxholes.

Men of the 9th (Rocket) Squadron, Parachute Regiment, put the finishing touches to their weapon pit, one of hundreds screening the border. Below: "Dear Mum: Well, here we are in Kuwait . . ." Pictures by *Daily Express Features Service*.

THEY WERE THERE

AMONG the major units which were rushed to Kuwait to keep the peace were: Headquarters 24 Infantry Brigade; 2nd Battalion, Coldstream Guards and 3rd Dragoon Guards; 1st Battalion, The Royal Inniskilling Fusiliers; 1st Battalion, The King's Regiment (Liverpool and Manchester); 2nd Battalion, Parachute Regiment; 11th Hussars; 7th Parachute Light Battery, Royal Horse Artillery; 42 Commando, Royal Marines; 45 Commando, Royal Marines; and 29 Field Regiment, Royal Artillery.

Vol. 16, No. 12

SOLDIER

FEBRUARY 1961

T H E   B R I T I S H   ✠   A R M Y   M A G A Z I N E

Libya, 4 piastres;   Cyprus, 40 mils;   Malaya, 30 cents;   Hong Kong, 60 cents;   East Africa, 75 cents;   West Africa, 9d.

Photographs: Sergeant W. J. TRICKETT, RAOC, Army Public Relations

Ready for any emergency, a patrol of The King's Own Royal Border Regiment, in jungle green, scouts ahead along an overgrown bush path near Kumba in the south.

★★★★★ ON GUARD IN THE CAMEROONS

British troops are chasing terrorists again, this time in the Southern Cameroons—once the feared White Man's Grave—where The King's Own Royal Border Regiment is keeping watch while the territory's people decide their future

IN single file, a patrol of British soldiers in jungle green crossed a flimsy wooden bridge over a crocodile-infested river and, fingers on the triggers of their self-loading rifles, hacked their way along a narrow track overgrown with creeper and tangled grasses.

A hundred and fifty miles away another patrol, soaked to the skin by torrential rain, painfully hauled themselves up a precipitous rock to an observation post overlooking the rolling grasslands 6000 feet below.

The men were from The King's Own Royal Border Regiment and they were hunting for terrorists as part of the Regiment's task of keeping law and order in the Southern Cameroons, a few miles north of the Equator in West Africa.

They were also making history, for this was the first time that a British regiment has been stationed in the Southern Cameroons— once known as the White Man's Grave— 3000 miles from Britain.

Vol. 17, No. 6

SOLDIER

AUGUST 1961

T H E   B R I T I S H   ✠   A R M Y   M A G A Z I N E

Libya, 4 piastres;   Cyprus, 40 mils;   Malaya, 30 cents;   Hong Kong, 60 cents;   East Africa, 75 cents;   West Africa, 9d.

Honest John leaps from its launcher, belching smoke and flame. Seconds later it exploded in mid-air four miles away. *Honest John* is a free-flight missile with a range of nearly 20 miles.

Picture: SOLDIER Cameraman ARTHUR BLUNDELL

THE ARMY BARES ITS TEETH

A WOODED hillside on Salisbury Plain erupted in smoke and flame as a creeping barrage of 25-pounder and 5.5-inch shells crashed down. *Centurion* tanks joined battle with their 20-pounders and Browning machine-guns and paratroopers and Infantry opened up with their three-inch mortars, *Wombat* anti-tank guns, 105-mm pack howitzers, their new general purpose machine-guns and self-loading rifles.

On the pitted hillside, tank after tank was knocked out and enemy forward positions were obliterated as the tremendous weight of fire swept every yard of ground. Then, as the barrage died, Royal Navy and Royal Air Force jet fighters and bombers screamed in to rocket and bomb the rear areas.

In those few minutes nearly a million rounds of live ammunition were fired, an auspicious opening to the first large-scale land-air warfare demonstration held by the three fighting Services in Britain and the largest concentration of weapons, machines and equipment since World War Two.

It was also the first time that the Army has been able to show at one demonstration the remarkable accuracy and lethality of its latest weapons—the *Honest John*, the 8-inch howitzer; the *Malkara*, mounted on its *Hornet* armoured vehicle; the *Wombat*, the pack howitzer; and the new machine-guns and self-loading rifles—and the increased mobility and striking power which its helicopters and light aircraft now provide.

Few, if any, of the 4000 spectators—high-ranking officers and cadets from all three Services, military liaison staffs from Commonwealth and NATO countries and Government officials—went away unimpressed

The Army showed off its new weapons and a million live rounds were fired at a dramatic demonstration of the hitting power of the three Services

The Infantry's latest anti-tank gun, the *Wombat*, in action. This weapon, which weighs only 650lbs, is carried in a long-wheel-based *Land-Rover* and can be manhandled across country on its own two-wheeled carriage. Four men are needed to operate it.

Above: Paratroopers give supporting fire with the 105-mm pack howitzer, the three-in-one weapon which can be used as a howitzer, anti-tank gun or field gun. Below: *Centurions* blast enemy tanks with their 20-pounders and Infantry with machine-guns.

Russian guards watch from the steps of their War Memorial in the British Sector as riflemen of the 2nd Green Jackets erect a barbed wire barricade to discourage demonstrations.

SPOTLIGHT

THE international searchlight suddenly switches its beam to Berlin where new restrictive measures by East Germany have evoked swift reaction in the Western sectors of the city.

Unruffled by the war of nerves, the British garrison took the heightening crisis in its stride. Putting their training smoothly into practice, Infantrymen moved up to the East-West border to begin armed patrols within a few feet of the newly-erected barbed wire on the East German side.

Backing them were *Centurion* tanks of the 4th Royal Tank Regiment. Royal Military Policemen patrolled the border-divided roads within bayonet reach of East German forces as the Infantry prepared to keep a clock-round vigil.

Near the Brandenburg Gate, other Infantrymen, watched by Russian guards,

Left: Two steel-helmeted Infantrymen stand behind their *Mobat* recoilless anti-tank gun sited in a wheatfield near the border between the British and Russian zones at Staaken.

ON BERLIN

Centurion tanks of 4th Royal Tank Regiment, followed by *Saracen* armoured personnel carriers, rumble along the West Berlin streets in an early morning "show the flag" exercise.

erected a barbed wire barricade round the Soviet War Memorial to discourage possible retaliatory demonstrations by incensed West Berliners.

In an alert exercise which started before dawn and lasted for four hours, 3000 men of the Berlin Infantry Brigade Group took up their battle positions. *Centurions*, armoured cars and Infantrymen of the 2nd Green Jackets, The King's Royal Rifle Corps, the 1st Battalion, The Durham Light Infantry and the 1st Battalion, The Welch Regiment, "showed the flag" as they manned the border under the close scrutiny of armed Communist guards.

● At home it was announced that a new strategic reserve division, some 12,000 strong and equipped with heavy tanks and artillery, is being formed. It will be based in Southern England and held ready to reinforce the British forces in Germany in an emergency.

Right: Maj-Gen Rohan Delacombe DSO, the British Commandant, inspecting troops. Across the street—and the border—is an East German recce car flying the Free German Youth flag.

THE STALWART GOES ON TRIAL

A LORRY that can travel at 50 miles an hour on roads and move across country like a tank is undergoing trials for possible use in the Army.

It is the *Stalwart*, a highly-manœuvrable six-wheeled vehicle which, the makers claim, has an even better cross-country performance than the *Saladin* or *Saracen*. It can cross a five-foot-wide trench, climb hills of nearly one-in-three, surmount vertical obstacles up to 18 inches high and turn round in only 45 feet.

Fitted with a Rolls-Royce B.81 220 bhp engine, the *Stalwart* is 20 feet six inches long and has an articulated chassis and a new type of non-slip differential which enables it to traverse any kind of country which a tank can cross.

The *Stalwart,* which is made by the Alvis Company of Coventry, is able to carry a load of five tons and its mechanical layout is almost identical to that of the *Saracen* and *Saladin.*

General Lauris Norstadt, the Supreme Allied Commander, Europe, commented favourably on the vehicle's performance when he saw it in action during a recent visit to Britain.

Above: Note the size of the six wheel suspended on an articulated chassis. Left Ploughing through deep water and mud.

THE ARMY TAKES LONDON

With eight internationals in its team, the Army won its annual contest against London's amateur boxers for the third successive year — this time by a bigger margin than ever before

Lance-Corporal Len Hobbs gets home with a left to Walker's chin and grimaces as a right hook grazes his face. Walker won on points.

Above: Corporal Larry O'Connell misses his bearded opponent with a right uppercut—but he went on to win decisively. Below: London's R. Pink ducks and runs slap into a hard left hand from the Army champion, Dvr Warwick.

FIFTEEN international boxers—eight of them soldiers—took part in the annual contest between the Army and London at Seymour Hall recently in which the Army scored a resounding victory by nine bouts to four.

It was the Army's third win in a row and brings the score since 1947, when the match was first held, to 7-6 in favour of London, with one match drawn.

This year it was a tough contest, each fight going the full distance, and in most cases only the barest margin separated the contestants at the end.

The Army began disappointingly when flyweight Driver Johnny Mallon, of 6 Training Battalion, Royal Army Service Corps— he has boxed for England—lost to Johnny Pattullo (Fitzroy Lodge). Mallon had an off night and could never disturb the imperturbable Pattullo whose ringcraft and hard hitting sometimes left his opponent floundering.

Private Lewis Mackay, of 14 Battalion, Royal Army Ordnance Corps, levelled the score in the next bout, soundly beating his bantamweight opponent, K. Hawkins (Napier); and Trooper Bobby Taylor, of 15/19th King's Royal Hussars, put the Army ahead by outpointing J. Mantle (Battersea) in a close-fought featherweight contest.

Rifleman John Head, 3rd Green Jackets, The Rifle Brigade, increased the lead with a good win in his featherweight bout with P. Cheevers (Fitzroy Lodge), but B. Whelan (Chiswick), a former Army boxer, reduced it with a fine victory in a fast-moving light-weight fight with Corporal Brian Ackery, of The Royal Fusiliers.

The Army won the next six bouts. Driver Paul Warwick, of 20 Company, Royal Army Service Corps, the Army lightweight champion, had no trouble disposing of R. Pink (Wandsworth) and Corporal Larry O'Connell (Royal West Kent Regiment) was always ahead in his light-welterweight fight with J. Davison (Fisher). But the Army welterweight champion, Private Jim Lloyd, of 14 Battalion, Royal Army Ordnance Corps, who won a bronze medal at the last Olympic Games, only just scraped through over Tony Lewis (St. Pancras). This was Lloyd's first contest since the Olympics and he was obviously out of form against a skilful and superbly fit opponent.

Army welterweight Rifleman Peter Morgan (3rd Green Jackets, The Rifle Brigade) was too good for E. Young (Lynn) and Driver Bill Monoghan (6 Training Battalion, Royal Army Service Corps) and Trooper J. Caiger (15/19th King's Royal Hussars) won their fights without difficulty.

The last two fights went to London, D. Pollard (Fitzroy Lodge) outpointing Private Len Pellant (Queen's Royal Surrey Regiment) in a light-heavyweight contest, and Billy Walker (West Ham) beating the Army's heavyweight champion, Lance-Corporal Len Hobbs, Grenadier Guards.

This turned out to be one of Hobbs' toughest ever fights. He was down for a count in the first round and took considerable punishment from a very fit and aggressive opponent.

● As SOLDIER went to press four of the Army's internationals, Private Lloyd, Trooper Taylor, Driver Warwick and cruiserweight champion Driver John Evans, of 6 Training Battalion, Royal Army Service Corps, were selected for the England team to meet West Germany.

They'll be specialist tradesmen in their units, but first and foremost they're soldiers—barrack square trained.

Soldier, Tradesman, Student, Citizen

IT was a great day for the Americans. The United States Army's only unit in Britain was holding its "colonel-making" ceremony—welcoming a new commanding officer—at its base near Harrogate.

Only a few hours earlier America's first astronaut had returned safely from space and her soldiers marched on to the parade ground with excusable jauntiness.

It was a great day, too, for the fledglings of the British Army—youngsters in the band of the Harrogate Army Apprentices School—as, sharing the occasion, they proudly led the seasoned American troops on parade.

The apprentices, in No. 1 Dress, typified the spirit of their School in their ebullient keenness, the smartness of their turnout and their precise drill. For the Army's appren-

tice tradesmen, whether at Harrogate or at the other three Army apprentices schools in Chepstow, Arborfield and Carlisle, are soldiers first and foremost.

Soldiering starts, in a mild form, in the first term at Harrogate, continues throughout the education and technical training which take up most of the three-year course, and takes precedence once more during the final term.

During their first six weeks the recruits settle down to Army life. Physical training

and games make them fit; talks and visits to the school laboratories give them an inkling of things to come. They are confined to camp, not allowed to salute until they can wear their uniform properly—and are away from "Mum" for the first time.

But there is always "Dad"—the Headquarter Company Commander, Major F. Parker, Royal Signals—at hand to solve their problems, and a busy six weeks soon goes by. Then comes the passing off parade, to which their parents are invited, and the recruits, still living in a separate part of the camp, begin to share more evenly the routine of the whole School.

Boys can join the School from 15 to 17 years old and most of them come in between 15 and 16½, signing on for nine years from their 18th birthday. The majority are from secondary modern schools, with a fair proportion from military families at home and abroad.

For the rest of the first term the boys learn simple foot drill and saluting, attend education and trade classes and spend a lot of time on the playing fields. Now they may

Left: Apprentice Tradesman RSM B. S. Dyer (right) talking to his CSMs. Above: The Reynolds twins, busy on shining parade, enlisted together.

SINCE the Army Apprentices School opened in 1947 it has maintained a close link with Harrogate. It supports the town on civic occasions and, as its gift on the Borough's 75th anniversary, the Sapper apprentices converted a cleaning cupboard in the Town Hall into a showcase for the other gifts of silver.

The Mayor and Corporation regularly visit the School and every year the Town Clerk (Mr. J. Neville Knox) and the chief officers give lectures on civic affairs to the final term apprentices. "The

boys are integrated into the town," says Mr. Knox. "Our only regret is that the camp is just outside our borough boundary."

But perhaps that may be put right when the spiders of Uniacke Barracks give way to new barrack blocks, classrooms and laboratories. Almost the whole of the camp is to be rebuilt by 1965, at a cost of £1½ million.

Perhaps by then, too, another "wrong" may have been righted and the School will be more appropriately named the Harrogate Army Technical College.

Pictures by
Capt P. E. Creedy, RAEC

Applied Morse instruction for the telegraph operators. Note the left-handed operator on the right of the picture.

Left: This apprentice line technician is delving into the mysteries of a complex multi-channel telephone terminus.

Right: A/T L/Cpl C. Garratt wears the Duke of Edinburgh's silver badge, long service stripe and an engagement ring.

The Apprentices' Band proudly leads the American troops and their Colour party on parade for the "colonel-making" ceremony at Memwith Hill. The Union Jack and the Stars and Stripes fly side by side at the camp entrance.

Below: Apprentice J. W. Smith, only 4 ft 10 ins tall, looks up in every way to the father figure of his Coldstream Guards platoon sergeant, Sgt Freeman, who stands 6ft 4ins tall.

smoke (if old enough—and many parents have to be reminded of the law on this) but may not drink alcohol.

For many years the Harrogate School taught Royal Engineer trades, too, but the last of the Sapper apprentices leave for the Chepstow School this month and in future Harrogate will teach only five Royal Signals trades.

After a year's basic course in the School's Signals Wing "A", the top tradesmen—line, radio, radio relay and telegraph technicians—sit a selection test, then go on to the "B" Wing to specialise in their chosen trades.

The telegraph operators—top trade of the Royal Signals operator group—remain in Wing "A," working up their Morse to 25 words a minute, a speed which will take them to Signals units all over the world and, after their service, land them posts in cable firms, motoring organisations, taxi fleets, or perhaps a £2000 a year job as a fishing fleet telegraph operator.

Civilian instructors, many of them ex-Servicemen, ensure a continuity of tuition, while military instructors keep the apprentices abreast of modern techniques and developments.

Brigadier R. S. Broke takes the salute as Centurion tanks thunder past during the Regiment's last spectacular parade.

SPHINX, BULL'S AND MERCER'S

After 22 years' illustrious service, 4th Regiment, Royal Horse Artillery, will soon disappear—but the identities of its three famous honour-titled batteries will live on

SELF-PROPELLED howitzers, Centurion tanks, Saracens and Champs, keeping perfect station, roared past the saluting base at Hohne in a dashing cavalcade of military might.

It was the first mounted parade held by 4th Regiment, Royal Horse Artillery, since it was equipped with the American 155-millimetre self-propelled howitzer in 1955.

And it was the last parade of its kind for next June the Regiment returns to Britain—after ten years' unbroken service in Germany—and merges with 33 Parachute Light Regiment, Royal Artillery, to form 7th Parachute Regiment, Royal Horse Artillery, and 4th Field Regiment, Royal Artillery.

The identity of the Regiment's three famous batteries—"F" (Sphinx), "G" (Mercer's Troop) and "I" (Bull's Troop) will live on in the Parachute Regiment.

But no gun in that proud display could compete in polish and the care lavished on it, with the ancient brass cannon which stands in place of honour outside the office of "F" (Sphinx) Battery. This was one of the guns lost in the disastrous retreat from Kabul in 1842 and which, with another, was recaptured in 1880 at Ghuzni by the troop that lost them. It is now a tradition that wherever the Battery goes the gun goes, too.

Earlier that day the 4th Regiment had been on parade for its annual administrative

Left: This famous brass cannon, lost in 1842 and recaptured 38 years later, is always placed outside "F" Battery office as a symbol of the Gunners pride and courage

inspection and the three batteries, flanked by their flags, were reviewed by Brigadier R. S. Broke MC, Commander Royal Artillery, 1st Division, who presented two Long Service and Good Conduct Medals. One went to Regimental Sergeant-Major W. P. Carthy, a Gunner since 1938—and the other to Armourer Quartermaster-Sergeant V. Farrant, Royal Electrical and Mechanical Engineers, who is attached to the Regiment.

Among those on parade was Battery Sergeant-Major C. J. Friend—the Regiment's longest-serving soldier—who joined "F" (Sphinx) Battery as a boy trumpeter in India in 1939 and has served with the Regiment ever since.

Born in Egypt in June, 1939, the 4th Regiment joined 7th Armoured Division on its formation, and in June, 1940, went into action against the Italians on the Egyptian frontier—the first British Gunners to do so. During Wavell's first desert campaign a Regimental observation post's report led to the capture of "Electric Whiskers"—the Italian General Bergenzola.

The Regiment also took part in Auchinleck's offensive in November, 1941, and fought at Sidi Rezegh—the hardest battle in its history—during which Brigadier Jock Campbell, leader of the famous "Jock Columns" and a former Commanding Officer of the Regiment, won the Victoria Cross. After the Battle of Sidi Rezegh the remnants of the Regiment were taken away in a 15-cwt truck.

The Regiment also fought at El Alamein, took part in the break-out from the Normandy beachhead, was in action at the Falaise Gap and in the attempted relief of Arnhem, crossed the Rhine and fought its way bitterly towards Hamburg. On the way it passed only a few miles from Hohne, the Regiment's home since 1950.

All three batteries have long and honourable histories and each zealously guards its traditions and identity.

"F" (Sphinx) Battery was formed in 1800 as The Experimental Troop, Bengal Artillery, and a year later was fighting the French in Egypt, dragging its guns into action by camel. For 40 years the Battery was caught up in various small wars in India and in both Afghan Wars. Two members of the Battery won the Victoria Cross in the Relief of Lucknow in 1843.

In World War Two, "F" (Sphinx) was the first artillery battery to be ferried across the Rhine in rafts and is the only battery to have served continuously with 4th Regiment, Royal Horse Artillery, since it was formed.

"G" Battery (Mercer's Troop) was formed in Ireland in 1801, also for service in the Napoleonic Wars, and has an unbroken history since then, although it joined "F" (Sphinx) Battery to form "F/G" Battery for eight months in 1939. It was in action in South America in 1807 and gained its present name at the Battle of Waterloo when its commander, Captain Mercer, disobeyed the Duke of Wellington's order to retire and, instead, engaged the French cavalry at point-blank range. Captain Paul Mercer, a direct descendant of the man who disobeyed the Iron Duke, serves with the Battery today.

"G" Battery (Mercer's Troop) had a magnificent record in World War One. In one action during the last desperate German offensive in 1918 all its officers were killed and a sergeant took command.

"I" Battery (Bull's Troop) was raised in 1805 under Captain Robert Bull and sent almost immediately to the Peninsula, where it took part in almost every major action. At Fuentes d'Onoro a section under Captain Norman Ramsay was cut off by French cavalry but charged its way out.

"I" Battery also fought at Waterloo, firing over the heads of British troops and taking great toll of the French. In the Second Afghan War it once mounted its guns on elephants to traverse difficult country. The Battery fought in most of the big Western Front battles in World War One, winning a formidable list of battle honours, and in the 1939-45 war escaped from Dunkirk, slogged through the Western Desert and Italy. It joined 4th Regiment in 1958.

4th Regiment, Royal Horse Artillery, will lose its self-propelled guns next June on its merger, for the new 7th Parachute Regiment, Royal Horse Artillery, will be armed with 4.2-inch mortars and eventually the 105-mm. pack howitzer, while 4th Field Regiment, RA, will have 25-pounders.

Above: Regimental Sergeant-Major W. P. Carthy, who joined the Royal Artillery in 1938, receives his Long Service and Good Conduct Medal.

Left: The men of "I" Battery (Bull's Troop) parade with tanks and self-propelled howitzers. In the Second Afghan War the Battery carried its guns into action on elephant-back.

Left: Warrant Officer C. J. Friend, longest-serving soldier in the Regiment, inspects the uniform and equipment of Captain Ramsay who led Bull's Troop in its famous ride through the encircling French cavalry at the Battle of Fuentes d'Onoro.

Right: Major B. P. Mcenroy, present commander of "F" Battery, inspects the list of his predecessors, dating back to 1801. The honour title "Sphinx" was granted for outstanding service in Egypt.

Side by side, the old Colours of the two uniting regiments are marched off parade while the men of the new Queen's Own Buffs, The Royal Kent Regiment, present arms in a final sad farewell.

The lowering of two flags and the unfurling of a new one signified the birth of the last amalgamated Infantry regiment, formed from two famous regiments which had nearly 600 years' service between them

THE BUFF AND THE BLUE UNITE

Left: Major-General Craddock DSO (left) and Major-General Talbot DSO, MC inspect the new Regimental Band, now 74 strong. Above: Major-General Craddock, formerly Colonel of The Buffs, inspects the guards of his old Regiment before they marched on parade to join those of The West Kents.

TO the sad strains of "Auld Lang Syne" two regimental flags—one buff, the other blue—were slowly lowered on a parade ground at Shorncliffe.

Suddenly, a trumpet fanfare split the air and high on its staff a new regimental flag —half buff, half blue and bearing the White Horse of Kent—was unfurled.

It was a poignant and a proud occasion. In that brief moment two famous Infantry regiments with 594 years' service between them—The Buffs (Royal East Kent Regiment) and The Queen's Own Royal West Kent Regiment—disappeared. And in their place a new regiment—The Queen's Own Buffs, The Royal Kent Regiment, was born.

It was a doubly historic moment, too, for it marked the end of the friendly rivalry between the two old regiments and was the last of the amalgamations of Infantry regiments in the Regular Army. The Men of Kent (The Buffs) and the Kentish Men (The Queen's) had joined forces to become Kent's only county regiment.

Appropriately, the ceremony was carried out in brilliant sunshine and began when two guards of each old regiment marched on and were inspected by the Colonels of the Regiments—Major-General R. W. Craddock DSO, of The Buffs, and Major-General D. E. B. Talbot DSO, MC, of The Queen's.

Then the Regimental Colour parties took post with the four Queen's and Regimental Colours and the symbolic act of amalgamation was performed by the raising of the new Regimental flag, after which the new Regiment, in blues and carrying self-loading rifles with bayonets fixed and led by their first commanding officer, Lieutenant-Colonel R. H. Dendy, formerly of The Buffs, marched past their Deputy-Colonel of the Regiment, Major-General Talbot.

Then came the saddest moment of all as the old Colours—bearing a host of famous battle honours from Blenheim to Belleisle, Malplaquet to Mons and Arras to El Alamein —were marched off parade for the last time.

The amalgamation of these two famous regiments will not mean that all trace of them will disappear. With the Saxon crown and sword of the Home Counties Brigade as its cap badge and on its buttons, The Queen's Own Buffs will wear a collar badge in the shape of the rearing White Horse of Kent, similar to The Queen's Own old cap badge, and the new Regimental motto is that of The Buffs: *"Veteri frondescit honore"* ("With its ancient honour it is evergreen").

Officers, warrant officers and non-commissioned officers of the new Regiment will also wear the royal blue lanyard with battledress, a former tradition in The Queen's Own; the new Regimental march is a combination of the two old ones; and the new Regimental Colours—to be presented later this year by King Frederik of Denmark, the Colonel-in-Chief of the Regiment—will bear the White Horse with "Invicta," the emblems of The Buffs (a dragon) and The Queen's Own (crown surmounted by a lion), both former regimental mottoes, and the battle honours of the two regiments.

Both old regiments had long and illustrious records of service and many of their traditions will be preserved. The Buffs can trace their origins to the year 1572 when Queen Elizabeth formed "a faire company of three hundred strong" from the trained bands of the City of London to help the

COVER PICTURE
SOLDIER's front cover, by Staff Cameraman PETER O'BRIEN, shows the Colours of The Buffs and The Queen's Own being marched past in slow time for the last time at Shorncliffe. Taking the salute are the Colonels of the Regiments, Major-General R. W. Craddock DSO, of The Buffs, and Major-General D. E. B. Talbot DSO, MC, of The Queen's Own.

The new Regiment receives its new Colours later this year from its Colonel-in-Chief, King Frederik of Denmark.

As SOLDIER went to press The Queen's Own Buffs was preparing for its first overseas tour —a six-months' stay in Kenya.

Major-General Talbot, Deputy-Colonel of the new Regiment, takes the salute as The Queen's Own Buffs march past. The new Regiment will continue its forebears' traditions.

Dutch against the Spaniards. They fought in the Netherlands for nearly 90 years until the Spaniards were finally defeated and took their title from the buff colour of their jerkins, breeches and hose.

In 1665, when war broke out between England and Holland, The Buffs became The Holland Regiment and fought their old comrades, and in 1689 became Prince George of Denmark's Regiment, fighting in Marlborough's campaigns. The Buffs were one of the regiments to fight in the last battle in which troops were commanded by a British monarch—at Dettingen, in 1743, when the Army led by King George II defeated the French.

In the Peninsular War, The Buffs earned one of their nicknames—The Nutcrackers— because of the number of French heads they cracked. They were also known as The Buff Howards and The Resurrectionists.

The Queen's Own Royal West Kent Regiment, recruited from London's southeast boroughs and west Kent, was formed in 1756 as The Queen's Own, fought as

Marines under Nelson, took part in the battle of Ushant in 1778 and helped to drive the French from Corsica, an occasion commemorated every year by the laying of a wreath at the foot of Nelson's Column. Originally numbered the 50th Foot, The Queen's Own won their nickname "The Dirty Half Hundred" during the Peninsular War because the men dirtied their faces when they wiped away their sweat with their black cuffs.

The amalgamation of these two fine old regiments has produced the strongest Infantry battalion in the Army. As SOLDIER went to press the 1st Battalion, The Queen's Own Buffs, was 1050-strong, including a band of 74 musicians.

Addressing the parade during the amalgamation ceremony, Major-General Talbot said there was a heartening determination to see that the best of both old regiments was preserved in their worthy heir.

There is no doubt that The Queen's Own Buffs, the last of the new Infantry regiments, will rise to the challenge.

Vol. 17, No. 3

SOLDIER

MAY 1961

T H E B R I T I S H ARMY M A G A Z I N E

Libya, 4 piastres; Cyprus, 40 mils; Malaya, 30 cents; Hong Kong, 60 cents; East Africa, 75 cents; West Africa, 9d.

Mr. Mayhew, a former major was dubious about selective service.	But Brig Sir Fitzroy Maclean said the only solution was some form of conscription.	Mr. G. W. Reynolds thought they should induce ex-National Servicemen to join the AER.	Mr. Marten confessed that he re-acted against "bull" but later it gained his respect.	Lieut-Comdr Maydon supported "spit-and-polish" in moderation.

RECRUITING, "BULL" and BUYING OUT

Round come the estimates— Parliament's annual opportunity to dissect the Army. This year's debate naturally spotlighted the problems of recruiting the new all-Regular Army. Why do soldiers buy discharges? Is there still too much "bull"? the MPs inquired

HOW is the new all-Regular Army to get all the recruits it needs? Is there still too much "bull"? Why do so many soldiers buy themselves out? Does parachute jumping teach leadership? Are the Army's digging methods out of date?

These were some of the problems which Members of Parliament discussed during the recent debate on the Army Estimates—their annual opportunity to say what they think of the Army. Rarely, however, do their comments get beyond the pages of Hansard or a very brief mention in the newspapers.

This year, with the end of National Service in sight, the major issue was: How can the Army achieve its target figure of 165,000 Regulars by 1963 and, if it cannot do so, should a system of selective service be introduced?

For his part, Mr. John Profumo, the War Minister, was confident that in two years' time the Army would have the men it needs and announced the following seven-point plan which he thought would bring success:

1. National Service radio operators, drivers, nursing orderlies, clerks and electronics tradesmen who sign on as three-year Regulars will receive back pay as Regulars from the date they were called up or 12 months in arrears, whichever was the shorter.
2. There will be an extensive publicity campaign on television, in the Press and by posters and films.
3. The Army will be kept in the public eye by stepping up displays and exhibitions.
4. The soldier's life will be made more exciting by sending him more often on overseas exercises.
5. More married quarters will be provided and units in Britain and Germany will be allowed to use caravans as quarters until permanent homes are built.
6. Soldiers will be persuaded to contribute to an Army scheme by which they can save for a home or small business on retirement.
7. Every effort will be made—including an overhaul of man-management and the elimination of "bull"—to create "a happy working atmosphere" which will induce soldiers to stay on.

Mr. Profumo, pictured here at his War Office desk, was confident, in announcing his seven-point plan, that by 1963 the Army will have the men it needs.

In the last 15 years costs have risen steeply. Pay and allowances have more than doubled since 1946.

Showing a willingness to buy from other NATO countries, and thus boost British products, the Army has ordered 17 French *Alouette* helicopters, to be used mainly for troop transport and casualty evacuation.

However, Mr. Profumo added a note of warning that if insufficient recruits were obtained all courses of action "including selective service" must be examined, "though I doubt if what is commonly known as selective service would be the right remedy." The Government would also consider alleviating the shortages by lowering medical and educational standards, recruiting overseas and further civilianisation.

Not surprisingly, these comments were greeted with scepticism in some parts of the House and Mr. Christopher Mayhew asked (without getting an answer) how a selective service scheme would operate. He doubted if the kind of soldier produced by selective service would contribute anything to the Army's sense of unity and purpose.

Many other members on both sides of the House were against any kind of conscription but Brigadier Sir Fitzroy MacLean, a former Parliamentary Under-Secretary of State for War, who thought the Army should be at least 200,000 strong, failed to see how some form of conscription could be avoided.

Mr. George Wigg, a former colonel in the Royal Army Educational Corps (his daughter recently joined the Women's Royal Army Corps), pointed out that the country had had selective service for many years in the shape of exemptions from National Service and claimed that "we have the right to ask young men to accept the obligations of service."

Mr. Emanuel Shinwell, War Minister 1947-50, rejected the idea of returning to National Service and described selective service as "simple nonsense." If the Army could not get its 165,000 it said it wanted, it would have to do with what it could get!

Brigadier Sir John Smyth VC, claimed that battalion commanders would rather have an under-strength unit of long-service Regulars than an up-to-strength one which included short-service conscripts.

Pleas for more recruits to be raised in Commonwealth countries, especially among the Gurkhas and in the West Indies, were made by Brigadier Sir John Smyth and Mr. Donald Chapman. The latter advocated the integration of Commonwealth recruits into British regiments and said that in Jamaica there were many young men, intensely pro-British and proud to serve, who would be able to take on the jobs for which the Army had many vacancies. He pointed out that the best recruit in The Royal Warwickshire Regiment last year was Private Foster, a Jamaican who had come to Britain at his own expense to join up.

A sailor, Lieutenant-Commander S. L. C. Maydon, suggested that one way out of the Army's manpower problem was to make more use of the reorganised Territorial Army and the Army Emergency Reserve which should be allowed to take part in overseas exercises with the Regular Army and be called up when necessary to fill the gaps. Mr. G. W. Reynolds pointed out that the 15,000 men in Category 1 of the new Army Emergency Reserve could be called out without proclamation and said everything should be done to induce ex-National Servicemen to join the AER.

MAIN DEPLOYMENT

OF THE SERVICES

UNITED KINGDOM

W. GERMANY

GIBRALTAR

CYPRUS

WEST INDIES

HONG KONG

MALTA

ADEN & PERSIAN GULF

LIBYA

WEST AFRICA

EAST AFRICA

SOUTH ATLANTIC

SINGAPORE & MALAYA

KEY

Army

Local Forces

R.A.F.

Royal Navy

"I must say, Fanshawe, I rather care for the look of the new Commanding Officer."

soldier humour

"It's all right for you padre, you've got friends up here!"

1962

Farewell to the National Servicemen

As the last of the National Servicemen struck off the days to demob on their "chuff charts", the British Army redoubled its efforts to recruit ever more regular soldiers to fill its rapidly diminishing ranks.

Regimental Recruiting teams toured far and wide and some even went overseas - to the South Sea Islands, and in particular Fiji, where they found an especially rich vein of interest in the British Army. Indeed, so successful was this campaign that more than 200 male and female soldiers were recruited to the British Army by the end of the year.

Whilst the majority of the Army busied itself with the myriad of tasks required of it at home, and with BAOR, others were involved in disaster relief in British Honduras after the colony was hit by Hurricane "Hattie". For some there was also a period of jungle bashing as well as riot control as violence flared again in Georgetown, British Guiana.

Other new and not so new changes were taking place among the Army's regiments and corps. Army Commandos, last seen during World War 2, were making a comeback. In order to support the new re-organised Royal Marine Commandos, 29 Field Regiment Royal Artillery was converted to the Commando role and stationed at the Citadel in Plymouth. In addition, other supporting arms and services were created to form a full-blooded and self-supported Commando Brigade.

On the downside this year was the realisation that with the departure of the National Servicemen, army sport would never quite be the same again. Indeed, during the National Service years such was the quality of the many professional and national sportsmen who graced regimental and corps ranks, that it had been almost impossible for a Regular soldier to gain entry to a regimental, divisional or army team. All that was now about to change.

Vol. 17, No. 12 **SOLDIER** FEBRUARY 1962

T H E   B R I T I S H   ARMY   M A G A Z I N E

Libya, 4 piastres;   Cyprus, 40 mils;   Malaya, 30 cents;   Hong Kong, 60 cents;   East Africa, 75 cents;   West Africa, 9d.

With fixed bayonets, soldiers stand guard outside a locked and shuttered wines and spirits store in Belize, the devastated capital.

IN THE WAKE OF HURRICANE "HATTIE"

When a 200-mile-an-hour hurricane shattered Belize, capital of British Honduras, British soldiers were the first to bring succour. More troops, flown from home, joined in the task of fighting disease, starvation and destitution . . .

IT was a night of horror and helplessness. Then the never-to-be-forgotten fury of Hurricane "Hattie" died down —and the battered people of British Honduras bewilderedly took stock.

Belize, their capital, lay devastated, the pathetic wreckage of thousands of wooden homes engulfed in the mud aftermath of tidal waves which followed remorselessly in "Hattie's" wake. The 30,000 people of Belize and thousands of others in the Central American colony faced epidemic, starvation and destitution.

But relief came quickly, spearheaded by British soldiers who, with their families, had shared that terrifying night. Within 48 hours they were reinforced from Jamaica by more men of their regiment and within a fortnight 1300 British troops—more than half of them flown the 4700 miles from Britain in the Army's biggest-ever mercy air-lift—were restoring life and hope to the colony as they fought disease, cleared debris, repaired buildings, reinstated public services and guarded warehouses and shops against looters.

First to bring relief to shattered Belize were men of "Z" Company of the 1st Battalion, The Royal Hampshire Regiment.

Vol. 18, No. 3   **SOLDIER**   MAY 1962

T H E   B R I T I S H A R M Y   M A G A Z I N E

Libya, 4 piastres;   *Cyprus, 40 mils;*   *Malaya, 30 cents;*   *Hong Kong, 60 cents;*   *East Africa, 75 cents;*   *West Africa, 9d.*

As Georgetown's Water Street blazes, the angry flames silhouette a gutted building

(Picture: *Guiana Graphic*)

FLARE-UP IN GEORGETOWN

SMOKE billowed over the waterfront of Georgetown, British Guiana's capital. Flames belched from the wooden shops, offices and warehouses lining Water Street, in the heart of the business area. Rioters, defying tear gas grenades, fought pitched battles with the police and drove back firemen with bottles and stones.

Within a few minutes of an urgent call for help, British soldiers of the Colony's garrison—"A" Company of the 1st Battalion, The Royal Hampshire Regiment—were driving the 30 miles from their camp at Atkinson Field, Guiana's airport.

In battle order, with fixed bayonets, the Hampshires helped to restore order, standing guard at street corners, rounding up looters and patrolling strategic points.

THE SAS IN THE

Guerillas led by men of the Special Air Service move in after ambushing a convoy in Exercise "Swift Strike II."

CLUSTERS of dark shapes emerged from the 14 American aircraft over the battle area. All at once, it seemed, 120 parachutes opened, and men of Britain's 22nd Special Air Service Regiment were descending on American soil. Soon they would become the first British soldiers to do battle on that soil since the "Redcoats" crossed the Canadian border 150 years ago, occupied Washington and burned down the White House.

This was "Swift Strike II," the first of three major exercises in which the British troopers fought alongside and against American troops in the forest-covered mountain regions of West Virginia and North and South Carolina.

"The most successful training we have ever done," is how Lieutenant-Colonel J. M. Woodhouse MC, who commands 22nd Special Air Service Regiment, describes the three-month visit, and Brigadier-General William P. Yarborough, Commander of the United States Special Warfare Centre at Fort Bragg, North Carolina, is equally enthusiastic.

The British unit visited Fort Bragg—"home" of the American airborne forces—at the invitation of its American counterpart, the Special Forces, so that each could benefit from the other's experience. Before getting down to large-scale exercises the two units exchanged lectures and

SOLDIER to Soldier . . .

NEXT month SOLDIER reaches another milestone in its 18 years' life. For only the second time the price of the magazine will be increased, from ninepence to a shilling, and for the first time since its production in this country—SOLDIER came home from Germany in 1953—it will have a new printer.

The price increase has been made reluctantly, but inevitably. The first two issues of SOLDIER were free. Then a charge of sixpence was made and 11 years ago the price was increased to the present ninepence. Since 1951, production costs,

particularly the major items of printing, paper and staff salaries, have risen continuously and considerably.

Offsetting these, advertisement revenue has remained constant while sales within the Army have naturally decreased as the Army has run down to today's strength. The gap between expenditure and income, falling on the tax-payer, must be closed. So SOLDIER goes into battle next year with a price increase, a new sales campaign and an advertising drive, all backed by a better-than-ever magazine which,

we think, will be as good a bobsworth as you can find anywhere.

And, in case any mathematician should draw attention to a 33⅓ per cent increase in the price, we are forearmed! We carefully looked up the pay of a soldier of 11 years ago and compared it with his pay today!

●

THE War Minister's statement that next year some "Ever-Readies" will fly out to Hong Kong, to train with Regular units there, gives a timely fillip to recruiting to the Territorial Army's new Emergency Reserve. This scheme, which will replace their annual camp for the selected men, will test mobilisation procedure and exercise these "Ever-Readies" in their role of individual reinforcements to the Regular Army in times of tension.

USA

High over the treetops of West Virginia a Special Air Service trooper ropes down from a United States Army H34 helicopter.

demonstrations, the British troopers particularly passing on the knowledge of jungle warfare they gained during the Malayan campaign.

Then came "Swift Strike II," in which the British regiment fought with 60,000 American troops, achieving its objectives without mishap—despite several treetop landings —and linking up with members of the Special Forces. After a two-day break came a 400-mile flight to West Virginia for a three-week anti-guerilla exercise in which some of the British soldiers fought alongside a company of the "Screaming Eagles" (101st Airborne Division).

The 900 square miles of Cherokee Indian country on the forest-covered slopes of the Smoky Mountains provided the setting for the final exercise. Ranged against the 120-strong British force, scattered all over this vast forest, were 2000 men of the "All American" 82nd Airborne Division.

The exercise lasted almost a month and showed the British force just how tough their guerilla role can be against first-class troops with strong air support. But the British troopers had their share of success with speedy ambushes of patrols and road convoys.

Free-falling back at Fort Bragg—described by a British trooper as an "All-American Aldershot"—and a spell with the United States Air Force's Air Commandos, brought the business side of the British unit's memorable visit to a close, but there was still the four days' leave to spend in Washington DC.

Throughout the visit the unit found American hospitality overwhelming, with a lavish barbecue, staged for the British troops by the Governor of West Virginia, among the highlights. A scrapbook of the visit, presented to the Regiment by the American Army, contains a message from General Yarborough praising the spirit of the Regiment, and adds: "Everyone you have met in the United States is proud to say he has known the 22nd Special Air Service Regiment and its men."

THE ARMY IN THE HOUSE

• • • • • • • • •

IN a statement on *Blue Water*, the surface-to-surface missile which the Army had hoped would replace the *Corporal*, the Minister of Aviation (Mr. Julian Amery) said the Government was keenly aware of the shock caused by the cancellation of *Blue Water*, particularly to the British Aircraft Corporation and its employees.

The Government's decision had been made because of the necessity for further economies in the defence programme, the increasing number and yield of tactical nuclear weapons which would be available in the later 1960's, and because hopes that *Blue Water* would be adopted by other NATO countries had not been realised. The efficiency of *Blue Water* was not in question, said Mr. Amery.

In reaching its decision the Government weighed very carefully the fact that commitments approaching £25 million had already been incurred on the development of the missile. But to have brought the weapon into service would have cost at least a further £50 million and possibly substantially more.

•

Replying to Mr. Roy Mason (Barnsley), the Secretary of State for Air (Mr. H. Fraser) said the Royal Air Force's transport force consisted at present of 23 Britannias, 11 Comets, 48 Hastings, 28 Beverleys, 12 Valettas, 10 Argosies, 12 Pioneers, 27 Twin Pioneers, 4 Pembrokes, 26 Whirlwinds, 10 Sycamores and 18 Belvederes.

•

Mr. Mason was told that in the year ending on 30 September, 1962, Royal Air Force Transport Command had flown 950 Servicemen home from the Middle and Far East for treatment of illness or serious injury. During the same period, 534 soldiers were evacuated by air from Rhine Army for medical reasons.

•

In reply to Colonel Sir Richard Glyn (Dorset, North) the War Minister (Mr. John Profumo) said that in the last ten years the Army had held three exercises involving two or more divisions and the use of tactical nuclear as well as conventional weapons. These were all in Germany. Exercises involving only one division had been more numerous. It was normal practice in exercises of this type for the umpires to assess casualties in relation to the weapons assumed to have been used.

•

Mr. Fraser told Mr. Mason that British United Airways had held, since 1 October, 1961, the contract for normal trooping between the United Kingdom and Germany and over the last 12 months an average of 314 flights per month had been made. During the same period it had been necessary to let some *ad hoc* charters for joint Service trooping to or from Germany to other airline operators. These firms, and the flights their aircraft made in the same 12 months were: Danair 63, Silver City 4, Derby Aviation 22, Cunard Eagle 5, Skyways 15, Lloyd International 9, Tradair 7 and BUA 4.

•

Replying to a number of questions by Mr. Mason, the War Minister said that in 1961 59 soldiers died in Germany, of whom 45 were buried there. In the Middle East 35 died, and in the Far East, 31. All but one of these were buried locally. During 1961 a total of 151 soldiers died in overseas stations. The cost of moving their bodies home by air would have been about £15,000, this figure not including the cost of providing coffins at the overseas stations, nor the cost of movement within the United Kingdom to the place of burial.

Perhaps the publicity given to Territorials spending their annual camp in Germany this year—the "Terriers" have long awaited the opportunity to train overseas—has tended to overshadow the "Ever-Readies", who have a most interesting and adventurous role. Potential recruits—who must necessarily be Territorials— have been unsure of the effect on their civilian employment of a call to service, and units have pondered how best to organise their "Ever-Readies" routine training. But more information has been given to employers, who are now giving their full support.

It is unfortunate that the widely publicised launching of this new Reserve was not more closely followed up. Within four months of recruiting opening, for example, 20 "Ever-Readies" of the West Riding Battalion, The Duke of Wellington's Regiment, flew to Germany to train with Regulars of the 1st Battalion,

The Prince of Wales's Own Regiment of Yorkshire. "Wouldn't have missed it for anything," "Send me again anytime" and "Shall we be going again next year?" are comments that sum up the Territorials' reactions.

Other "Ever-Readies" have enjoyed similar experiences and, more recently, men of The Queen's Royal Rifles and London Rifle Brigade Rangers practised combined operations with the Royal Navy, and helicopter assault techniques. It will not be long before the word spreads and applications to join this corps d'élite outnumber the vacancies.

•

Tailpiece: A Territorial Sapper found he had planned his honeymoon for the same time as his annual camp. He decided to forego the honeymoon. There's keenness for you!

SOLDIER
to Soldier

FEBRUARY, 1962, will be the beginning of a new and challenging era in the Army's history, for later this month the Government will announce Britain's defence plans for the next five years.

Not the least vital part of the new five-year plan is expected to be a decision on whether Britain should retain all, only some, or none of her overseas bases—a subject on which controversy has long raged in Parliament and Press.

For months past politicians, leader writers and military correspondents have been urging their own pet schemes. Some say that the Army cannot do its job properly if it does not hold on to all its present bases which, in any case, are politically necessary; others that all overseas bases should be abandoned before Britain is forced to quit; yet others that only a few, like Singapore and Aden, should be retained. Field-Marshal Viscount Montgomery advocates scrapping all overseas bases and replacing them with seaborne Commando groups based in Gibraltar, Aden, Perth (Australia) and either Singapore, Hong Kong or North Borneo, leaving the bulk of the Army in Britain as a mobile reserve.

In SOLDIER's view overseas bases will always be vital to Britain's strategy. They provide areas of British influence, are places where heavy weapons and equipment can be stock-piled and from which "fire brigade" forces can go quickly into action (as they did from Bahrain and Kenya during the recent Kuwait operation) in sudden emergencies. They can never satisfactorily be replaced by long-range air-transported forces which can carry with them only light weapons.

This does not mean, however, that the ability of the Strategic Reserve to fly anywhere in the world at short notice and in large numbers is not equally vital. Significantly, and presumably looking ahead to the time when some of Britain's present bases will have to be surrendered, the Defence Minister, Mr. Harold Watkinson, has said: "We must devise a new strategic policy, based on a flexible mobile force, more independent of the fixed installations on which we rely today."

★

A SOLDIER flown to torrid Aden from wintry Britain will suffer almost no ill effects from the heat if he is first artificially acclimatised.

This is one of the remarkable discoveries revealed by the heat acclimatisation tests carried out on 54 volunteer soldiers by the Medical Research Council in its "hot box" at Hampstead (see SOLDIER, December, 1960).

But, say the scientists and doctors who carried out the trials, there is one important proviso: for the treatment to be fully effective, the soldier must carry out his normal military training while being conditioned. It was the absence of such training at Hampstead that resulted in more men than was expected suffering from heat exhaustion when they went to the Middle East.

The 54 volunteers were divided into three squads, one going to Scotland, where they trained in cold, damp conditions, the second sailing to Aden so that they became acclimatised naturally during the voyage and on arrival. The third squad remained at Hampstead, spending four hours a day in the climatic chamber (temperature 104 degrees Fahrenheit, humidity about 70 per cent). After a month all the men were re-assembled at Hampstead, medically checked and flown to Aden where their military training included route marching and load carrying. Two weeks later they were flown back to London for their final scientific examinations.

During the trials in Aden very few of the men who had been naturally acclimatised went down from heat exhaustion and, as expected, the squad from Scotland suffered most (about three in every four). But of the men who had been through the "hot box" in Hampstead only two out of five were affected. Had they been able to carry out their normal military training while undergoing treatment, say the scientists, their acclimatisation would have been much more effective.

It is estimated that a week's climatic chamber treatment, plus normal military training, would produce 50 per cent acclimatisation, two weeks about 80 per cent and three weeks a somewhat higher percentage. The long-held belief that too much water is bad for a man in a hot climate was also disproved. Some of the men in Aden (who in Britain normally drink three pints of liquid a day) consumed more than three gallons each day.

There are obviously many important lessons which the Services will be able to learn from the Hampstead experiment. And not only the Services, for some of the findings will be passed on to industry and the sporting world.

LEARNING

"**N**O lights—no noise" were the orders. Sentries and listening posts took up their positions. As the desert night quickly closed in, the men of 4 Platoon withdrew into a deep *wadi* and waited . . .

In the early hours of the morning the terrorists attacked the Platoon's earlier position. The men of 4 Platoon lay silently alert, undetected in their new hide. Two hours later the terrorists attacked again, but with no more success.

Only three days previously these men of 4 Platoon—cadets

The men of 4 Platoon made their advance unseen along the bed of a deep *wadi*. Now, in two waves, they close in for the final assault on the terrorist defences.

LEADERSHIP IN THE DESERT

of the Royal Military Academy—were sitting in their classrooms at Sandhurst studying the theory of war. Now they were soldiering in the lonely wastes of the Libyan Desert, learning to live hard, to patrol in difficult country and to hunt down an elusive hit-and-run enemy.

This was "Beau Jest," Sandhurst's second overseas training visit and an exercise, in a setting not unlike that of the Kuwait operation, designed to give the cadets opportunities to show their leadership and endurance. In "Beau Jest's" second phase the 480 cadets, fighting as company groups in a battalion, attacked a "second class" enemy and then withdrew to a defensive position.

In the first phase the cadets fought as self-sufficient platoons, each with a sector of desert to clear of enemy terrorists. Typical of these groups was 4 Platoon, commanded by Junior Under-Officer Rufus Gunning and made up of senior cadets and the intermediate junior term of Sandhurst's Marne Company, with a section from Ypres Company commanded by a Southern Rhodesian cadet, Junior Under-Officer Glanville Raubenheimer.

Left: A section of the Platoon makes its way up the side of a *wadi*. Right: Advancing into the jebel. The stretcher bore a "casualty" on the 15-mile return march to Tarhuna base.

Vol. 18, No. 7

SOLDIER

SEPTEMBER 1962

T H E   B R I T I S H   ARMY   M A G A Z I N E

Libya, 4 piastres;   Cyprus, 40 mils;   Malaya, 30 cents;   Hong Kong, 60 cents;   East Africa, 75 cents;   West Africa, 9d.

Sixteen years ago the Army lost its Commandos. But today an Army badge again rests firmly on that proud green beret. Men of 29 Regiment, Royal Artillery, in their new role of supporting the Royal Marines, have become . . .

GUNNER COMMANDOS

THE Marine Commandos needed artillery support. They needed Gunners equally as fit and agile as themselves, capable of scaling the same cliffs, fording the same rivers, ploughing through the same bogs—and bringing their guns with them. It was a job for Commando Gunners.

Already part of the Strategic Reserve, 29 Regiment, Royal Artillery, was given the job, learning of it on the way back from the "fire brigade" action in Kuwait. It meant a complete reorganisation, with changes in role, training techniques and in armament. It meant that every man in the Regiment would have to tackle the punishing Commando course at Lympstone, 40 miles from the Regiment's new home in the Royal Citadel, Plymouth.

After a brief work-out, an advance party of three officers and a dozen non-commissioned officers, including all the physical training staff, went to Lympstone, took the Marines' Commando course and became the Gunners' Commando instructors. The five-week course was streamlined to three weeks for the Gunners. Pruning was achieved only by cutting out lectures and practical tests on Infantry subjects. All the tough, physical tests of courage and endurance were retained but packed into the shorter period.

Eighty Gunner officers and men were sent on the first Army Commando course since 1945. With little or no build-up they were flung into the most stringent man-made test of physical endurance and courage known to the Services. This diverse cross-section of the Royal Artillery, with its various ages, temperaments and Service backgrounds, donned its denims, gritted its teeth, and set out to show what it was made of.

Inevitably the course had its tragedies. Sometimes, though the spirit was determined, muscle-power was drained and weary feet pounded to a standstill. One of the Regiment's fittest and finest soldiers, a successful heavyweight boxer, burned up the course until it came to the heights, where he reluctantly accepted his most bitter defeat and retired to await his posting.

But there were triumphs too. Bombardier George

Without any cliff-scaling experience, Gunners have this decent to master after a few brief tips. It is just one hazard en route to the green beret.

GUNNER COMMANDOS continued

At a Larkhill demonstration the Gunner Commandos showed how they bring a 105-mm down a cliff. They had the gun down, assembled and ready for firing in under 14 minutes.

The fastest method of carrying a gun from ship to shore is slung under a helicopter.

Smith, aged 47, a veteran of 26 years' service, tackled the course with the best of the young ones. Only once—on the 30-mile trek across Dartmoor—did he need the ten per cent leeway allowed for those over 35.

Of the 79 Gunners on that first course, 51 came through, and of the 28 casualties, 15 succeeded at a second attempt. The second course, in March, showed a similar ratio. After the third and largest course—104 men —came the Regiment's big day.

Here the Gunners' versatile 105-mm, cocooned against the sea, enters an LCT on an amphibious exercise to France with 145 (Maiwand) Commando Battery and 43 Commando.

Bdr George Smith who, at 47, tackled the rugged Commando course with the fittest.

THE GURKHAS DROP AGAIN

AS a *Beverley* bumbled over Sembawang airfield on Singapore Island the doors opened, the red light turned to green and the despatchers roared: "Stand in the doors . . . GO!"

It was a history-making moment. For the first time for 17 years the Gurkhas were parachute jumping again. Two at a time from each of the two doors 20 men of the 1st Battalion, 10th Princess Mary's Own Gurkha Rifles flung themselves into space to float gently down to the dropping zone.

Every man made a perfect landing which, said Flight Lieutenant L. W. Brown, the chief instructor, was not surprising. "The Gurkha, with his light, compact body and strong legs, is ideally built for the job. He is probably the best natural paratrooper in the world."

The Gurkhas were students at the Royal Air Force's Far East Parachute and Survival School at Changi and the first of their countrymen to parachute since 153 Gurkha Parachute Brigade was disbanded in 1944.

Above: GO! and a Gurkha steps out into space, rapidly followed by a comrade while the Royal Air Force despatcher stands by. Below (left): The first Gurkha to parachute since 1944 swings gently to earth on Sembawang airfield.

Before jumping the Gurkhas had to become accustomed to their equipment. Here one gets the feel of a billowing parachute and learns how to collapse it.

After nearly five centuries of service in Portsmouth the Royal Army
Ordnance Corps is leaving to set up a new home in Blackdown

Thousands of troops began their Army service here in the Hilsea Barracks where once 15,000 soldiers paraded for an execution.

FAREWELL
AFTER 469 YEARS

The last sack of clothing is heaved aboard the last Corps lorry to leave the Hilsea Barracks.

IT was a sad and historic occasion when, a few days ago, the Royal Army Ordnance Corps' flag was lowered at Hilsea Barracks, Portsmouth, for the last time. It marked the end of the Corps' 469-year-long association with one of the Army's oldest garrison towns.

For nearly five centuries the Royal Army Ordnance Corps and its predecessors have served continuously in this great naval base and for the past 41 years Hilsea Barracks has been the Corps' spiritual home through which all but a few of its present members have passed. Now, the Regimental Depot there has left to join the Corps Training Centre at Blackdown, the Corps' new home.

The first home of the Ordnance in Portsmouth was at The Point, where, in 1493, the Board of Ordnance established an office and a wharf in which military stores were kept for King Henry VII's "most nobel armie on the *See* against His auncyient enemies and rebelles of Scotland."

For many years after that the Ordnance Depot in Portsmouth, second largest in Britain, was the base for expeditions against the Continent. One of its first tasks was to take charge of "sheefes of arrows, billes, bowestrings, serpynte powdre, sacres, falcons and fauconettes."

Later the Ordnance Wharf became the Gun Wharf (now HMS *Vernon*, the Royal Navy training school) and it was from there that the Board's officers and men—then civilians appointed by the Master-General of Ordnance—re-supplied British ships

In the 1700s the Board of Ordnance ships at Portsmouth bore the Ordnance Ensign and seal in the shape of a shield on which were three cannon and three cannon balls-the forerunner of the present-day Corps badge.

A tablet erected in 1708 bearing the cannon and balls *(right)* is still to be seen at Fort Blockhouse, once part of the Ordnance depot.

Several public houses in Portsmouth were also named after the Board of Ordnance and its activities-among them "The Three Guns" and "Ordnance Arms."

KEEPING

Sappers of the postal service, on their regular round of London's main stations, pick up another late-night batch from Kings Cross.

THE tempo at Mill Hill is quickening. The heart of the British Army Postal Service is beating faster, coping with the mounting flow of Christmas mail pouring into the London rail and air termini, and speeding it to British Servicemen all over the world.

Inglis Barracks, at Mill Hill in North London, house the Home Postal Depot, Royal Engineers, a fully-operational military village, streamlined and geared to match the new mobile Army of the Sixties and carry its mail swiftly to the four corners of the earth.

This Christmas, only the second at the new Mill Hill centre, the men and women of the postal service are out to see that 23717980 Private Smith, J. gets his Christmas cheer from home more quickly and certainly than ever before. A mechanical handling system that is second to none in Britain, and a keen and efficient staff, are ready to take the Christmas mail avalanche in their stride.

This will mean receiving, sorting and dispatching some

Army needs a slick and adaptable postal service.
at Mill Hill is geared to the Army's postal needs

THE ARMY POSTED

33 million items over the lengthy seasonal period, compared with a normal weekly turnover of about half a million.

Even that normal weekly figure represents an unceasing flow into the sorting office, a vast former anti-aircraft ordnance workshop, now the centre of a gigantic web, throbbing with movement by land, sea and air.

The magic letters "BFPO" take an item, wherever posted in the United Kingdom, into a mailbag bound for Mill Hill. When that bag arrives at one of the London rail or air termini, the Army takes over.

Three-tonners of the postal service call every two hours at London's stations, airports and main post offices collecting mail—intended for Army, Royal Air Force and sometimes Naval personnel overseas—for the Mill Hill sorting office. Here the mail begins a short but vital stage of its journey —by hooks attached to an endless belt that weaves round the lofty sorting office.

The secret of this part-manual, part-mechanical channelling of the mail to the sorting points lies in a simple arrangement of coloured hooks. The Sapper unloading the mailbags attaches each one to its appropriate coloured hook—green for letters, blue for parcels, yellow for insured parcels and red for the "final letter bag" containing registered items and dispatch instructions. As each bag arrives above its sorting point the hook releases the mail and detailed sorting begins.

The staff of the Depot work in three eight-hour shifts. Busiest shift is through the night when 60 per cent of the mail is sorted and sped on its way. A staff of 50, including 29 Women's Royal Army Corps personnel, work on the night shift, many of them permanently. During the day the sorting staff is cut to 35—but not at Christmas-time!

Day and night, strict schedules are maintained. Sapper drivers and couriers, speeding the outward mail on its way, are a familiar if unobtrusive sight at all airports and docks in the London area.

Unobtrusive, too, is the word for the men of the courier service, who provide a reliable and confidential link between Army commands and the War Office.

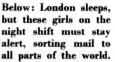

Right: Cpl Babs Jolley has had four years in Army postal work. She goes out to Hong Kong in March to help the Army Post Office there.

Below: London sleeps, but these girls on the night shift must stay alert, sorting mail to all parts of the world.

Above: Cpl William Sim (courier) and Cpl Stan Smith (guard) board the express at Kings Cross for Edinburgh.

Left: A quick slice of the knife frees more parcels to add to the avalanche for sorting.

Vol. 18, No. 1

SOLDIER

MARCH 1962

THE BRITISH ARMY MAGAZINE

Libya, 4 piastres; Cyprus, 40 mils; Malaya, 30 cents; Hong Kong, 60 cents; East Africa, 75 cents; West Africa, 9d.

A SOUTH SEAS

They're like overgrown Gurkhas, these men—and women—who have come from the Fiji Islands to join the British Army. They're keen, eager to become good soldiers and have quickly settled down to Army life. But they miss the sun!

BREEZE IN THE BARRACK ROOM

MIKAELE KILINIO YASA is cheerful, well-built, close on six feet tall and well-spoken. Only a few months ago he was an assistant land agent in his homeland of the Fiji Islands. Now he is a Rifleman in the Green Jackets, one of 200 Fijian men—and 12 women—who have travelled halfway across the world to join the British Army.

Of all the overseas recruits—there are West Indians, Seychellois and men from British Honduras, British Guiana and other parts of the Commonwealth helping to bring the Regular Army up to strength — the Fijians have stolen the limelight and, unaffected by publicity, endeared themselves to civilian and fellow soldier alike.

Nor is this merely because the Fijian recruit comes from a remote and romantic Pacific island group—nor because he can play a rattling good game of Rugby. It is because he is such a naturally cheerful and friendly character, intensely proud of being British and, as a soldier, possessing the same virtues which have earned for the Gurkha the deep respect of friend and foe.

Rifleman Yasa had a good, well-paid job but when an Army recruiting team visited Fiji he immediately applied to join up, simply for the opportunity to serve his Queen and country. This loyalty to the Crown, stemming from the days when Fiji's chiefs proudly asked Britain to take the islands under her wing, and exemplified by the service of Fijian troops during World War Two and in Malaya against the Communists, spurred hundreds to volunteer.

The recruiting team, led by Captain S. W. Hardcastle, Royal Artillery, a personnel selection officer at The Yorkshire Brigade Depot, tested more than 800 men and 50 women, all of them unmarried. The 200 men selected were mainly in the 18-21 age bracket and consequently half of them were students, as Fijians normally attend school to 18 or 19 when they then sit for the Senior Cambridge Certificate, a credit in

which is equivalent to Ordinary Level in the General Certificate of Education.

Of the other men, half were in Government service as Post Office workers, clerks and Public Works Department employees, and half in farming or such jobs as clerks, shop assistants and mechanics. Policemen and Regulars of the Fijian Military Forces were not recruited, with the exception of two soldiers who were just completing their initial service, but some of the older recruits have served in the Fijian Territorial Army or the now disbanded Fijian Navy.

Rifleman Yasa is more fortunate than most of the recruits. He went to Poona University and is one of the few—some studied in New Zealand—who had previously been abroad from Fiji. After the recruits had been shown films and given a talk on the Army by the recruiting team, they were asked to make a choice of three arms or corps.

In gay shirt and sulu *a Fijian burlesques the* hula. *He and fellow recruits in the RASC and RE were giving a concert of songs and dances.*

THE TATTOO THAT GROWS

THE reaction of members of the old Bath United Services Club to the first Bath Searchlight Tattoo must have been similar to that of Jack's mother when, after throwing the bag of beans out of the window, she awoke to find the beanstalk.

Eight years ago, when the club's finances were desperately low, a crisis meeting was called of leading Service personalities in the city—and someone suggested a tattoo. That first one-day event cost £300 to stage and

THE man but for whom there would be no Bath Tattoo is Colonel G. D. Kersley, present chairman of its executive committee. Colonel Kersley, then president of Bath United Services Club, called the original meeting at which the idea of a Tattoo was first voiced.

Captain Aubrey Jackman, a staff captain at HQ 43 (Wessex) Division, TA, has been Tattoo Director since its inception. After World War Two he formed and directed the Band of 138th Infantry Brigade in Austria, and after leaving the Army was for several years a theatre stage director.

it made a clear profit of more than £1,000.

Every year the Tattoo has expanded until it is now the largest to be presented annually in England. This year's Tattoo, to be staged later this month in the attractive tree-fringed arena in Royal Victoria Park, Bath, has cost £12,000—40 times the cost of the first one —and for the first time it is being recognised by the three Services.

While heavy costs have killed similar events in recent years, the Bath Tattoo flourishes. Bookings have poured in, not only from all over the West Country, but from as far as Germany, Holland, and the Scandinavian countries. Since 1956, when the event was taken over by the Bath United Services Charities Appeal, many Service charities have benefited.

Overhead expenses have been kept down by an immense amount of voluntary work under a committee of serving and ex-Service men and women of all three Services. Sub-committees handle site lay-out, erection of stands, seating, tentage, lighting and publicity. A team of ten housewives deals with hundreds of postal bookings and distribution of tickets to agents, staffs a full-time booking office in Bath and mans the ticket offices at the Tattoo gates.

Lighting is controlled and manned by

members of the Electrical Engineering Division of the Admiralty's Ship Department at Bath. The Signals Section of Bath Civil Defence Corps provides telephone and wireless communications and the Auxilliary Fire Service mans a fire station on the site, with firemen forming an arena working party.

The Civil Defence Welfare Section staffs the canteen, where there are free meals for all troops taking part, and the Women's Voluntary Services have other canteens on the site.

The Bath Tattoo has been lucky with its weather and one bad year—1958—proved a blessing in disguise. Until then the Tattoo had been staged on a recreation ground where county Rugby matches are played. But in 1958 constant rain softened the turf and the Tattoo committee had to pay £1,000 for returfing. As a result the event was transferred to the Royal Victoria Park.

Last year's Tattoo brought in a record profit of more than £2,000, but expenses are increasing while the audience capacity is unchanged. Professional impressarios would hesitate to stage an outdoor event which required a 75 per cent capacity attendance to break even. But the Bath organisers are convinced they can put on a fine show and still make a profit for charities.

THE "VIKINGS" ON

ADOPTING THE NICKNAME, "THE VIKINGS," THE 1ST BATTALION, 1ST EAST ANGLIAN REGIMENT, IS COMBING ITS HOME COUNTIES, IN A CAREFULLY-PLANNED MILITARY OPERATION, FOR THE RECRUITS IT NEEDS

This striking notice dominates the entrance to Dovercourt Camp. The Viking's head flash, once worn by East Anglian District, has now been adopted by the 1st East Anglian Regiment.

THE VIKINGS

"CORPORAL SMITH, take your section to 'The Crown and Anchor' and send a couple of chaps along to the coffee bar. Corporal Brown, I want your men to spend the evening in the public bar of 'The Fox and Hounds' and call at the fish and chip shop later."

Driving men to drink, you say? Hardly that, but certainly an unusual detail for a soldier although it is one to which Regulars of the 1st Battalion, 1st East Anglian Regiment, have become accustomed.

Not long ago the Battalion was in Berlin, well under strength and demobilising men faster than it received recruits. Then the War Office ordered: "Come home, go out and get recruits and bring yourselves up to

Canoes have been popular as a "try-it-yourself" feature of recruiting sorties. They attracted a good deal of attention on Oulton Broad when simultaneously capsized. Here "A" Company "shoot a bridge in Lowestof

Men of Support Company set up a *Wombat* anti-tank gun to cover Soham's 0 main street. Only schoolboys stop to watch but they are potential recruits!

Photographs:
SOLDIER Cameraman
FRANK TOMPSETT

In the recruiting operations room Maj E. W. A. Power (left) and Capt S. G. Beck, Battalion public relations officer, discuss the campaign.

Normal training goes on—sometimes in odd settings—when the men are out on sorties. Here's a mortar problem viewed from a stove-warmed park seat.

THE MARCH AGAIN

establishment. You have a year in which to find 350 men."

Accepting the challenge, the Battalion started by making its new name known at home—people in its recruiting areas were still thinking in terms of the pre-amalgamation Royal Norfolk and Suffolk regiments—as a prelude to an all-out recruiting operation.

Taking command of the Battalion in Berlin, Lieutenant-Colonel A. F. Campbell MC opened his campaign by appointing Captain S. G. Beck, helped by a sergeant, as public relations officer and sending Lieutenant R. D. Gowing, a company sergeant-major and a corporal to the East Anglian Brigade Depot in Bury St. Edmunds to initiate a publicity drive at home.

The Battalion adopted a nickname—"The Vikings"—which caught on as quickly with the soldiers as with the local newspaper editors, television and radio teams who were invited out to Berlin, and which strengthened the ties with East Anglia where the original Vikings raided and settled between the 6th and 10th centuries. The "Vikings" went all out for success in work and sport and there was plenty of material for the Press from activities in the crisis city, ski-ing in Germany and Austria, climbing in Bavaria, sailing and canoeing in Norway and a training visit to Denmark. "The Viking Bulletin," the Battalion's own news sheet, kept local papers up to date.

As part of the eight-month "softening-up" campaign, the Band and Drums and a demonstration platoon of 50 men were sent home from Berlin to tour Norfolk, Suffolk, Cambridgeshire and the Isle of Ely, publicising the Battalion and gleaning information for the main recruiting drive to come. The detachment's Viking military pageant, which included a Viking raid, a World War One scene, a World War Two patrol and a display of modern warfare, played to village audiences and to 20,000 people at Oulton Broad Regatta.

When the 1st East Anglian Regiment came home to Dovercourt Camp, Harwich, an enormous amount of goodwill had already been created and the "Vikings" were accepted as friends and not as a new and unknown battalion.

From their embarkation leave the "Vikings" brought back more information —about local reactions to an Army career and local employment conditions—and the names of 90 likely recruits. All was ready for the third stage, of showing people the Army at work.

The Battalion reorganised into four companies. Headquarters Company took on the administrative work and the Regular soldiers of "A" Company and Support Company were to go out on sorties. National Servicemen were put into "C" Company to remain in Dovercourt with a mixed programme of camp duties and military training.

This was the first time an Infantry battalion had been relieved of all other commitments to carry out a recruiting drive and the first time recruiting had been tackled as a military operation.

A recruiting operations centre was set up in Dovercourt Camp and here Major E. W. A. Power and his staff plotted the 1200 contacts, from town clerks to barbers, ex-soldiers and Territorials, whose help had been enlisted by the home recruiting team. The Battalion's intelligence section took over the collection and collating of recruiting information and case histories were prepared for every potential recruit.

here's nothing like a game of dominoes and a glass of good ale for breaking the ice when you're wooing likely recruits in the "local."

Meanwhile, back at the Depot—in the East Anglian Brigade's display workshop— L/Cpl R. T. Codling works on a diorama. NB: The soldier (left) has NOT fainted!

MILITARY MEDLEY

The eight old Colours of the Royal Lincolnshires and Northamptonshires are trooped for the last time—on the square of the 2nd East Anglian Regiment at Osnabruck.

The Mayor of St. Albans (Mrs. I. E. Stebbings) with General Sir Evelyn Barker DSO, MC, Honorary Colonel of 286 Regiment, Royal Artillery (Territorial Army) (The Hertfordshire and Bedfordshire Yeomanry) at the ceremony of granting to the Regiment the freedom of entry to the city. The Regiment paraded with its guns and light vehicles, the Mayor taking the salute.

FAREWELL TO THE OLDEST COLOURS

IT was an occasion without precedence and unlikely to be repeated when eight Colours of the 1st Battalion, 2nd East Anglian Regiment (Duchess of Gloucester's Own Royal Lincolnshire and Northamptonshire), were trooped for the last time at the Battalion's barracks in Osnabruck, Germany.

The eight Colours included the oldest in service, those of the 2nd Battalion, 10th Foot (Royal Lincolnshire Regiment), now 103 years old, and those of the 58th Foot (Northamptonshire Regiment), only a year

younger, and the last Colours to be officially carried into action by a British regiment —at the battle of Laings Nek on 28 January 1881. The third set, of the 1st Battalion, 10th Foot, were in their 100th year of service, and the fourth set, of the 48th Foot (1st Battalion, Northamptonshire Regiment) in their 73rd year.

Their place was taken by new Colours presented by the Duchess of Gloucester, Colonel-in-Chief of the new Regiment and formerly of The Northamptonshire Regiment.

Men of the 1st Battalion, Scots Guards, made history when their company, due to take part in an exercise with cadets from Ardingley College in Sussex, moved from Milton Barracks at Gravesend to Elizabeth Barracks at Pirbright. Instead of travelling by road or rail the 100 Guardsmen flew to Surrey in RAF *Belvederes.*

A scorer's eye view of the scene on Folkestone Cricket Ground when Prince Frederick IX of Denmark, Colonel-in-Chief of The Queen's Own Buffs, The Royal Kent Regiment, presented new colours to the 1st Battalion. Queen Ingrid and Princess Marina, Colonel of the Regiment, also attended this historic ceremony.

1963

Professionals again

Despite the Arctic weather conditions that heralded the arrival of the New Year and brought most of the country to a standstill, 1963 was a hot and busy year for the British Army.

The heat came largely from the "Borneo Emergency" which was a rather nasty confrontation with Indonesian forces on the borders of Borneo, Brunei and Sarawak in the Far East. The emergency had begun at the latter part of the previous year when this part of the British Empire had been granted independence and neighbouring Indonesia expressed territorial ambitions over various parts of the new Federated sovereign states.

Whilst this emegency kept several thousand troops busy, others were involved in the many overseas and BAOR based exercises that made up the annual training year. Some were also very busy assisting with disaster relief work in Libya. Indeed, apart from the wide range of overseas garrisons that were spread around the world, British troops could be found exercising as far afield as Thailand, USA and Norway, thus living up to their new "professional" status and advertising slogans of "see the world with the British Army".

Finally, 1963 was the year that saw the very last of the National Servicemen depart and the scrapping of the Troopships that had carried so many of them so far. The very last of the line - HMT "Nevassa" was withdrawn from service after her final voyage during the early part of the year bringing troops home from East Africa. From now on "Air trooping" - a whole new concept in travelling, would be the way the "professional" regular soldiers of the British Army and their families would see the world.

RAID ON TEBEDU

Major-General W C Walker DSO, Commanding British Forces in Borneo, had forecast weeks before that the next rebel attack would be at Easter. And Good Friday was only two hours old when the raiders, after a four-month lull since Brunei, struck in Sarawak. SOLDIER'S team was on the spot to report on the classic British "fire brigade" action

Commando reserves, called forward from Kuching, emplane in *Wessex* helicopters on the flight deck of the Commando carrier, HMS *Albion*. The carrier had sailed from Singapore with men of the 2nd/10th Gurkha Rifles.

Royal Marines of "L" Company, 42 Commando, and civil police, visited houses and shops, asking occupants to produce their shotguns and ammunition. The police wrote out details of weapons, then issued official receipts.

CORPORAL John Remek, Sarawak Police, 30-year-old father of four boys, sat alone at his desk in the charge office of Tebedu Police Station, three miles from the Indonesian border. He was about halfway through his night's duty when the raiders burst in. He made a dash for the passage behind him to sound the alarm, but covered only three strides when the shot rang out, and he reeled as the fatal bullet hit him.

Another band of raiders burst into the nearby sleeping quarters. As Corporal Joseph moved to resist, a bullet snicked his right ear, another cut through his hip. As Constable Anyau moved in support, he was shot in the arm.

The shots awoke Inspector Reginald Chimbon, head of the station, in his separate accommodation within the compound, and shots missed him narrowly as he dashed out. He fired back from beneath his stilted quarter then leapt for cover into a water tank.

The raiders had entered stealthily via an open drain running beneath the ten-foot wire fence. At the rear of the compound they had simply uprooted the fence and crawled beneath it. Having stripped the armoury of its *Bren* gun and 11 rifles they left boldly, "shooting up" the nearby bazaar, looting, and finally disappearing into the jungle.

The first militant action in North Borneo since the Brunei flare-up in December was ended. It was not to be the last—but next time British forces would be waiting.

Word reached Lieutenant-Colonel

2nd Division and the Gurkhas into the more remote 3rd Division. *Albion* was anchored off shore with a company of 40 Commando aboard and the big *Wessex* helicopters of 845 Naval Air Squadron were standing by to speed them wherever they might be needed. Six *Whirlwind* helicopters of 846 Naval Air Squadron had flown in to Kuching in impressive formation, the day after the raid, to reinforce 656 Squadron, Army Air Corps. Headquarters of 3 Commando Brigade also moved in and Brigadier F C Barton took over command from Colonel Strawson.

Tebedu had been the spark that alerted British military forces in North Borneo, but it was not the sole reason for the moves. The raid could easily have been a signal for united action by subversive forces inside and outside North Borneo at a time when progress towards Malaysia was reaching a critical stage.

Evidence had been pouring in of preparations for an armed resistance by the secret Communist organisation of Sarawak, the CCO. Groups of young Chinese had been disappearing from their homes and establishing camps in the jungle, learning jungle survival and receiving elementary arms training. In at least one instance a group received training in the use of automatic weapons

COVER PICTURE

SOLDIER's front cover this month shows a corporal of the Royal Corps of Signals—he is a radio technician, heavy—working on an E 10 transmitter at the Royal Signals Experimental Station, Droitwich.

which must have been brought in from outside Sarawak.

J M Strawson, The Queen's Royal Irish Hussars, Military Commander, West Sarawak, 68 miles away at Kuching, by 4 am. Six Troop of 40 Commando, Royal Marines, under Lieutenant Douglas Keelan, set out from Serian, covering the tortuous three-hour, 30-mile drive in the Hussar's *Land-Rovers*, organising the local home guard and arranging defences.

Confirmation reached General Walker at Brunei soon after dawn. By 8.30 am the Command's "fire brigade" force— "A" Company, The King's Own Yorkshire Light Infantry—was alerted. By lunchtime the advance party was aboard a Royal Air Force *Valetta* heading for Kuching.

After top-level conferences it was decided to reinforce from Singapore rather than from Brunei, and 40 Commando and "L" Company of 42 Commando were flown in while the 2nd Battalion, 10th Princess Mary's Own Gurkha Rifles left Singapore aboard the Commando ship, HMS *Albion*. From Brunei a Royal Army Service Corps tank landing craft, diverted from its normal Labuan-Brunei run, sailed for Kuching with transport and supplies for the "fire brigade" company, and with men of Lloyds Troop, 20 Regiment, Royal Artillery, on board.

The Commandos and "C" Squadron of the Hussars moved into the 1st Division of Sarawak, "A" Company of the Yorkshire Light Infantry into the

Men of The Queen's Royal Irish Hussars check a lorry at a road block on a bridge near Kuching.

Story by **PETER DAVIE:**

Cpls Curly Couperthwaite, Royal Signals, and Frank Barrett, Royal Canadian Signals (arms up), worked together throughout the visit. Here Sgmn Pete Hardman watches as they erect an aerial.

A dust haze shrouds th rolling wooded countr side of Canada's Gagetow Camp as vehicles and me move stealthily forward

The rare luxury of bein able to chop down trees in spired The Queen's Ow Buffs to build a camp e picturesque log cabin

Pte Tommy Corbett selec the chicken stew out of Canadian ration pack, a the handy petrol stov heats water for a "brew.

LOGGING INDUSTRY

In an old farmhouse in the heart of the exercise area a highly specialised team of defence scientists, officers and men, all from the Canadian Army Operational Research Establishment, set out to record the whole of the ten-day Exercise "Tribulation" in detail.

After recording "everything that could be measured" and collecting the operational logs of every unit involved in the exercise, the team returned to Ottawa to begin months of sifting and analysing to produce statistics that will help give a commander in the field the probable result of almost any given encounter.

"We are not trying to run a soldier's war from the back room," said

Pictures by **PETER O'BRIEN**

Lieutenant-Colonel Donald Holmes, who led the field unit, "but we do aim to provide him with a fair summary of the odds in a given situation. Then he can play it from there."

The Establishment has an arrangement to exchange information with similar organisations in Britain and America.

Training with a BITE

MOSQUITOES bit, boots pinched, and the rain deluged down. Soaked and weary, a rifle platoon trudged on over miles of rough Canadian bush while their comrades laboured to fashion storm-proof and gnat-proof bivouacs that were to be their homes for the next six weeks. The views of the men of The Queen's Own Buffs varied only in depth of feeling: If this was Canada, the Canadians could keep their great big cotton pickin' country!

Kent's County Regiment, part of Britain's Strategic Reserve, had flown to Canada to share the Canadian Army's summer training at Camp Gagetown, the thickly wooded 427 square miles of training area in New Brunswick. They chose to plunge straight into training, each rifle platoon setting off on a tough 20-mile marching exercise within 24 hours of arrival. Plunge was the word for one rifle company, which suffered a constant ten-hour downpour.

The ferocity of the mosquito attack took the British Battalion Group completely by surprise, and also surprised the Canadians who have built up some natural protection against the virus. Bites swelled alarmingly, about half a dozen British troops needed hospital treatment and many more were treated by the Royal Army Medical Corps detachment with the Battalion.

To add to all this the entire Battalion was breaking in new boots. To save the indignity of boarding and leaving the Royal Air Force *Britannias* wearing plimsolls and with their studded boots—studs are banned aboard *Britannias*—slung round their necks, The Queen's Own Buffs acquired their supply of the new welded rubber sole boots just before departure. The resulting equation: New boots plus rugged Canadian bush equals blisters!

But finally the sun came out, blisters healed, gallons of repellent began to keep the gnats at bay and British troops began to see the brighter side of Canada. Choppable trees were an unaccustomed luxury giving a new dimension to bivouacking. Eminently habitable log cabins sprung up all over the bivouac area, and the Battalion's vehicles became the most lavishly camouflaged in Canada.

The British boys found too that they were getting on famously with the Canadian Army, mess visiting mess, troops exchanging visits, and, at work, the British troops learning to fight alongside Canadian armoured units, use Canadian vehicles and support weapons, and fit into Canada's 3rd Infantry Brigade Group just like any Canadian battalion.

The training area itself—at first dismissed as a "Salisbury Plain with trees"—proved full of interest and challenge. After coming successfully to terms with it—despite the blisters—the Battalion switched to all-arms training with the Canadians, practised night and day assaults with Canadian tanks, learned to use Canadian assault boats and to build and launch a Canadian Infantry assault bridge.

Exercise "Blind Man's Buff" (a neat tribute to The Queen's Own) saw the Battalion giving a good account of itself in an anti-guerilla operation in which men of the famous Royal 22e Regiment (the "Van Doos") from Quebec formed the enemy. The British soldiers' experience in this kind of warfare gave them the edge in this and the Canadians admitted to picking up a few wrinkles on deployment and on the handling of prisoners.

But naturally the British Battalion Group, training with 11,000 Canadian troops—a fifth of the Canadian Army—profited greatly from the exercises. The Royal Army Service Corps detachment—"A" Platoon of 1 Company—drove *jeeps*, three-quarter tonners (for which they had nothing but praise) and the "deuce and a half," on the right-hand side of the road in strict dusk-to-dawn black-outs which permitted only a pinpoint of side and rear light.

Five men of the Royal Signals linked the British Battalion with its Canadian Brigade headquarters, working closely with Canadian signalmen, and men of "A" Company, 1st Battalion, 3rd East Anglian Regiment, found parts of the training area equally as rugged as the Malayan jungle they had left 12 months before. (The East Anglians joined The Queen's Own Buffs for the trip, adding a rifle platoon to each company to match the Canadian battalions.)

The *Oxfordshire*—last of a long line of troopships. Fitted with many of the amenities of an ocean liner, she was the Army's finest trooper.

Above: The scene that has faded into the past. Loaded with equipment, soldiers file up a gangway on to a troopship. Below: A pontoon school on the troopdeck. Hammocks were later replaced by comfortable bunks.

In World War Two even the *Queen Elizabeth* carried troops. Here 14,000 American veterans cram her decks.

THE LAST

TROOPSHIPS HAVE CARRIED BRITISH SOLDIERS ROUND THE WORLD FOR THREE CENTURIES. NOW THE LAST NOSTALGIC VOYAGE HAS BEEN MADE.

OF THE LINE

A HEAVING line snaked from the proud white bows looming above the quayside at Southampton. In the gathering dusk a military band played carols as the giant ropes were pulled ashore. A long blast from the siren on the yellow funnel echoed round the docks as the tugs churned away. Troop Transport *Oxfordshire* was safely berthed. Another historic chapter in the annals of the British Army had ended.

For troopships are finished. The *Oxfordshire*, 20,586 tons, the fastest, biggest and best trooper the Army ever had, was also the last. Her arrival at Southampton from Malta with the 1st Battalion, The Royal Highland Fusiliers, signified the end of an era. With her charter prematurely ended, the *Oxfordshire* has been returned to her owners. All trooping is now by air—it is both quicker and cheaper.

The Pipes, Drums and Bugles of the Fusiliers had struck up as the ship entered the Solent. The stirring sound drifted across the channel and prompted an occasional cheery wave as the *Oxfordshire* nosed into Southampton Water. Appropriately, the daylight faded as she nuzzled up to her berth and the last red glimmerings of a pale winter sun silhouetted the stark dockyard skyline.

As the tugs nudged the great white ship into place, 500 soldiers let out a roar that must have been heard in their home towns of Glasgow and Ayr. The 156 families and 520 officers and men were more concerned about being home after three years abroad than being on the voyage that ended an era. But for her crew and the old soldiers aboard, it was a sad day.

On the quay a small welcoming party waited and listened to the carols. Cranes lifted the cumbersome companionways and linked the ship with the shore in the last symbolic act of berthing the last troopship after its last voyage. Welcoming officials, including the Provost of Ayr, stepped aboard and messages were read from Princess Margaret, the Colonel-in-Chief of the Regiment, the Lord Provost of Glasgow and Provost William Cowan of Ayr. The *Oxfordshire*'s last nostalgic voyage had ended quietly without pomp or ceremony.

Throughout the voyage, soldiers on all decks had maintained a constant argument about the merits and demerits of future trooping by air. It was an argument that will continue in barrack room and mess for many a year.

Colour-Sergeant Robert Atkinson estimated that half the Battalion were very much in favour of air trooping and the other half equally against it. Regimental Sergeant-Major Noel Kisbee was looking forward to trooping by air. . . . Major Denis Halstead swore they would all regret the change. Sergeant George "Sailor" Watson, who once served in the Royal Navy, was surprisingly glad that sea trooping had ended . . . while Lance-Corporal Murdo Nicholson bemoaned the end of shipboard friendships. So the arguments went on ceaselessly into the night as *Oxfordshire* steamed home.

Lieutenant-Colonel John Harrington MC, Ship's Commandant of the *Oxfordshire* during her last year (and very much against air trooping) retired after her last voyage.

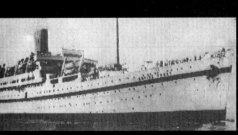

EMPIRE FOWEY

DUNERA

NEVASA

EMPIRE CLYDE

DEVONSHIRE

EMPIRE ORWELL

EMPIRE KEN

DILWARA

ASTURIAS

There's a breathless hush...
As the boot comes down—
Not a thundering crush
That would shake a town,
Nor a steel-shod heel,
On a crisp right wheel,
Clattering and sparking on a concrete square.
For the leather sole has gone
And there's rubber welded on—
Silence is the order now, so stamp who dare!

THERE'S A CLAMP ON THE

AN unfamiliar silence is descending on the Army's drill squares. The familiar crack of countless studded boots being brought down smartly on concrete parade grounds is on the way out. For the first quantity deliveries of boots with rubber composition soles have been made—and the sound of marching feet is fading fast.

Rarely has a change of equipment provoked so much public emotion. It is almost a year since the Army announced that leather-soled boots were to be replaced—and the indignation lingers still.

Drill sergeants turned purple at the news . . . Chelsea pensioners shook their heads sadly . . . and old soldiers throughout the country blanched at the thought. Only the Guards put their foot down firmly and announced that, despite the march of progress, they would continue to wear old-fashioned LOUD boots for duty. It was some small consolation.

But rubber-soled boots had to come. They are cheaper, last longer and are more comfortable. So despite public opinion the Army stood firm and ordered 417,140 pairs.

The ancestor of today's Army boot was introduced in 1913. Before this, handsewn *Bluchers* (old-fashioned high shoes named after a Prussian field-marshal) were issued. But with the world on the brink of a war these could never be manufactured in sufficient quantities, and the mass-produced Army ankle boot was born.

Perhaps unlike any other item of their equipment, soldiers regard their boots with something approaching affection. The great, black, stiff things that crippled raw recruits soon became supple enough for them to march for miles without discomfort.

At home and abroad, in the greatest wars the world has ever seen, "boots, ankle, general service" stood up to the test. During World War Two, 70 million pairs were made in Britain's blacked-out factories and three million pairs were supplied to the Russian Army.

An old encyclopedia describes a boot as "one of a pair of coverings for the lower extremities of the body." But it's not quite that simple. The Army has boots, mountaineering; boots, marching, ski; boots, ankle, patrolling; boots, rubber, jungle; boots, cold, wet; boots, motor cyclist; boots, rubber, thigh, and a host of others. Special footwear for special jobs makes the British Army one of the best shod in the world.

An immense amount of research and experiment goes into the production of the Army's footwear and the War Office has now accumulated such a wealth of experience that foreign attachés frequently ask for advice on design, manufacture and supply of Service footwear.

Old soldiers can recall being first issued with a pair of brown boots of untanned leather which had to be blackened, while more recent recruits remember toiling with candles, irons and bone handles to remove the wretched, persistent pimples on a pair of chrome leather boots.

No National Serviceman will forget evenings of melted polish, spit, small circles, aching forefingers and the frus-

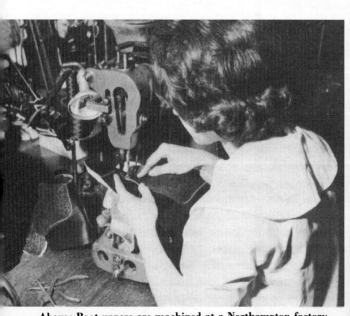

Above: Boot uppers are machined at a Northampton factory.
Right: This craftsman has about 20 tacks in his mouth all day.

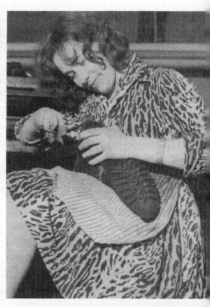

Beauty and the boot? After welding the rubber sole is trimmed by hand.

The Brigade of Guards put its foot down firmly in a stand against the new boots—and still wears old "loud" boots on duty.

CLUMP!

trations involved in getting that mirror-like finish that seemed just about the most important thing in their lives. Much of the blame for thinking up that lot can be laid at Beau Brummel's door—when serving in the 10th Hussars he insisted that soles of boots should be polished and discovered that the most brilliant shine was obtained by mixing boot blacking with finest champagne.

The first mass-produced boots of 1913 have remained basically unaltered except for minor modifications like ammunition boots, which were made with reinforced toecaps and studless boots so that drivers' feet would not slip on pedals.

During the Korean campaign a new *mukluk* boot was introduced, made of water repellent canvas with rubber soles for dry, cold weather. In Malaya, the 1st Battalion, The Loyal Regiment, wore out 10,000 pairs of jungle boots. Gurkhas, also fighting terrorists in the Malayan jungle, wore hockey boots in preference to jungle boots when they found that hockey boots left the same imprint as the terrorists' boots.

Rubber-soled boots made their appearance in the Army during World War Two when Commandos used them for night raids—ordinary boots were too noisy. The major difference now is that the composition rubber sole is vulcanised direct on to the upper.

The new boots underwent extensive trials in different climates and terrain all over the world. In England they were tested artificially in hot and cold chambers while, on a boot track, soldiers "marched them" over different surfaces to test their durability.

Soldiers should feel the benefit of the new boots in that they are more comfortable, do not need "breaking in" and the toecap and heel counter are of smooth leather—no more boning.

At John White's factory in Northamptonshire, where more than half the new boots are being made, production has reached 6,000 pairs a week. The boots start as a "side" of leather; the upper components are cut out, stitched together and fixed on a last and finally the sole is vulcanised direct to the upper.

During the whole operation only one

job is done by hand—by a man who spends his days with a mouthful of tacks spitting them out and hammering the upper to the last. The inevitable did once happen when one of these men nonchalantly crammed a handful of needle-sharp tacks into his mouth . . . and gulped! He swallowed the lot, but apparently soon recovered.

A major problem in the development of the new boot was its effect on the health of the feet. Porous leather soles allow ventilation; composition soles do not. The problem was overcome by providing a porous nylon sock in the boot which allows air to circulate around the foot.

So despite the scarlet expletives of purple drill sergeants, "quiet" boots are here to stay. The Duke of Wellington once declared: "The most important item of equipment for a soldier is first, a good, serviceable pair of boots; second, another pair of boots; and third a pair of half soles." Half soles won't be needed now but, loud or quiet, the new boots should fill the bill as the soldier's most important item of equipment.

Off and on-duty footwear. Incredibly, soldiers wear either without discomfort.

And this is how the new boots should NOT end up. These worn soles would produce some harsh words from an NCO.

THE Scots dreamed up a novel use for boots, in the sixteenth and seventeenth centuries, as an instrument for extorting confessions. Made of iron, they were fixed to the victim's feet and legs and a wedge was driven between the boot and the leg. If the luckless victim refused to answer, the wedge was driven in deeper with a mallet. In 1591 this torture was described as "the most severe and cruell paine in the world."

Stories from reports by
Michael S Simon, pictures by
Sergeant M Parsons, Army
Public Relations, Libya.

FOCUS ON

The British garrison in Liby
but our troops, still plague
sand, find life remains f

Banking and climbing high over Wavell Barracks, Benghazi, home of the 14th/20th King's Hussars, an *Auster* of the Regiment's new Army Air Corps section leaves on another mercy flight over the Libyan Desert. Since the Hussars became airborne earlier this year with the delivery of two *Austers* and promise of a third, the versatile aircraft have flown hundreds of miles to evacuate casualties hurt on exercises deep in the desert. Though the Regiment had no previous knowledge of aircraft, the section has been built up from scratch. The Flight Commander, Captain Henry Joynson, 16th/5th Lancers, who is starting his second tour with the Army Air Corps, hopes to train men from each squadron of the Hussars in aircraft techniques.

Men of the 14th/20th King's Hussars are spending much of their spare time excavating a Byzantine fort, probably built around AD 300-400. Well-preserved walls and staircases have been found and the entrance to the fort uncovered. The structure is about 65 feet square and it is believed that the walls were between 16 and 20 feet high. The Commanding Officer of the Regiment, Lieutenant-Colonel G A L C Talbot (in trilby), is shown visiting the site at Tika, ten miles from Benghazi.

Latest recruit to the 14th/20th King's Hussars' Army Air Corps Section is Private Cassius—a donkey. Cassius was bought for £7 from an Arab trader by Corporal Michael Wilcox, an aircraft technician in the section. After Corporal Wilcox had gained special permission to keep Cassius (christened after boxer Cassius Clay) the donkey was given a billet on the airstrip and has become a firm favourite with the section. Corporal Wilcox comments: "I wanted a camel, but it was too expensive!"

LIBYA

no longer a big one
the same flies and
interest — and news

Men of "C" Company, 1st Battalion, The Green Howards, had the Libyan Desert for a stage and an audience of Libyan Army officers. The play, commissioned by the Libyan Government, was a 48-minute demonstration of platoon attack supported by armoured personnel carriers and *Ferret* scout cars of the 14th/20th King's Hussars. The two Benghazi-based units rehearsed for ten days to ensure that the action, staged at El Charruba, battle ground of former desert campaigns, was slick and realistic. The audience was given a commentary in Arabic, and also heard orders being passed between the armoured vehicles.

Acting Number Two in this Green Howards' mortar crew is Sergeant O Turner, from Michigan. Sergeant Turner was one of a detachment of United States Marines which travelled from Naples to Tripoli to share the 1st Battalion of the Yorkshire Regiment's celebrations for Alma Day. As well as taking part in weapon demonstrations, the Marines— 14 of them—marched with The Green Howards in the anniversary parade, for which Marine Sergeant Lewis E Cunningham took over a drum major's mace that the Marines had presented to The Green Howards 36 years ago when the two Regiments served together in the Shanghai Defence Force. The Americans spent a week with the Yorkshiremen, who provided a non-stop programme of training sessions and social events. In return the Marines entertained the officers and other ranks of The Green Howards to a cocktail party.

Corporal Louis Devey, helped by his three-year-old daughter, checks his car at the entrance to the Tripoli Services Car Club. Motoring in Libya, where the donkey cart and the camel are still the biggest road hazards, is an economical proposition for Servicemen as they have no purchase tax to pay. As a result, the two-year-old club has doubled its membership over the past 12 months—and 90 per cent of the 200 members own new cars! The club has its own ramp, bought with a gift of £250 from the Nuffield Trust, enabling members to maintain their cars cheaply and efficiently.

The weapon is a smoke-making machine; the enemy—millions of germ-carrying flies. Staff-Sergeant Alan Hecks, Royal Army Medical Corps, is attacking the suspected cause of a polio outbreak which had already killed two and paralysed 35 people. Lieutenant-Colonel R J P Blyth, Deputy Assistant Director of Army Health, called in by the Libyan health authorities, discovered the epidemic coincided with a rapid increase in the fly population. He promptly sent Warrant Officer Clifford Edwards, Staff-Sergeant Hecks and Sergeant Grant Davies, of 2 Hygiene Wing, Royal Army Medical Corps, Tripoli, on a fly-killing mission. Their first "fog" assault was estimated to have eliminated half the flies. The Colonel's next move was to intensify the immunisation campaign and 100,000 doses of British Trivalent oral vaccine were provided.

One of the many famous footballers in the Army—Frank Blunstone.

Brian Hewson set up a mile record that will still take some beating.

Albert Quixall is congratulated by Gen Crocker at an Army Cup Final.

SPORT

NATIONAL SERVICE LEAVES ITS MARK

The Army is going to miss its two year champions

NATIONAL Service brought the aristocrats of sport into the rank and file of the Army — men like John Charles, Bobby Charlton, Ted Dexter, Tony Lock, Joe Erskine, Henry Cooper, Brian Hewson, Ken Norris. . . . In football, National Service brought a golden era; in athletics, records tumbled regularly; the Army boxing team could battle with the best. . . . Now the Army has lost its conscripted sporting specialists—and the loss will be felt for some time.

Especially in football. Since the war the Army team had been made up entirely of National Servicemen, most of them professional footballers. There was also a second, largely professional side and a third, all-amateur team. Not a single Regular soldier made even the amateur side during conscription.

One of the Army's team of stars—Ronnie Clayton.

George Cooper (left) punishes Joe Erskine with a fierce left cross during an Army bout in 1953.

But this was not surprising, with a choice of such stars as Trooper John Charles, 12th Lancers; the late Duncan Edwards, a lance-corporal in the Royal Army Ordnance Corps; the late Tommy Taylor, a Gunner; Lance-Corporal Bobby Charlton, Ordnance Corps; Albert Quixall, Cliff Jones, Ronnie Clayton, Frank Blunstone, Jim Baxter and many others. With their help the Army played such sides as Everton, Aston Villa, Glasgow Rangers and Dundee, and put Army football in a very comfortable financial state.

Today's all-Regular side, after taking a few hidings as a result of that in-

herited fixture list, is starting from scratch with a revised programme, and is slowly finding its feet. But the stars are still sorely missed in matches against other NATO countries still benefiting from conscription.

In athletics the National Serviceman has built a formidable fortress of records that could stand firm for years. Brian Hewson's mile in 4 minutes 5 seconds in 1955 will take some beating by a Regular soldier. Bombardier Hewson, who, with National Service pending, signed for three years, was Army half-mile champion in 1953-54-55, setting up a record 1 minute 52 seconds in 1954, a time equalled only by another National Serviceman, Welsh international Driver Anthony Jones, in the 1960 Inter-Services Championships. In the same year Private Robin Woodland, Royal Army Ordnance Corps, set up the existing 440 record of 48.8 seconds.

During 1953-54, Signalman Ken Norris twice set up new Army three-mile records, but his 14 minutes 7 seconds lasted only four years

GOODBYE
To Them All
– and Thanks

IN a remote and unimportant corner of Asia called Korea, 280 National Servicemen, few of them old enough to vote, fought and died alongside their Regular soldier comrades. They died helping a small country resist a powerful aggressor, and helping the United Nations meet the first real challenge of its young life.

Later, in the conflicts of Malaya, Kenya and Cyprus, National Servicemen stood up bravely, in nerve-racking fighting conditions, winning through against a ruthless guerilla enemy. Through 24 years packed with events that have changed the course of history the British conscript has made his mark

insight into the make-up of their fellow men.

For many, even among those who had looked forward to it, the first days and weeks of National Service came as a shock. The discipline, the countless things to remember, having to wear a uniform and a properly-angled hat, pocket buttons to keep fastened, masses of kit that seemed to be more a responsibility than an asset—"Lose a button-stick and you're for it!"—and quite impossible to cram into a kitbag. . . . It seemed to the young National Service-man that he would never last the day without finding himself on a charge for some technical oversight. Many's the young recruit who has walked three

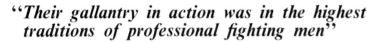

"Their gallantry in action was in the highest traditions of professional fighting men"

FIELD-MARSHAL SIR GERALD TEMPLER

both on those events and on the traditions and customs of the force with which he has served.

This year, 1963, the British Army will become all-volunteer for the first time since July, 1939, when 34,000 men were conscripted to the Militia in its one and only intake. During the war it was just one army with an urgent job to do. But since then the relationship between Regular and National Service-men has been that of partners, with give and take on both sides. Now they part company on the best of terms.

And as the Army strives to fill the yawning gaps—left by being virtually cut in half in under three years—it has bid a nostalgic farewell (not at all what is traditionally expected from the soldier) to those two-year troopers, while millions of ex-Servicemen look back with affection on those two distinctive years of their life and forward with a broader viewpoint, a squarer stance and a deeper

times the necessary distance to avoid the nervous strain of having to salute an officer!

Then there were the rumours. Even now the Army is only just learning that rumour is an enemy to be feared and must be dealt with ruthlessly by keeping all ranks informed of decisions as early as practicable. To the fresh National Servicemen, about to be tested, trained, vaccinated, posted . . . the rumours were alarming.

So what with the hard beds, early rising, the kit, the rumours, the dictatorial corporal (what an exalted rank that seemed at first) and most of all the feeling of being, from the time he is allotted it, just a number, the National Serviceman at first found Army life just too much for him.

Yet through it all there was the knowledge that everyone else was in the same boat and the problems, so shared, diminished. When the first ten days or

HERE is your "New Look" SOLDIER — at the new price of a shilling.

★ This is the first issue to be printed by The Forces Press at NAAFI's up-to-the-minute works in Aldershot. The litho-offset process gives a cleaner and easier-to-read text and sharper pictures, enhanced by a new, whiter and smoother paper.

★ Within the same format, SOLDIER has been streamlined and modernised. The ever-popular letters pages, covering a wide range of topics but representing only a fraction of the queries answered by SOLDIER's letters service; the reviews of military books; the "How Observant" teaser, for this month specially elevated to prize competition status; the "SOLDIER Humour" pages, next month drawn by Larry, of "Man in Apron" fame — all these regular features will remain, with two important additions.

★ Every month one of the Army's famous regiments, its glories and tragedies, customs and eccentricities, will be mirrored in "Your Regiment," and another new series, "The Army's Old Boys," will present personalities among the 400 In-Pensioners of The Royal Hospital, Chelsea. The sports pages will spotlight each month one of the Army's sports.

★ To help you find these features, plus SOLDIER's world-wide coverage of the Army in well-illustrated articles, there is a contents list on Page 3. And on the next page SOLDIER's new printers herald, in their advertisement, the introduction of colour inside the magazine.

★ From this issue, SOLDIER costs a shilling. As explained last month, the magazine has cost ninepence since 1951. But over those 11 years costs have steadily risen while sales have diminished as the Army has decreased. SOLDIER knows that its readers will not begrudge the extra threepence a month, nor would they wish their magazine to be heavily subsidised.

★ You can help SOLDIER and help yourself by filling in the subscription form on Page 30 and having the magazine posted direct to you — and to your friends and relatives. Send a cheque or postal order for 13s. 6d. per year, payable to Command Cashier, and SOLDIER will be sent direct, anywhere in the world, post paid.

★ No more scurrying for copies, no more disappointments! You can't afford to miss the "New Look" SOLDIER!

Into the Army's assembly belt

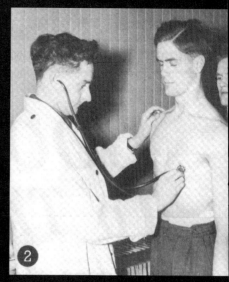

1 This is it. Home is far behind and ahead lies a new life in the Army . . .

2 And at first it seems to be a life of continual queuing, the doctor . . .

3 The tailor—and if he says it's a good fit, then it's a perfect fit . . .

continued from Page 5

so—they seemed like months—had passed, and the Army felt that its new recruits were just about fit to be let out of camp in the Queen's uniform, friends had been made and Army life became a little more tolerable.

Later it became clear that early misgivings could be blamed simply on changing to a new way of life. Once the adjustment was made the bright young National Serviceman made friends with the Army and took the same pride in its traditions as the Regular soldier. While, for some, National Service remained simply an intrusion on their life, for most, who accepted it as a duty to their country, it was also a wonderful opportunity.

Here were two years in which to do something quite different and see something of the world. For many wise young men it provided a breathing space in which to take stock of their lives. For those who had found themselves in the wrong job after leaving school, here was the chance to make the break and work towards a new career.

To the Army, National Service, at its peak, meant thousands of men on its doorstep every fortnight, 23 times a year

(twice a month except December which had just one intake) all to be kitted, drilled and trained.

The National Serviceman served in practically every branch of the Army, including the Guards and the Household Cavalry (though as a rule the ceremonial duties were done by the Regulars), and fitting square pegs into square holes was

"They have become competent Signalmen in less than half the time normal before 1939. We have every reason to be proud of them"

"The Wire," Journal of the Royal Corps of Signals

one of the Army's main preoccupations. It was no easy task. While there was the skilled tradesman who wanted to continue in a similar line during his service, there were others who sought a change. Imperial Chemical Industries was one major British firm which advised its employees to look for something different during their service. On the other hand the Army could meet the wishes of the recruit only within the strict confines of supply and demand.

4 And then a lesson in packing a load of strange objects into a kitbag . . .

5 And, suddenly, it all clicks into place and you're nearly a soldier . . .

6 Arms swinging, heads up, shoulders back and marching like a veteran.

The Royal Army Service Corps was a popular choice among the thousands who hoped the Army would teach them to drive. Inevitably many such candidates found themselves in the less popular Infantry, yet often found driving opportunities there. But many solicitors and accountants chose Gunner or Infantry roles rather than follow their colleagues into commissions in the Army Legal Service or the Royal Army Pay Corps.

University graduates were automatically considered as potential officers but by no means all of them had the necessary qualities of leadership. However, the Army tried hard in these cases not to waste willing brains and they were usually seconded to a special branch. Many such back room boys made a considerable contribution to Army planning during their two years. The Army Operational Research Group, the Military College of Science and the Atomic Weapons Research Establishment benefited greatly from conscripted talent. Secondment to the Ministry of Supply on armoured development and research was another useful avenue for the conscripted boffin. Some even taught at Sandhurst!

Few people realise that conscription,

even during the war, never applied to Northern Ireland. The Army tried to meet the requirements of the Northern Irish Regiments from Irishmen domiciled in this country or from men of Irish extraction. Since the war, however, men living in Northern Ireland could volunteer for two years' service if they wished.

From the first conscription in 1939 until it ended in 1960, 3,800,000 men were called to the Army compared with one million to the Royal Air Force and half a million to the Royal Navy. The post-war figures show an even more striking Army predominance. The Army found it needed large numbers of men simply to train others who would be lost to the Service in a comparatively short time. National Service was uneconomical. It would have to go.

The decision to end National Service

"It is outrageous that the youth of today should be subject to this tedious, squalid and regimented discharge of an imaginary duty"

The late Mr. GILBERT HARDING

left the Army with a major task of re-organisation and recruiting. These part-time soldiers made up half the Army and had become an integral part of it, not a separate section that could be closed off like the wing of a mansion. It meant the urgent replacement by volunteers of three-quarters of the strength of some sections of the Army. Signals were hit badly and many regiments faced the prospect of losing the majority of their men.

Many informed critics, weighing these facts, said the Army would never do it. Mr. George Wigg, MP, writing in the "Sunday Pictorial" of 14 May, 1961, stated baldly: "Face this fact, and face it now: Some form of call-up . . . is going to be necessary *soon*. The recruiting drive . . . is not going to get the minimum number of volunteers. . . ." And political considerations apart, Mr. Wigg had many allies, with considerable evidence to support their case.

In 1952 there were 223,000 National Service other ranks in the Army compared with 181,000 Regulars. From then on the Regular and National Service figures began to drop, with the National Service share becoming slightly

Goodbye Parades!

THE Army's farewell to its National Servicemen became a personal, individual affair with units choosing their own way of saying goodbye. There were scores of small informal presentations—from units and from Regular comrades—and other bigger occasions which caught the attention of the Press.

The Duke of Wellington's Regiment honoured 94 departing National Servicemen with a parade in their honour when the Commanding Officer, Lieutenant-Colonel Barry Kavanagh MC, shook hands and chatted with every man. More than 200 Regulars presented arms and the Regimental Colours dipped in salute as the 94 men marched off with a military flourish and the band played "Auld Lang Syne."

The fierce parade-ground expression of Regimental Sergeant-Major Robert Cox actually softened to a smile as Private Henry McGanity, last recruit to pass through the Royal Army Ordnance Corps Depot at Blackdown, was presented with a clock. "I'm sorry to see him go," said the sergeant-major. "The National Servicemen have been a grand lot."

The last three conscripts to serve with 38 Corps Regiment, Royal Engineers—Lance-Corporal Peter Murphy and Sappers Mark Sharp and Walter Morris—were presented with inscribed tankards by the Commanding Officer, Lieutenant-Colonel D. J. Willison.

Gunner Bob Bruce, last of the line on the staff of the School of Artillery, Manorbier received a silver cigarette case from his Regular comrades, presented by his battery commander at an all-ranks dance.

At Shorncliffe, the 1st Battalion, The Royal Sussex Regiment, paraded with Band, Drums and Colours in a stirring tribute to their last 20 National Servicemen.

With a handshake and a word of thanks, Lieut-Col A. B. M. Kavanagh MC says a personal farewell to his National Service "Dukes." Below: It's the last detail–handing in one's kit.

smaller each year. By the end of 1959 the Army's total other-rank strength had dropped to fewer than 235,000 and more than 100,000 of those were two-year men. A year later, with only 79,000 conscripts left in the Army, the Regular strength had dropped even further, to under 130,000 other ranks, 153,000 including officers.

The Army was faced with the formidable task of reversing a downward trend before it could begin to build up its strength to the required 165,000 by the end of 1962, a figure below which it was agreed the Army could not function

> "*Many lost their lives and we shall always remember them with great pride*"
> EARL MOUNTBATTEN

efficiently. Should a crisis occur, more men would be needed.

The critics had strong grounds, but they made the mistake that greater men had made before them—they underestimated the British Army!

But as the Army drive began to gain impetus, Berlin upset the balance. Rhine Army needed strengthening to meet the threat and, after various alternatives were considered, National Servicemen in Rhine Army were called upon to serve a further six months. This affected only 9000 of the greatly reduced intake during the final six months of conscription (which ended in November, 1960). Strangely it did not affect the National Servicemen closest to the trouble—those in the Berlin garrison—as the garrison is not a part of Rhine Army.

In the event the Army topped the 165,000 all-Regular mark with six months to spare. On 30 September last the Army had 168,416 officers and other ranks—plus fewer than 12,000 National Servicemen. Present indications are that the new, all-Regular British Army will have reached its long term ceiling of between 175,000 and 180,000 by autumn, just a few months after saying goodbye to its last National Serviceman.

Two years have passed and the final parting with those once strange items of equipment is a goodbye to old and trusted friends.

SOLDIER
to Soldier

LONG after Parliament has curbed the latest Army game—discharge by by-election—soldier and civilian alike will still be chuckling. Prospective candidates with purely party and political ambitions have viewed the invasion with alarm and Members of Parliament have been no less serious in their opinions. In reply, the War Minister (Mr. John Profumo) has urbanely tried to preserve the true perspective of an infinitesimal percentage of the Army being involved in all this.

But in retrospect it has all been a delightful piece of chicanery snowballing into a Quixotic tilt at the very roots of democracy. A lieutenant started it all in West Middlesbrough with the aim of getting out of the Army to further his studies. The rest, just wanting to get out, weighed a possible £250 discharge against the £150 of a lost deposit, and jumped on the band waggon. And the cleverest contrived to get out and stay out—but not pay out.

Column dodgers of all three Services made up the bulk of over 200 applicants for nomination papers in the Rotherham and Colne Valley by-elections. Newspapers and their cartoonists have had a field day and local government in Rotherham, a solid Yorkshire town with now an assured place in any chronicle of the year's events, found itself in overwhelming demand by the Press. Solemnly, joining the august body of bulletin-issuers, an overworked Town Hall staff had to announce that figures of application papers would in future be issued weekly instead of daily.

Should all 200 applicants put up some form of fight—and in the last series of by-elections not all the ex-Servicemen were content to treat the matter as a formality —Rotherham would have an interesting time. Would there be sufficient rooms for meetings? Would the local printers cope? Would the ballot papers look rather like emperor-size football coupons? And would it be a wise precaution to ensure that the Town Hall balcony would safely accommodate a couple of companies for the declaration of the result?

Spare a thought, too, for radio and television—the difficulties of interviewing 200 candidates, the problems of the television pundits analysing possibility and probability, and the problem of the BBC whose duty is to name every candidate in the field.

At this rate, of course, a General Election could, in theory, denude the Army of ten or so brigades. In fact, any increase on the Rotherham and Colne Valley figures, or on the normal small percentage of misfit soldiers who buy themselves out—there were 462 trained soldiers in the six months up to last September—is as likely as one of the 200 ex-Service applicants being elected to Parliament.

And one Member of the House will be watching the whole campaign with a keen personal interest. Brigadier Fitzroy McLean did all this, but in reverse. He joined the Army to get out of the Foreign Service.

But the Army's problem is not merely one of numerical strength. The Royal Signals will still be missing the National Servicemen next autumn, with a strong likelihood of a shortage of certain technicians. The Royal Army Medical and Dental Corps will both be short of nursing assistants and there will be gaps, too, in the Army Catering Corps.

The need for senior non-commissioned officers will be most marked in the technical branches while the departure of the two-year men has left many gaps among junior ranks. So there will be no lack of opportunity in this all-professional force, especially for young men with technical ability.

The Army will be a better place without the National Serviceman. It is already more compact, better paid, better fed and housed and it will soon be composed again entirely of men who have chosen to make the British Army their career.

But the professional soldier who has served with the National Serviceman will miss him. The tight net of conscription put a wonderful cross-section of characters into khaki, each one playing his part in watching over the interests of his home and country, each one coming to terms with Army life in his own way, and leaving his mark.

Without him the Army will never be quite the same again.

PETER J. DAVIES

"Ah hates playin' poker with the general—he's such a damn bad loser."

"Can we do three hundred and eight dainty teas?"

"Your transport's outside, Sergeant!"

1964

An African Sunset –
and Mediterranean mayhem!

Events in East Africa were to the forefront of British Army operations in 1964 as the British Garrison prepared to depart from the newly independent Kenya. Before this took place however, British troops were required to quell mutinies by troops serving in the Kenya, Tanganyika and Uganda Rifles as well as bring law and order to a restless civilian population.

This piece of nostalgic withdrawal from Empire however was overshadowed by fresh violence in the former colony of Cyprus where Turkish and Greek islanders were yet again engaged in open hostilities with each other. Not surprisingly perhaps, such violence captured most of the international and national headlines. Other areas where troops were involved in operations included the Arabian Protectorate of Aden where dissident tribesmen of the "Red Wolves" faction were attempting to seize control.

In addition to all this action, earlier in the year soldiers had been sent Skopje in Yugoslavia to assist with rescue work after massive devastation by an earthquake in the area. Others were more fortunate and had the bonus of some sunshine too. In June several hundred British troops were moved to Swaziland to assist the civil authorities with law and order.

By the end of the year however, they, along with those from East Africa finally bid farewell to yet more of Britain's African Empire. The year ended with the bulk of Britain's new Regular Army looking forward to the introduction of other welcome improvements to their conditions of service, as well as the gradual withdrawal from many other "sunshine postings" that remained part of Britain's diminishing Empire.

PEACEMAKING
on the Island of Hate

POLITICIANS who engineered the truce in Cyprus would be the first to admit that it could never have been done without the extraordinary talent of the British soldier to keep his head when all about him are losing theirs.

The hot-headed young Cypriots who grabbed their guns shortly before Christmas and rampaged through the island in an orgy of hate, slaying and arson, were cooled off by British soldiers acting with a natural tact and diplomacy that would have staggered the *Corps Diplomatique*.

When a shouting, gesticulating crowd of trigger-happy Cypriots pulled out their guns, a sergeant marched into the centre of them and said: "No shooting here. Calm down. Nobody's going to be hurt." When men, women and children were frantically looting a big food shop, an officer stalked in and

ordered: "Stop this nonsense. Leave it!" When Turk and Greek Cypriot policemen faced each other and cocked their rifles after an argument, the Royal Air Force Regiment drove between them and stayed there until the dispute was settled.

During the days of tension, it required only one soldier to put a foot wrong to set guns blazing again all over the island. No one did. And yet many soldiers have bitter memories of Cyprus. Not long ago a British uniform was a target for a bullet in the back. It says much for the character of the British peacemakers.

Four days before Christmas, after weeks of mounting tension, the first shots were fired, sparked off when Greek Cypriot police demanded to see the identity cards of a crowd of Turkish Cypriots. The gun battle which followed left two people lying dead in the street.

Within hours, gunfire was heard throughout the island. Streets in Nicosia emptied; schools were closed; shops put up their shutters and police were issued with weapons.

On Christmas Eve, Rifleman Gordon Baldwin, 3rd Green Jackets, died after being machine-gunned in the seaside town of Larnaca. With a friend he had tried to cross into the Turkish quarter to rescue a besieged Greek family. Later the same day three British airmen were wounded while on patrol in Nicosia.

Servicemen and their families in the British bases at Dhekelia and Episkopi rapidly cancelled Christmas plans and prepared for celebrations in the safety of their own communities.

Fighting between Greek and Turk became steadily worse; each side accused the other of worse atrocities. In one village all Turkish homes were

Below : Security forces moving into Nicosia on Christmas Day.   Above : The first British patrol moving into the neutral zone.

Island of Hate continued

A flag-draped lorry leaves the Ledra Palace Hotel, emergency headquarters of the Glosters.

burned to the ground; at least a dozen people were killed in street gun battles in Nicosia. A cease-fire was negotiated—and immediately violated.

On Christmas Day, while fighting continued unabated, a truce force was set up under Major-General Peter Young, commanding Cyprus District.

Back in Britain, during the early hours of Boxing Day, men of the 1st Battalion, The Sherwood Foresters, were being recalled from Christmas leave. Later that day one company of the Battalion was on its way to Cyprus, where 1st Battalion, The Gloucestershire Regiment, and 33 Field Squadron, Royal Engineers, had moved into Nicosia. The task of the truce force was to enforce the cease-fire, disperse "irregular" fighters and organise food, water and medical assistance.

British patrols visited Service families trapped in residential areas by fighting between Greeks and Turks. A squadron of *Ferret* armoured cars of 14th/20th King's Hussars arrived from Libya to help with the patrolling and all British troops were ordered not to fire unless absolutely necessary.

Mr Duncan Sandys, Commonwealth Relations Secretary, flew in on a trooping flight from Britain and while the remainder of the Foresters arrived, the Glosters took over Greek Cypriot strongpoints on the border of the Turkish-held area. One of their patrols was fired on near the Kyrenia Gate in Nicosia but did not return the fire.

While Mr Sandys met Cypriot leaders, fresh shooting broke out near the residence of the British High Commissioner. The 3rd Green Jackets moved into Nicosia with 33 Field Squadron under command in an Infantry role.

Burned-out houses, bullet-scarred walls, blood-stained streets, heavily sandbagged windows, road blocks and the sun glinting on the barrel of a home-made gun—this was Christmas in Cyprus.

By New Year's Eve, British troops occupied a neutral zone between the Greek and Turkish communities in Nicosia. With the easing of tension, the Hussars began making long-distance patrols while 3 (LAA) Wing, RAF Regiment, 3rd Green Jackets and the Glosters continued patrols within the city. A NAAFI van, under armed escort, took badly needed food supplies to British families besieged in the northern suburbs.

The 2nd Regiment, Royal Artillery, arrived from Britain equipped as Infantry and the Foresters established four-man mobile patrols in the Larnaca area. But when it seemed the situation was quiet, two Greek monks and a boy novice were brutally murdered in the garden of their monastery. Later that day more houses in Nicosia were put to the torch in revenge—British troops were called on to help fight the blaze.

The newly arrived Gunners took over the Episkopi base and 1st Battalion, The Parachute Regiment, which arrived the following day, took over the Dhekelia base. Included in the huge air lift with the Battalion were Headquarters, 16 Parachute Brigade Group; 1 (Guards) Independent Parachute Company; 216 Signal Squadron; 21 Recce Flight, Army Air Corps; 23 Parachute Field Ambulance; 16 Parachute Ordnance Field Park; 16 Parachute Workshops, Royal Electrical and Mechanical Engineers; 16 Parachute Brigade Provost Unit; 63 Parachute Company.

Cpl Malcolm Foulkes, 3rd Green Jackets, takes over a control post from a Greek "irregular."

EAST AFRICAN ALERT

FOUR MUTINIES IN FIVE DAYS SPARKED OFF A COLOSSAL MILITARY OPERATION

REBELS overthrow a government; soldiers mutiny, sack their British officers and rampage through towns terrorising civilians including British women and children; three African leaders appeal for help. It all happened within a few days and initiated the biggest military operations since Suez. It was a hectic month for an already extended British Army Strategic Reserve. Here is the diary of that month:

DAY ONE

About 600 armed rebels overthrew the government on the tropical island of Zanzibar about 20 miles off the coast of East Africa. Britons barricaded themselves in their homes as mobs raided police armouries, cable offices, the radio station and airfield. A request for British troops to be flown in was refused.

DAY FOUR

One company of 1st Battalion, The Staffordshire Regiment, flew from its barracks in Nairobi to Mombasa and embarked on the Royal Navy frigate *Rhyl* which sailed immediately for Zanzibar with orders to assist in the evacuation of Britons if necessary.

DAY SIX

The coup was complete. About 150 Britons, mainly women and children, left the island.

DAY SEVEN

Soldiers and sailors on HMS *Rhyl* gave 62 pints of blood to a Zanzibar hospital where hundreds of injured natives were being treated.

DAY NINE

Flare-up Number Two. Soldiers of 1st Battalion, Tanganyika Rifles, mutinied over pay and promotion at their barracks near Dar-es-Salaam, forcing their British officers and non-commissioned officers to leave for Nairobi immediately by air. Mutineers rampaged through the town setting up road blocks and taking over the radio station. To protect British nationals the aircraft carrier *Centaur*, with 500 Royal Marines of 45 Commando aboard, sailed from Aden, and HMS *Rhyl* left Zanzibar, the ships meeting off Dar-es-Salaam. The 2nd Battalion, Scots Guards, cut short a training exercise in Aden and immediately returned to barracks in Kenya.

DAY TEN

Men of 2nd Battalion, Tanganyika Rifles, 400 miles away, joined the mutiny and sacked their officers, who were similarly flown to Nairobi. The destroyer *Cambrian* left Aden for the East African coast.

DAY TWELVE

Flare-up Number Three. In neighbouring Uganda, men of 1st Battalion, Uganda Rifles, kidnapped the country's foreign minister at their barracks at Jinja and forced him to authorise substantial pay rises. British officers and non-commissioned officers were confined to their quarters and no one was allowed to approach or leave the barracks. Mr Milton Obote, the Prime Minister, appealed to Britain for help

---

Above: Scots Guards leap from a truck to take over an airport in Uganda shortly after the third mutiny

and within 45 minutes seven aircraft left Nairobi carrying men of 1st Battalion, The Staffordshire Regiment, and 2nd Battalion, Scots Guards. They landed at Entebbe and set about securing the airfields and other strategic installations.

DAY THIRTEEN

Flare-up Number Four. Men of 11th Battalion, Kenya Rifles, mutinied, seizing weapons and ammunition. In the confusion one man was killed before scout cars of 3rd Regiment, Royal Horse Artillery, arrived at the barracks at Lanet, 100 miles north of Nairobi, and

Mutinous troops of the Tanganyika Rifles are marched off at gun point by a Royal Marine commando.

Tanganyikan mutineers hand over their weapons to British troops after being captured in the bush.

restored order. The Gunners secured the armoury, set up road blocks and took over the officers' mess where the British families had gathered. In Nairobi the remaining company of the Scots Guards took over key positions and 8th Independent Recce Flight, Army Air Corps, moved its aircraft further away from the capital for safety.

Meanwhile troops were moving fast. About 680 Royal Marines of 41 Commando left Lyneham for Kenya. HMS *Rhyl* and the survey ship *Owen*, with a company of Gordon Highlanders on board, arrived in Mombasa harbour. The company of the Staffordshires which had been aboard HMS *Rhyl* throughout the crises was flown to Nairobi. In England, 26 Regiment, Royal Artillery, was placed on short-notice alert at Shoeburyness as spearhead unit of the Strategic Reserve. The 1st Battalion, The Duke of Edinburgh's Royal Regiment, in Malta; 39 Infantry Brigade Headquarters, Northern Ireland; and 1st Battalion, The Cheshire Regiment, in Rhine Army, were all put on 72 hours alert and 1st Battalion, The Devonshire and Dorset Regiment,

in Northern Ireland, and 6th Infantry Brigade Group in Rhine Army, were placed on seven-day stand-by.

DAY FOURTEEN

Dawn in Tanganyika. While HMS *Cambrian* fired her guns as a diversion, 60 Royal Marine commandos landed by helicopter from HMS *Centaur*. They were led by Brigadier Patrick Sholto Douglas MC, the British commander of the Tanganyika Rifles, who had been in hiding since the mutiny. They moved quickly to the mutineers' barracks, rushed the guardroom and took over the camp while most of the soldiers were asleep. The remainder of 45 Commando were ferried ashore by helicopter to assist in rounding up the mutinous battalion.

Dawn in Uganda. One platoon of the Staffordshires, armed with *Sten* guns, stormed the guardroom and arsenal at Jinja Barracks. By the time the African soldiers were awake, Staffordshires and Scots Guards were in complete control. British women and children were evacuated and the African soldiers disarmed.

Dawn in Kenya. Royal Horse Artillery

scout cars were fired on when they approached the mutineers' barracks at Lanet. They returned the fire and finally crushed the mutiny after Mr Jomo Kenyatta promised to investigate the army's pay and conditions.

DAY FIFTEEN

The mutinies had crumbled. Arrangements were made to disband the Tanganyika Rifles; 500 men of the Uganda Rifles were sacked after another pre-dawn raid on their barracks by the Staffordshires; and investigations started in Kenya.

Then followed the post-mortems, the investigations, recriminations, dismissals, arrests, trials and above all, from the three African leaders, sincere thanks and praise for the conduct of the British troops.

And while the situation slowly returned to normal, Mr Duncan Sandys, Commonwealth Relations Secretary, speaking in the House of Commons, congratulated the three Services for the "promptness and efficiency with which they discharged these difficult and unusual tasks."

With fixed bayonets, two men of the Royal Horse Artillery guard prisoners in a football goal net after the Kenya Rifles' mutiny.

COVER PICTURE

When men of the 2nd Battalion, Scots Guards, went into action to quell the mutiny in Uganda they had to leave behind Unita and Fortior, the twin lion cubs they have adopted as battalion mascots. SOLDIER's front cover picture, taken by an Army Public Relations photographer in Kenya, shows Unita giving a friendly pat on the cheek to Regimental Sergeant-Major Campbell Graham. Unfortunately it probably won't be many months now before the cuddly twins are a little less cuddly and a lot less friendly!

REBUILDING A TORN CITY

S/Sgt Jeff Richardson and Sgt Alan Milner confer on a siting problem, while (left) Cpl Peters and L/Cpl Lenny Leonard draw up building plans on the Butel school site.

Above: L/Cpl Ian Atkinson helps a Yugoslav to fix a ramp to a hut, and (left) Sgt Steve Hambrook uses a surveyor's level.

British *Nissen* huts provide a safe shelter amid the cracked and tottering structures.

TEN enormous lorries and trailers, piled high with *Nissen* hut components, packed into the central Tito Square in Skopje. On each one in bold letters was "British Aid for Skopje: London—Skopje: Britanska pomoc Jugoslavia." People of the earthquake-shattered town emerged from their tents and tarpaulin shelters to welcome the giant convoy. Among them were seven British Sappers who had travelled ahead from Germany to see the huts built. They didn't speak—just grinned at one another. At that moment there was no one more proud of being British.

SKOPJE

continued

With the help of an interpreter, Capt Charles Brodley talks to an elderly resident of Skopje.

The Sappers, first British Army detachment to visit Jugoslavia since the war, were still marvelling at this remarkable break in the daily routine of life within 11 Engineer Group at Osnabruck. Corporal John Crankshaw had just climbed into bed the previous Saturday when the door flew open and a voice said: "Start packing, lad, you're off to Skopje."

There were, in fact, 72 hours before Corporal Crankshaw and six fellow Sappers, led by Captain Charles Brodley, 35 Corps Engineer Regiment, boarded the Trans-Europa Express at Dortmund for the 36-hour journey to Belgrade. They made for Skopje's town park where the city council had set up offices in temporary rushwork structures. It was here, among rows and rows of tents, that the party sorted its seven tons of stores and built bivouacs for the night.

The convoy, carrying components for 24 *Nissen* huts, arrived three days later and the huts were immediately earmarked for use as schools. The earthquake had left the city without a single school and replacements were urgently needed. The *Nissen* huts, with their large floor space—66ft by 24ft—were the only buildings on offer that filled the bill. They were to form three schools, eight huts to each school, on sites in different parts of the city.

Within 24 hours the Royal Engineers' task was doubled. The British Government offered 20 more *Nissen* huts and these were immediately earmarked for two more schools. Four more Sappers left Osnabruck, this time travelling by road, bringing two *Land-Rovers* to ease transport problems and towing trailers bearing 1600lb of tinned food.

But work on the first three schools had already begun, with Sappers supervising Jugoslav labour. Each of the nine or ten settlements in the area was being administered by a separate authority—in Djorce Petrov they worked for the Skopje Council, in Butel for the Macedonian Government, at Madari for the Zagreb Council—and civic pride turned the work into a friendly race.

Yet another *Nissen* hut takes shape. Spr Paddy Moore helps Jugoslav workers secure the frame.

Pictures by Sergeant GEORGE TOLLEFSON, British Army Public Relations

OUT ON A LIMB

Dust swirls from a packed earth road as men of A Company leap from a three-tonner during practice of ambush drill.

IN SWAZILAND

SINCE being rushed into Swaziland during internal disturbances last November, "home" for the 1st Battalion, The York and Lancaster Regiment, has ranged from a cattle show ground to a school with two houses—one named York and the other Lancaster!

But this month the Regiment is due to move from its temporary lodgings into the newly built St George's Barracks at Matsapa—the first permanent barracks in Swaziland for British troops.

Since taking over from 1st Battalion, The Gordon Highlanders, the "Tigers" have been very much cut off from their homes and the rest of the Army. It has been seven difficult—but rewarding—months during which, apart from their official role of assisting the police to keep the peace, they have made many friends.

In the capital town of Mbabane a multi-racial boxing club has been formed and twice a week the Battalion boxing team gives instruction to local Swazi boys. Sergeant Harry Brooking, of the Corps of Drums, has been teaching the Swazi police band and helping its drummers to improve their stick work.

The Regimental Band has been fantastically popular and Bandmaster Mike Sumner and his men have played in almost every township in the country, everywhere being received with wild enthusiasm by the natives, some of whom walked miles to see

them. On one occasion a Swazi who had served in the Swazi Pioneer Battalion during World War Two turned up for a parade resplendent in his preciously preserved wartime battledress, complete with medals.

Nearly 2000 miles from the nearest

L/Cpl Mike Connel and a Swazi warrior discuss the merits of using a glockenspiel as a shield.

ordnance depot, the Regiment faces formidable supply problems. Stores are either flown in by the Royal Air Force or delivered by sea to adjoining Mozambique. The tiny airfield at Matsapa is manned by the Signals Platoon and Captain Barry Smeeton, the Regimental Signals Officer, had to step in as airfield controller and learn the mysteries of cloud base, airspeed and barometric pressure.

Stores arriving by sea in Mozambique are collected by a road convoy commanded by the Quartermaster, Captain John Cooper. All wearing civilian clothes and armed with a sheaf of visas, the drivers tackle roads of packed earth and arrive back covered from head to foot in red dust.

With newspapers taking more than a week to arrive from England, the Tigers have avoided feeling too cut off by starting their own broadcasts from the local radio station. Tiger Radio goes on the air every week with taped programmes of messages and requests from England—it's a regimental "Family Favourites" which has an ever-increasing number of listeners.

And in between work and play many of the men have found time to give blood to the local hospital—a gesture that is making them even more welcome friends to the people of Swaziland.

From a report by Captain D G Rowe, RAEC, 1st Battalion, The York and Lancaster Regiment.

Canadian uniforms to wear winter and summer.

FIGHTING FIT for the FUTURE

BOFFINS play an increasingly important part in the running of an army and always one of their most important tasks is to ensure soldiers are dressed properly.

Modern uniforms must be comfortable, practical and protective against the hazards dreamed up by modern man. Experts from many different fields are involved in producing such a uniform.

In **BRITAIN,** boffins at the Chemical Defence Experimental Establishment have developed special clothing and equipment that soldiers of the future will need to combat bacterial warfare.

It is a lightweight protective suit (pictured right) worn over normal battle-dress. With gloves and the latest type of mask, the soldier is completely covered from head to foot—not a square inch is in contact with the atmosphere.

CANADA has recently perfected new all-weather uniforms which can be worn everywhere from the Arctic to the tropics. Issued to the Canadian Army in Germany, they comprise a shirt-coat, jacket and liner, winter and summer trousers and eight-inch high waterproof boots.

Parts of the jacket and trousers are rubberised and both can be treated with a silicone spray to make them completely waterproof. Diagonal pockets in the shirt each hold a 20-round magazine for the FN rifle. The new boots have moulded soles and are unusual in that their wearers are ordered NOT to polish them—the only maintenance required is an occasional treatment with a silicone compound.

The new uniforms give protection in temperatures as low as 22 degrees below freezing and are perfectly comfortable in temperatures as high as a sweltering 80 degrees.

At the army technical laboratory in **FRANCE,** the boffins have come up with a new battle-dress made of "Satin 300," a synthetic material which is very difficult to contaminate by radio-activity.

Unlike the Canadians, they favour completely different uniforms for summer and

A French soldier wearing a polythene overall (above) looks fearsome when putting it on (below).

This may be the appearance of a soldier of the future in a uniform to combat bacterial warfare.

winter, each with several different styles designed for men with specific jobs.

They have also developed a special polythene overall—like an enormous bag—which the soldier can pull over his battle-dress to give the same sort of protection as the British uniforms.

Not far from the French army laboratory, the world's leading women's fashion designers work in their Paris salons. But it is very doubtful that they put more effort or forethought into their designs than the men who design uniforms for the soldier.

Tony Nash and Capt Robin Dixon speed to golden victory in the two-man bob.

A GOLD
FOR THE GRENADIER

ON the one British golden moment of the Winter Olympics, when hats were flung high in the air and perfect strangers embraced in delight, at the centre of things, with a half share in a gold medal, was a soldier, Captain the Hon T Robin Dixon, Grenadier Guards, brakeman on Britain's number one bob. He and driver Tony Nash—introduced to bobbing while serving with The Royal Dragoons in Germany seven years ago—had won the first British Winter Olympic gold medal since Jeanette Altwegg took the figure skating in 1952. Before that there had only ever been two, won by figure skater Madge Sykes in 1908 and the ice-hockey team of 1936.

It was a spectacular, nerve-tingling win by the blink of an eye (twelve-hundredths of a second) over the British team's great friends, rivals and mentors, the Italians, who came second and third. The British pair led the Italians by thirteen-hundredths of a second after the second run, and were behind (by a 20th of a second!) after the third.

After a fast start on the final run, the British bob hit the side and practically zigzagged down the final straight. The two Britons were pessimistic. Then their nearest rivals, the Italian number two team, made a similar error and finished with a slower time. There was only Eugenio Monti, six times world champion, to come. He too had an unsteady spell and finished third.

It was a close thing and the Britons had that little slice of luck to add to the hours, weeks, months of application over the past three years. They deserved their success for their consistent performances over the four runs, emerging as the only team to break 1min 6sec each time.

But a share of the credit must go to the great Eugenio Monti, who brushed aside congratulations after his second run to leap to the aid of the British pair, who were brooding over a sheared axle bolt. Monti hurriedly grasped a spanner, whipped the part off his own bob, rushed it to the top, helped fit it to the British bob then watched it sweep down the run into the lead.

The gesture robbed Italy of the chance of their only gold medal of the meeting, but it will be remembered long after many gold medal performances are forgotten.

BUT ECLIPSE FOR OUR BIATHLETES

NO one can be more disappointed with the British placings in the Olympic biathlon than the competitors themselves, who have literally lived and breathed biathlon for the past two years. During that time the seven men who had emerged clearly as Britain's best biathlon prospects improved enormously, benefiting from the best of coaching, from being plunged into hard international competition—and from their own hard, punishing efforts over mile after mile of featureless snow. And their results up to and including the Olympic event reflect the hard work that had been put in.

In a field of 51, Lieutenant Robin Dent, 40 Regiment, Royal Artillery, came 29th in a time of 1hr 36min

Lieut Robin Dent, who put up a great show for Britain, but still finished well down the list.

27.2sec, which includes a six-minute penalty for missing the target only three times. This was great shooting considering that the unfamiliar icy conditions offered no "cushion" for the elbows.

And the running time? Twelve months ago Lieutenant Dent won the British Army Biathlon Championship, after 12 months of intensive training, with an actual running time of 2hr 2min 7.1sec. He covered the Olympic course more than half an hour faster! Both comprised 20 kilometres ($12\frac{1}{2}$ miles) of rugged cross-country skiing.

Corporal Alan Notley, 3rd Green Jackets (current holder of the Queen's Prize at Bisley), was 37th, his 1hr 46min 10.3sec including five misses at the ranges—a ten-minute penalty; Captain John Moore, 17 Regiment, Royal Artillery, was 40th, his 1hr 47min 49.4sec including a 20-minute penalty (ten misses), and Lieutenant Rod Tuck, Royal Marines, 43rd in 1hr 51min 55.5sec, including 18 minutes added for nine missed shots.

SPORT

DESTINATION TOKYO— TARGET GOLD

THIS month the attention of sporting enthusiasts throughout the world is focussed on Tokyo, scene of the 18th Olympic Games. Soldiers will be watching with a special personal interest the fortunes of Army athletes representing Britain at this supreme contest.

Without National Service champions, the number of military competitors is smaller than for many years, nevertheless Britain is pinning many of her hopes on soldiers.

Already a soldier has helped win a gold medal for Britain—at the Winter Olympics earlier this year Captain the Hon T Robin Dixon and Tony Nash sped to victory in the two-man bob event to gain Britain's first Winter Olympic gold medal for 12 years.

This month in Japan other soldiers will be striving to follow that golden lead. Their chances may be slim and the experts are pessimistic—but experts can be wrong.

In the pentathlon event, Britain is leaning heavily on the Services. Captain of the British team is Sergeant Mick Finnis, 1st Battalion, The Middlesex Regiment, a brilliant all-rounder and one of the best-known athletes in the Army.

Supporting him will be Lance-Corporal Jack Fox, Royal Electrical and Mechanical Engineers, a comparative newcomer to pentathlon who astounded experts by the speed with which he became a champion.

Third member of the team is a civilian, Roy Phelps of Gloucester, with Captain R F Tuck, Royal Marines, as the reserve. When the classical Olympic Games were held in Greece, the winner of the pentathlon was the supreme champion of the meeting— this is what Finnis and his team will be striving to attain.

No one deserves a ticket to Tokyo more than Staff-Sergeant Instructor John Pancott, Army Physical Training Corps, who is half of Britain's two-man gymnastics team.

While serving in Singapore he hitch-hiked to Tokyo to attend the pre-Olympic Games so that he could get the feel of the place. A soldier for 16 years, he is reigning British champion for the high bars, rings and parallel bars.

In the British athletics team will be champion steeplechaser Lance-Corporal Ernie Pomfret, 10th Royal Hussars, who has seldom been out of the news this season with success after success. The other military member is a Territorial soldier, Private Alan Dean, 6th/7th Battalion, The North Staffordshire Regiment. He will represent Britain in the 800 metres. Private Dean plays soccer for his Battalion and earlier this year won the Territorial Army Cross-Country Championship.

Another Territorial, Lance-Bombardier Hugh Wardell-Yerburgh, of 883 (Gloucestershire Volunteer Artillery) Locating Battery, Royal Artillery, will be sculling at Tokyo in Britain's coxless-four crew.

Only two soldiers won medals at the Rome Olympics and one of them, bronze medallist Captain Michael Howard, Royal Pioneer Corps, will again be fencing for Britain this year and making his third Olympic appearance. With him in the team will be British foil champion Major H W F Hoskyns, North Somerset Yeomanry/44th Royal Tank Regiment, Territorial Army, who has so far had an outstandingly successful year.

Sergeant R McTaggart, 1st Battalion, The Glasgow Highlanders, better known as Dick McTaggart, Britain's greatest amateur boxer, will be battling against the world's finest light-welterweights to try and bring home a medal.

Two Regular soldiers will be competing in the three-day equestrian event—Captain J R Templer, Royal Artillery, on M'Lord Connolly, and Sergeant R S Jones, King's Troop, Royal Horse Artillery, on the Troop's Master Bernard.

The eyes of Great Britain will be on its team during the next few weeks—and the soldier competitors will know that 250,000 men will be personally cheering them.

Four soldier champions at Tokyo this month. Top is British foil champion Maj H W F Hoskyns, a Territorial Army officer. Above (left to right) are Sgt Mick Finnis, captain of the pentathlon team, L/Cpl Ernie Pomfret, the champion steeplechaser, and L/Cpl J Fox, a brilliant new pentathlete.

Story by RUSSELL MILLER ☆ ★ ☆ **Pictures by ARTHUR BLUNDELL**

IT'S THE POWDER-PUFF BARRACKS

Bright green bedspreads, dressing tables, colourful rugs on the floor and only four beds to a room—the living accommodation is a far cry from the barracks of yesterday.

They may be soldiers, but they are girls too, and in their own club there is a fully-equipped hairdressing salon.

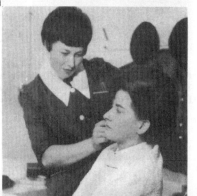

YELLOW and blue baths ... special basins for hair shampooing ... sun lounges ... cocktail bars ... dustbins screened from view by coloured bricks ... even the electricity sub-station is lilac and grey!

This is the £1,000,000 barracks with the feminine touch—Queen Elizabeth Barracks, Guildford, new home of the Depot and Training Centre, Women's Royal Army Corps.

It's a revelation and a revolution. The first barracks ever created specially for girls, it kills stone dead the popular image of bleak, forbidding buildings grouped round a desolate square.

With colour, imagination and forethought, the new barracks lets girls be girls AND soldiers. It is new thinking that bodes well for the future of the Women's Royal Army Corps. The old training centre was in wooden huts at Lingfield, Surrey—now raw recruits nervously facing the Army for the first time will do so in surroundings that even their Mums will envy.

The living accommodation is built in lilac, orange and grey bricks with light and dark blue fibre-glass panels separating the picture windows. Each block houses a complete company with separate rooms for the non-commissioned officers and four-bed rooms for the privates.

They are furnished with the new-style Army furniture, in use for the first time. Each girl has her own dressing table and a two-tone wooden wardrobe (no more steel lockers). Bedside lights and cupboards are built in above each bed, there are coloured rugs on the blue linoleum, bedspreads, a table and four chairs in each room and big sliding windows.

A completely new idea is to screen off the wash-basins with lockable cubicles giving privacy to every girl. In addition the wash-rooms have special wide bowls with hand showers for hair shampooing, all the baths are either yellow or blue and there are stainless steel bowls for washing "smalls."

Informally positioned so that every bedroom catches the morning and evening sunlight, each block has a rest room comfortably furnished with carpet and armchairs where the girls can sit and chat in their curlers.

If the girls don't want to spend their spare time in the privacy of their own lounge, they can go off to the splendid Junior Ranks' Club a few minutes' walk across landscaped gardens.

There they can entertain their boy friends, have a drink in the tavern (if they are old enough) or a meal in the canteen, watch television, play games or just sit and read in one of the quiet rooms.

The rooms at the club have folding partitions to make the accommodation flexible for parties and the monthly dance.

Above: Bright colours create a comfortable, informal atmosphere in the dinning hall. In the medical centre (below) patients are treated in quiet wards fitted with every modern facility.

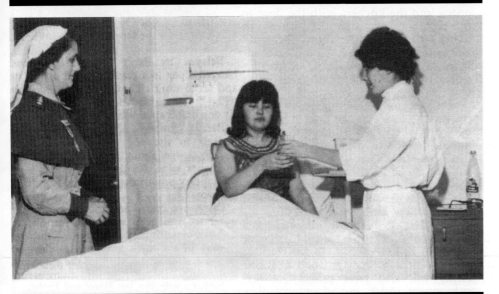

Left: From the balcony of their sun lounge corporals watch roller skating– the most popular hobby among the girls. In the Junior Ranks' Club (below, left) girls can entertain their boy friends. Startling feature of the dining hall (below) is the attractive folded slab roof.

SOLDIER to Soldier

By reducing the enlistment age to 17 and introducing the Junior Army Association to cater for interested boys before they are old enough to join junior units, the Regular Army has now bridged the gaps during which potential recruits were apt to lose their enthusiasm.

Now the Territorial Army comes into line with the Regulars, and with the earlier maturity of adolescence, by also allowing the enlistment of 17-year-olds as young soldiers. For the six months until they come on to normal Territorial service they will receive minimum training pay at the same rate as 17-year-old Regulars undergoing basic training, but will be liable for service only at home unless they volunteer for overseas and parental permission is given.

Their training, clothing and equipment will be on the same scale as adult volunteers but, because of their age, they may not enlist (for two, three or four years) without the written consent of parents or guardian. Similar consent is required for inter-unit transfer or parachuting.

This should all help considerably both Regular and Territorial recruiting. Adventure, excitement and technical equipment have a much stronger appeal to the teenager than the sense of duty and the camaraderie which attract the older man, and many a youngster keenly interested in the Army has had to be reluctantly turned away at a display with the suggestion that he comes back when he is old enough.

A still bigger fillip to Territorial recruiting is likely to emerge from the increasing opportunities to train overseas. A few years ago Territorials went out to Singapore and Malaya for their annual training—but they were parachutists. Others have been fortunate enough to train with Rhine Army units but for the majority it has been the usual routine fortnight's camp at home.

Last month, however, nearly 3000 men of the Reserve Forces took part in "Travel Man," an exercise which tested the reinforcing in emergency of Rhine Army and also gave the part-time soldiers valuable training experience with modern weapons and equipment alongside Regular soldiers. And airtrooping, by now "old hat" to most Regulars, is still something of a novelty, and a new technique to learn, for most of the Reserve Army.

After "Travel Man" the Territorials will be keener than ever to train overseas and keener still to have their equipment brought up-to-date and in line with the Regulars alongside whom, in emergency, they would take their place.

Det hse, f furn, 1 sit, 2 beds, k and b, sep wc, mains svces—
DELIVERED COMPLETE!

BY the end of next month, 150 new modern mobile homes—more than 700 tons of housing—will have been shipped from Huddersfield to Germany to help ease Rhine Army's pressing housing problem. The homes, 50 square feet larger than the caravans bought for Germany two years ago, are designed for couples with two children. More than half will go to Osnabruck.

They come from the factory completely furnished, including full-size refrigerator, cooker, bath, separate toilet, heated airing cupboard and towel rail, ventilated food store and extractor fan. The floor, walls and roof are lined and the windows double-glazed to give an insulation the makers claim is twiçe as good as a normal small bungalow.

Priced at under £1000, the mobile home is regarded as useful temporary family accommodation to ease the current shortage. More may be ordered during the coming financial year.

The home is permanently mounted on a steel "ski" chassis so it can be lifted, moved and sited easily on firm, level ground ready for connection to mains services. Cooker and water heating unit are powered by propane gas, and the plumbing for kitchen, bathroom and toilet, and the wiring for lighting and heating are both ready for connection to the mains.

The door of the 36ft by 9ft home opens into the kitchen, with the door to the bathroom opposite. The 13ft by 9ft living-room is on the right, the main bedroom beyond, and the second bedroom, with its bunk beds, at the far end. The height from floor to ceiling is nearly 8ft.

A settee in the living-room can be converted into an additional double bed, and there is a sideboard, folding dining-table, two easy chairs and four dining-chairs. The War Office's strict fire-resistance requirements are met by the extensive use of plasterboard internally, and large windows in bedrooms and kitchen allow emergency escape.

The first 48 homes were earmarked for Osnabruck, the second 48 for Hameln, 14 for Verden, 10 for Herford and the final 30 for Osnabruck. Rhine Army will also have priority in any subsequent order and afterwards they may be seen in Britain.

Soldier's wife Mrs Iris Morse and Penny, her daughter, examine the roomy fridge.

One of the mobile homes on show to the Press at Wellington Barracks, London. The rounded ends of the "ski" chassis enable the homes to be slid into place.

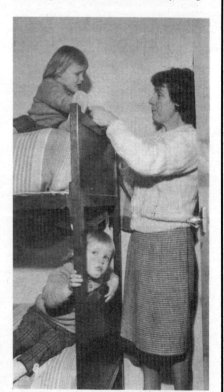

Penny and her twin, Catherine, try out the bunk beds. These are big enough for adults.

THE YOUNGEST SUBALTERN LOWERED THE FLAG

THE wheels of time turned full cycle for the George Cross island of Malta when the youngest subaltern of 1st Battalion, The Royal Sussex Regiment, Lieutenant S C Thorpe, hauled down the Union Jack to mark the end of 164 years of British rule. In 1800, the same Regiment raised its King's Colours after capturing Fort Ricasoli, Napoleon's last stronghold on the island. Today, those same Colours, the island's first British flag, hang in a place of honour in the Palace Armoury in Valletta.

Representatives of the three British Services and other NATO countries played a large part in the island's independence celebrations. In a two-hour tattoo, watched by a crowd of 60,000, men of The Royal Sussex Regiment, dressed in the uniform of the period, recalled the scene on the Fort's ramparts in 1800 with a tableau "The First British Flag"—one of five tableaux depicting major events in Malta's history.

The Regiment's Band and Corps of Drums, with the bands of The Duke of Edinburgh's Royal Regiment and the Royal Malta Artillery, were featured in a massed band display of marching and counter-marching.

During his stay on the island as the Queen's representative at the celebrations, the Duke of Edinburgh paid his first visit as Colonel-in-Chief to his own Regiment. After inspecting a Guard of Honour, Prince Philip strolled round the barracks chatting with all ranks and meeting wives and families. He said he hoped the Battalion was enjoying its stay in Malta as much as he did during his service in the Royal Navy.

Dazzling white uniforms were the order of the day for men of the Royal Malta Artillery when they were inspected by Prince Philip —one of the many military events during the island's independence celebrations.

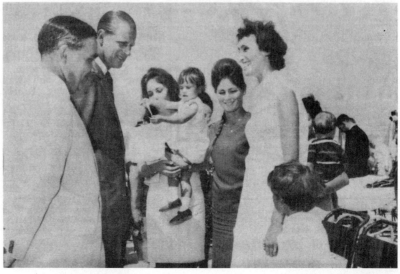

Thrill of a lifetime for wives and children — the Duke of Edinburgh stops for a chat during a visit to his own Regiment in Malta.

HAPPY IS THE DAY!

JOIN the Army and see the world —in your own car! All-round increases in pay from the 1st of next month bring the old recruiting slogan right up to date and lift most of the Army's married sergeants into the £1000-a-year class.

The biennial pay and pensions review, recommended by Sir James Grigg's committee in October, 1958, has given the Services a total average increase over two years, in rates of pay, allowances, pensions and gratuities, of just under seven and a half per cent. Previous reviews were in 1960 and 1962.

Weekly increases fatten the soldier's pay packet by the following amounts: Private between 7s 0d and 14s 0d, lance-corporal 10s 6d to 14s 0d, corporal 10s 6d to 17s 6d, sergeant 14s 0d to 21s 0d, staff-sergeant and warrant officer, class II, 17s 6d to 28s 0d, warrant officer, class I, 24s 6d to 31s 6d.

Some increments for long service are up, and parachute pay has been increased by 1s 6d to 7s 6d a day.

Annual increases for officers are: Second-lieutenant £46, lieutenant £46 to £55, captain £64 to £82, major £100 to £109, lieutenant-colonel £146 to £164, colonel £274, brigadier £438, major-general £566, lieutenant-general £712, general £912 and field-marshal £1077. Medical and dental officers get increases, following awards to their civilian counterparts, and new pay scales

recognise the special circumstance of officers in the Army Legal Services Staff. Increased, too, are officers' parachute pay and special qualification pay for officers in the Royal Engineers, Royal Signals and Royal Electrical and Mechanical Engineers.

The new rates of retired pay and pensions will apply to officers retiring on or after 1 February, 1964, and to soldiers discharged on or after 31 January, 1964. Retired pay and pensions for the Women's Services, like their pay, are again at about 85 per cent of equivalent men's rates.

Some gratuities have been increased and there are new rates of gratuities payable to widows of Regulars who are not eligible for a Service widow's pension. These will apply where deaths occur on or after 1 February, 1964.

Marriage allowance has been increased by between £54 and £77 a year for soldiers, and between £64 and £82 for officers. Married Servicemen in Britain living in private accommodation will benefit by the full amount of the increase in marriage allowance, but for those in quarters there is an apparent "Irishman's rise" for they will have to pay, after allowing for tax, about the same increase in rents.

The explanation is that while both marriage allowance and quartering charges have remained unchanged since 1958, there has been a very steep

increase in civilian housing costs since then. During this time the married man in quarters has not, on the whole, suffered financially, but the lot of the married man out of quarters (representing a significant percentage of the Army's married men) has steadily become worse over the six years.

The new quartering charges, says the War Office, represent the average expenditure on housing, basic furnishings and household effects (the equivalent of a furnished quarter) of civilian families of comparable income groups. But because income groups' expenditure varies widely, quartering charges are being varied by rank so that the lower ranks are not penalised.

A special adjustment has been made so that the net increase in marriage allowance for non-commissioned ranks meets the higher quartering charges, but, warns the War Office, there is always the possibility that in a future review, should there be a steep rise in housing costs, quartering charges may have to go up by more than marriage allowance.

In handy, tear-out form, the next three pages give in detail the majority of the new pay rates, allowances, pensions and gratuities.

Pay rates for chaplains, Royal Army Educational Corps, veterinary, legal, medical and dental officers, quartermasters and Sapper quantity surveyors will be given in next month's SOLDIER.

1965

More Jungle Bashing!

1965 began with the swift deployment of troops - in the shape of the Queen's Own Buffs and members of the Royal Artillery - to British Guiana, where a politically inspired terrorist war was being waged between rival factions in the Colony.

Other operations worldwide - such as the UN peace-keeping force in Cyprus, and the terrorist campaign in Aden, continued during the year with no immediate signs of a settlement. Despite these activities, British troops managed to exercise in some fairly exotic places - such as Jamaica and the Bahamas and gain a good deal of experience - not too mention enjoyment, from the visits.

Jungle operations however were very much to the fore this year. In Malaysia, operations continued in the non-stop struggle to protect the borders of this new Federation from trigger-happy terrorists.
Despite the claims of President Sukarno's neighbouring Indonesia to crush the new Federation quickly, British soldiers- the same men who just a few years back won the long and bitter campaign in the same jungles against an equally determined enemy - patrolled day and night the long and dangerous borders between Malaya and Thailand, as well as those of Borneo, Sarawak and Sabah that joined with Indonesia.

Assisting the troops with this thankless task were two new "vehicles" that were undergoing trials by the Army in the Far East. They were the first of the Hovercraft that would eventually be used worldwide by a whole variety of Armed Forces. At the time they were much appreciated by both the trials team and all those fortunate to use them.

IN A POLITICALLY-INSPIRED TERRORIST WAR ONE MAN, ABOVE ALL OTHERS, IS INVALUABLE TO HELP FIGHT IT. HE IS THE BRITISH SOLDIER

Alert and ever-watchful, soldiers on round-the-clock patrols guard "targets" ranging from a factory to a sleeping child.

THE PROTECTORS

PIERCING screams rent the humid night air in a tiny palm-fringed village in British Guiana. Nearby a patrol of The Queen's Own Buffs swung into action. Bursting into a house the Buffs found a terrorist slashing a terrified 16-year-old girl and her three-month-old baby sister with a sugar-cane cutlass.

The soldiers jumped on the man, tore the cutlass from his hand and dragged him off to the police while the girl and baby were rushed to a hospital where their lives were saved.

It was a sickening, heart-searing incident—but a routine job for "The Protectors," the 1200-strong force of British soldiers who are keeping the peace in the turbulent sugar colony on the northeast coast of South America.

Gritting his teeth and smothering his personal emotions like no other soldier in the world can, the British soldier is helping local police in their war against political extremists who have killed nearly 200 people, injured 1000 and burned 1500 homes and other buildings in a wave of terror that has gripped the colony for nearly a year.

It is not a pleasant job and British Guiana is no tropical paradise—it is flat, hot and hostile. The colony's uneasy peace crumbled early last year when politically-contrived racial violence between

the Indian and African residents resulted in wide-spread brutal murders of civilians and burning down of property.

Only the urgent arrival of British troops restored calm and now it is their unbending vigilance, tact and perserverance which keep the place calm.

Last month the 1st Battalion, The Queen's Own Buffs, finished its tour of duty in the colony and returned home in time for Christmas. The Buffs were replaced by 1st Battalion, The King's Own Royal Border Regiment, who flew out to join 1st Battalion, The Devonshire and Dorset Regiment.

With 43 (Lloyd's Company) Medium Battery, Royal Artillery, serving in an Infantry role, the two Infantry battalions are dovetailed with other minor units into a security force, under the command of Colonel Robert de Lisle King, which includes the colony's armed civilian police and the baton-carrying Home Guard, recruited and trained by the Army.

In humid temperatures which seldom fall below 80 degrees Fahrenheit, round-the-clock patrols keep constant vigil in the streets of the capital, Georgetown, in wood hut villages and over fields of rice and sugar cane dotted along the 500-mile palm-fringed seaboard. They guard "targets" ranging from a sprawling factory to a sleeping child.

It is at night that the real danger exists. Steel-helmeted, their bared bayonets glinting in the moonlight, the patrols watch and wait for the spark that could flare into another outbreak of killings similar to recent incidents when two Africans were machined-gunned and an Indian family of four was wiped out by a political fanatic with a rifle.

Last year arsonists, as well as burning homes, destroyed a church, cinema and hospital and within a few weeks damaged £400,000 worth of sugar cane—the colony's main export.

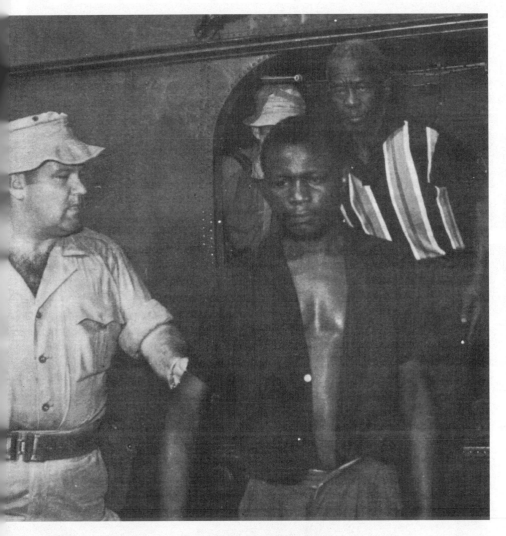

A tragically familiar sight in Georgetown –a father and his seven children died in this house at the hands of an arsonist.

Continuing ceaselessly is the search for illegal arms, ammunition and explosives. Home-made shotguns have been discovered in hollow trees or beneath the water of dykes—even the tops of the swaying palms are searched.

One operation was a raid on a house being used as an "arms factory" where rifles were made with crudely carved butts and barrels of old bicycle frames. The spring action of one gun was a mousetrap and the hammer and trigger of another had been taken from a toy revolver.

Much of the Protectors' work is routine. Platoons are scattered as far as 70 miles apart to take charge of selected trouble spots, showing the flag with constant patrols and snap searches of houses, vehicles and river ferries.

One of the Army's great deterrents is the surprise heliborne assault. In one dawn swoop along a 15-mile stretch of riverside settlements, more than 40 murder and arson suspects were captured.

Patrols landed from Royal Air Force and Royal Navy helicopters while *Alouettes* of 24 Recce Flight, Army Air Corps, hovered overhead ready to chase any suspects who made a run for it.

At the same time, more patrols blocked the river, searched all river traffic and commandeered small craft to ferry suspects to a rice mill for interrogation. The skipper of one boat who failed to stop when challenged hurriedly changed his mind after a burst from a *Bren* across his bows. Inland, mounted patrols rounded up suspects in the denser parts of the operational area.

Helicopters can have a hypnotic effect on the locals. Two murder suspects stood transfixed outside a small wood burner's hut in a jungle clearing while six assault pioneers of The Queen's Own Buffs were winched down from a hovering helicopter. The suspects were hooked on to the end of the winch cable, hauled up and flown off for questioning.

FOCUS ON MALAYSIA

Largely surrounded by hate, Malaysia continues the non-stop struggle to protect her borders from incursions by trigger-happy terrorists. President Sukarno of neighbouring Indonesia has so far failed to meet the much-publicised deadlines by which he will have crushed the new-born Federation of Malaysia. His optimism is staggering, for watching the borders of Malaysia are British soldiers, the same men who just a few years back won the long and bitter struggle in these same jungles against an equally desperate enemy. They may be from the other side of the world, but the jungle is no stranger to them and, while they quietly get on with their job, Malaysia, after a difficult birth, grows strong.

Right: Men of 1st Battalion, Scots Guards, patrol the Thai-Malay border, constantly on the watch for Communist terrorists infiltrating into Malaysia. The Guards, now part of 28th Commonwealth Infantry Brigade Group, took over from 3rd Battalion, The Royal Australian Regiment. Above, Maj Sir Gregor McGregor (right) discussing tracks in the remote border area with two departing Australians, Maj A Argent (centre) and Capt G Warland.

Above: A Gurkha and a Royal Ulster Rifleman share a sandbagged dugout facing the Indonesian border in Sabah. Their alert expressions were not posed—for only about 300 yards away Indonesian troops were reported to be massing

Left: Unusual Transpot for the 4th Royal Tank Regiment. A few months ago they were fighting the Red Wolves in the Radfan mountain area of Arabia—now they change thier *Ferret* scout cars for a longboat on a jungle-fringed river in Sarawak. Ignored by the woman doing her family wash, the patrols carry out house-to-house searches for hidden arms in riverside villages

Above: Sergeant Mick Lines, 4th Royal Tank Regiment, checks identity cards at a surprise road block in Sarawak—a routine task that sometimes snares unsuspecting Indonesian agents

Left: Working as quietly as possible and communicating only by signs, men of 2nd Battalion, The Parachute Regiment, ferry equipment across a muddy river in Johore State during jungle warfare training. Makeshift rafts of sticks and groundsheets will even carry heavy guns. The Red Devils were among the British reinforcements flown out to Malaysia when a full-scale attack from Indonesia was threatened a few months ago

In famous battles past, the British Cavalry's spirited charges shattered enemy armies weakened by the Infantry. Now the Cavalry, minus bugles and pennants, plus the *Malkara* missile, is set to jump and fight beside airborne Infantry

MAILED FIST AND RED BERET

THE buccaneers of a new airborne Cavalry unit have lifted the dash and drama of old-time horse soldiering into the 20th century. Men of The Parachute Squadron, Royal Armoured Corps, wear the red beret with a "mailed fist" cap badge and sport the motto "Go anywhere, do anything" with a touch of the Balaclava spirit. Their weapon is *Malkara*, long-range destroyer of tanks.

This two-hundredweight missile is launched and guided from a lightly armoured *Hornet* vehicle by a crew of three. It is phenomenally accurate and will deliver a high-explosive deathblow to any tank in the world.

After an initiation ritual that began a year ago at the Airborne Forces Depot, Aldershot, the Squadron has been fully integrated in 16 Independent Parachute Brigade Group. The vital operational role is to protect a brigade landing with an anti-tank weapon capable of neutralising enemy armour.

The three launcher troops are equipped with the *Hornet* and are supported by administrative and reconnaissance troops and a Royal Electrical and Mechanical Engineers workshop. Last month one of the

Story by JOHN SAAR
Pictures by FRANK TOMPSETT

Charge of the height brigade. Troopers from many tank and Cavalry regiments jump from a *Hastings* in a Parachute Squadron practice drop.

back to airborne forces an armoured unit which will give us a strong anti-tank capability immediately after landing."

A blast of cold air from the *Beverley's* boom aperture jostles the swaying stick of *Hornet* crews. The snow-covered Salisbury Plain looks as dreary as Korea as the plane runs in on the Everleigh dropping zone at 1400 feet.

In the confusion of the wind rush the troopers go through their aircraft drill with the nonchalance expected of crewmen used to intricate manoeuvres in the cramped innards of tanks.

The green has barely lit and the first man is dropping through the floor into the slipstream. With the last man clear by seconds, the navigator electrically releases a 21-foot extractor chute to drag the six-ton *Hornet* from its nest in the freight bay. The *Beverley* trundles along trailing its entrails from the cargo maw until the eight-ton load of the launcher on its medium-stress platform somersaults free.

While the parachutists glide down to plop neatly into the snow, their battle chariot hangs under six 66-foot chutes and steams into the ground at 18 miles an hour. The 12 airbags explode on landing and when the deriggers race up to slacken off the festoons of chains they find the sturdy launcher and its complex guidance system intact.

The dropping zone flares are still smouldering when the vehicle is driven

Cyclops Squadron men wore wings and the RTR's tank. The new Squadron has drawn volunteers from Cavalry and tank units.

into the rally area ten minutes later. The signaller-loader and driver-loader mount missiles on the twin launcher booms and store two more in rear bins. The commander-controller—a sergeant, corporal or lance-corporal—checks the circuits on the missiles.

Right: A *Hornet* ready to fire. The practice rockets have dummy warheads and can be destroyed in mid-air if they go "rogue."

Below: The rocket-propelled missile outranges every known tank gun. No tank has enough armour to resist the deadly warhead.

Cold nights and scorching, sweating, thirsty days. Grit in everything, dust everywhere. Sharp-thorned bushes, sharper stones and the shifting sand that turns a mile into four. Desert soldiering is hard—ideal training for soldiers whose global trouble-shooting role may take them anywhere

Libya 1 Across the Sahara

BUZZING over the Sahara Desert for long, tedious hours, an Army Air Corps *Auster* reconnoitred the route for a 14th/20th King's Hussars 4000-mile expedition to the Tibesti Mountains.

Captain Henry Joynson of the Regiment's Air Troop clocked 58 flying hours, including a 780-mile emergency flight to Tripoli for a spare part, in ten days. From the air he spotted a pass invisible to the 17-man ground party in their four three-tonners and two long-wheelbase *Land-Rovers*, and led them to a region not previously penetrated by vehicles.

The arduous double crossing of the Sahara took the party, led by Second-Lieutenant John Smales, from the Regiment's station at Benghazi to the Libyan-Chad border 1500 miles due south. Three easy days on the 760-mile metalled road to the Fezzan town of Sebha gave the adventure training trip a gentle start.

But from Sebha, the rapidly deteriorating route headed south-east across the Sahara

Above: in the barren Sahara wastes, lone trees are mapped and footprints are landmarks.

Left: A three-tonner crests a dune after being dug out yet again by the sweating soldiers.

Above: Desert stalemate. Bogged again, and only sand channels and shovels will free it.

Below: A 14th/20th King's Hussars' *Land-Rover* cooling off near the Tibesti Mountains.

and the party sweated in the relentless heat with shovels and sand channels as the vehicles bogged down repeatedly in soft sand.

Although water was rationed to one-and-a-half pints a day—little enough when the mercury is nudging the 100 degree mark!—none of the party came near to obliging a white vulture circling hopefully overhead.

Arriving at the oasis village of Waw El Kabir to replenish water stocks, the expedition found a fully-fledged ghost town with houses abandoned though intact, and a deserted "Beau Geste" fort.

A base camp was established at the desert paradise of Waw En Namus, the crater of an extinct volcano, which boasted a bamboo plantation, palm trees, wild duck and several million white-man-eating mosquitoes.

Two hundred and fifty miles south lay the fantastically wind-blasted sandstone heights of the 10,000-foot Tibesti mountains. Here, wary contact was made with the Tibu—men of the rocks. These tribesmen are of uncertain temperament and carry two throwing knives, but they proved friendly.

Among the mountains, the expedition found neolithic rock paintings of giraffes, lions and gazelles and flint arrowheads.

From a report by Michael S Simon, Army Public Relations, Libya.

THEY call it air mobility. What it meant for 100 Guardsmen was a chameleon switch from the great-coated immobility of duty in London to the hot, hard grind of Infantry soldiering in North Africa.

The Guardsmen flew from London to Germany to rejoin 1st Battalion, Coldstream Guards, and found themselves in the middle of preparations for Exercise Long Stop which was to lift the Battalion from the frost and snow of Germany to the dust and sunshine of the Libyan desert.

Soon after, the complete Battalion flew with vehicles and support weapons to El Adem and moved to Bomba Bomba camp. In the extensive desert training area between Derna and Tobruk the companies field-fired and practised assaults with "live" support from the mortar platoon.

WATERLOO

1200 hours. British Troops make a temporary withdrawal behind a cloud of blanco.

THE WELCH IN CALYPSO LAND

West to freezing Newfoundland and then due south to the sweltering Caribbean—it was a 10,000 mile training adventure for 450 Welsh soldiers

A FOUR-MONTH drought in the Caribbean island of Jamaica ended with the arrival of The Welch Regiment. The skies of the "island in the sun" darkened and the Welshmen were welcomed with a home-from-home downpour.

One young Welsh soldier, peering through the sheets of rain, was even sufficiently moved to remark: "You know what, man? It reminds me of Cwmgwdi." Columbus, who discovered the island 500 years ago, may not have agreed; but Dylan Thomas would have understood.

It was Exercise Calypso Hop—a 10,000-mile iaunt for 450 men of 1st Battalion,

The Welch Regiment, to practise a quick move by air over a long distance. Royal Air Force *Britannias* flew each company for a fortnight from the British spring to freezing Newfoundland, where six-foot snowdrifts surrounded the airport, and from there to sweltering Kingston in Jamaica.

The untypical rain did nothing to dampen the spirits of the Welsh lads, whose first task was to winkle out the "insurgents" causing trouble in the hills in the north of the island.

These daredevil fighters, comfortably ensconced up-country, were played by a platoon of The Welch Regiment and a platoon of the Jamaica Defence Force.

Organising the exercises was an American officer, Major "JB" Tower, who commands a Welch company as US Liaison Officer at the School of Infantry, Warminster, where the Welch are the demonstration battalion.

The first exercise started at midnight after a briefing by "JB" attended by two officers of the 3rd Battalion, The Jamaica Regiment, who were observers. Lieutenant John Williams, who settled in Jamaica 12 years ago and claims a Welsh great-grandfather, took a look at the country the soldiers had to cross and commented laconically: "There'll be plenty of bruises tonight."

To hit the enemy simultaneously at two

Above: In an idyllic millionaires' playground setting, men of The Welch Regiment take time off on a Jamaican beach.

IN CALYPSO LAND

In the bar at Gander Airport, Newfoundland, Corporal Tommy Thorne, on his way to Jamaica, was having a quiet drink and thinking that the barman looked strangely familiar. "Haven't I seen you somewhere before?" he asked. "You're durned right," drawled Bill McMahon, "in Tobruk, 1941." Tommy and Bill were drinking pals in besieged Tobruk during the 1941 desert campaign. The reunion was a short one, for the *Britannia* was quickly refuelled. "See you in about 20 years' time," quipped Bill McMahon as he waved goodbye.

Reunion in the bar at Gander Airport, Newfoundland, when Cpl Thorne (right) met a war-time comrade (second from right) for the first time since 1941.

In pouring rain Captain John Ayres (above) briefs his men before setting off on a reconnaissance. Below: On one of the many exercises a patrol of the Welch races across a field in north Jamaica.

points at first light, the soldiers had to trek across razor-sharp volcanic rocks in pitch darkness for five hours. The battle started rather disconcertingly with half the leading Welch platoon assessed as "casualties," but when the supporting platoon took over, things improved and, dodging from tree to tree, they rooted out the "insurgents."

The last few hours of the battle were fought, of course, in pouring rain.

Back at Cotton Tree Camp, Moneague, the soldiers dried out, only to be soaked again on the next exercise. On the church parade, the local minister, sheltering under a huge black umbrella, informed his drenched congregation: "I know you won't appreciate the sentiment of my remarks, but we really need this rain."

But the sun did break through for recreational afternoons on the north coast beaches—the millionaires' playgrounds of Ocho Rios and Montego Bay.

Undoubtedly the man who had the most enjoyable stay in Jamaica was Lance-Corporal Brian Dingle—he was on leave. He married a Jamaican girl ten years ago and his Battalion agreed to let him go on the exercise and spend his leave with his wife's family.

TRANSPORT OF TOMORROW?

TWO *Hovercraft* are being used with spectacular success in Malaysia's near-war against Indonesia. They could be pioneering a whole new transport concept for the Services.

Exuberantly piloted (?) by four British officers, the *Hovercraft* are in use operationally for the first time. And the evaluation of their use in Borneo will play a major part when the time comes to make the big decision—useful or useless?

The men of the *Hovercraft* Unit Far East have no doubts about the matter. Major Roger Harris, Royal Corps of Transport, who commands the unit, says: "In my view the *Hovercraft* will certainly come into use. Here in Borneo we can skim along rivers at a phenomenal speed carrying big loads of men or materials. We can do things beyond the capability of any other known form of transport."

It certainly would be ironic if this British invention—already apparently exploited on a civilian net by foreign countries while Britain made up her mind—were used first on a large scale by some other army.

The *Hovercraft* Unit is based in a small camp on the banks of a wide river in Tawau. Here are kept the two Westland SRN5 *Hovercraft*, painted in jungle green with a Union Jack on each rudder.

A gentle slope from the camp across a sandy beach and mud flat to the water, allows the *Hovercraft* to drive straight in and out of the camp on their daily missions.

Since early this year, both machines have been used extensively in operations against Indonesian guerrillas infiltrating across the border in the sprawling complex of waterways that surround Tawau, but to date the machine-gunner who sits warily through a hatch in the roof of the *Hovercraft* has never been needed.

Twenty-five men comprise the unit, about half of them Army and half Royal Navy. There are four "drivers" (one problem the Unit still has not solved is what to call them—suggestions range from the racey "hoverpilot" to the pedantic "operator") all of whom were trained at the Inter-Services Hovercraft Trials Unit in England.

Above: Rising in a roaring cloud of spray on to its cushion of air, a *Hovercraft* prepares to return to base after a routine mission near the border.

Story by RUSSELL MILLER/Pictures by FRANK TOMPSETT

SOLDIER

SEPTEMBER 1965 • One Shilling

Cover Picture

In Tawau, Malaysia, one of Britain's two *Hovercraft* in the Far East roars along a jungle river. It is returning from a routine detail to ré-supply Serudong Laut, a company position further up river right on the border with Indonesia. The machine-gunner can be clearly seen poking up through a hatch in the roof. This picture was taken by SOLDIER cameraman Frank Tompsett from a *Whirlwind* helicopter of the Royal Air Force.

Top: Malay children scream with delight as the SRN5 moves off. Above: Major Harris, boss of the units, talks to a driver during weight trials.

Left: Mammoth *Hovercraft* capable of high speeds could make that cargo ship useless in a few years.

Below: The SRN5 at speed on the open sea. The unit has completed several long journeys in all weathers at average speeds of over 50 knots.

calm sea it is just like sitting in a noisy car, but negotiating the twisting rivers of Borneo certainly provides a thrill—it is similar to a four-wheel drift in a car.

Approaching the bend, the driver points the nose into the turn and the whole machine literally slides round at a skidding angle which is corrected after the bend. The other heart-lurching experience is to see the driver rush towards sandbanks in the river—it is difficult at first to accept that you are merely going to skim over them.

A sheet of spray briefly ruffles the South China Sea calm as L/Cpl Carl Butler skids into a turn.

Playtime on BLAK

THE cheapest water skiing in the world is among the attractions offered at a beach run by a handful of soldiers on Blakang Mati, an island off Singapore. Ten years ago it was just another deserted beach; today it is an informal playground with facilities that would not shame the French Riviera.

Ski at 3s 6d for a quarter of an hour; hire a canoe for 1s 2d an hour or a boat with an outboard motor for 4s 8d; eat lunch served under an umbrella on the beach for a few shillings with an iced drink from the bar (open all day); swim in the warm South China Sea or just lounge in the shade of the green trees that fringe the golden sand.

All this is offered by the Canoe Club of 30 Battalion, Royal Army Ordnance Corps, stationed in Singapore. It's enough to make Billy Butlin green with envy.

"Discovered" in 1955, the beach has been developed entirely by the effort and interest of a successive chain of soldiers. A thatched lean-to became a wooden hut, changing rooms were built, tables, chairs and umbrellas added, then a boat-house, kitchen, bar and verandah.

Manned entirely by volunteers, the beach attracts a good crowd every weekend throughout the year. Visitors pay up to 2s 4d beach fees and these "paying guests" plus the profit from the bar have brought more than £300 into the Canoe Club kitty.

One of the pleasant aspects of Blakang Mati is that it is completely informal with very few restrictions. There is none of the martial discipline often imposed on European beaches when hiring a boat or canoe.

The 16 locally-built canoes at the beach are treated with cheerful abandon and often capsize, but so long as no one paddles too far out, no one bothers much.

Even very small children hire the canoes and have a fine old game in them. If they swamp them and submerge then it is so much the better—they pretend they are in a submarine.

But the freedom is far from reckless and on the verandah of the bar some helper is inevitably standing scanning the area with binoculars.

Four Malaysian soldiers run the boat hire. Corporal Sharif, a battalion clerk, looks after the bookings while Corporal Tex Suhaimy, Lance-Corporal Ramly and Private Majio drive the speedboat and

Above: Maj A G Gill, RASC, leaves a sparkling wake and the island's waterfront behind him.

Below left: As the sun goes down on the Blakang Mati beaches, a sampan glides back to Singapore.

Below: The children hate leaving their island paradise, so re-embarkation can take a long time.

"Daddy always says that Combined Operations are risky, but *who* is that rocking our boat?"

NG MATI !!! Story by RUSSELL MILLER / Pictures by FRANK TOMPSETT

organise the water skiing. Regulars behind the bar are Corporal Tony Thompson and Private Jim Martin. All the helpers get their expenses paid, but no wages.

An Indian contractor runs the kitchen, somehow producing quite good meals from his little tin shack, and a harassed waiter with all-gold teeth rushes up and down the beach serving food.

The general running of the beach is now the responsibility of a three-man committee—Major Harry Higgins, Warrant Officer Graham Belfield and Staff-Sergeant Harry Vincent. Mrs Belfield and Mrs Vincent usually collect the beach fees—wearing bikinis and bus conductor-type cash bags.

Most families get to Blakang Mati by hiring a sampan for a few shillings in Singapore to take them across in the morning and pick them up in the evening. It makes an excellent day out.

Blakang Mati beach is a superb example of unselfish enterprise by a few soldiers and has reached such a stage of prosperity that it even finances regimental charities.

And, unfortunately, it is the sort of facility that all too often is taken for granted by soldiers and their wives.

Beach fees which pay for the club and leave something over for charities are collected by the two bikinied ladies in the centre of the picture, Mrs Audrey Belfield (left) and Mrs Audrey Vincent.

Below: Informal committee meeting. Left to right: S/Sgt H Vincent, Maj H Higgins, WOI G Belfield.

WATERLOO

1131 hours. First French casualty.

THE WINDMILL THAT HASN'

IT is probably the most famous canteen in North-West Europe. Its distinctive shape, looming out of the fog or the night, has brought comfort to millions of weary troops.

The menu aspires to nothing more adventurous than sausage, two eggs and a cup of tea. But every week thousands of soldiers swear that cup of tea at the Windmill YMCA on the autobahn in Germany is the best they have ever tasted.

For 18 years the Windmill has been dispensing cups of tea and comfort to everyone from the Commander-in-Chief downwards. Almost all troop movement in Germany involves using the autobahn on which it stands—and every soldier who has ever served in Germany must remember with affection the "good old Windmill."

Originally used as a café by the Germans, it was closed when Hitler built the autobahn and remained empty until 1947 when

it was taken over by the YMCA. Since that time countless tired soldiers have pulled their vehicles off the autobahn after exercises or a long drive, clattered up the central spiral staircase and slumped at a table with a steaming cup of *char*.

Open from seven in the morning until eleven at night every day of the year except Christmas Day, the Windmill has changed little from when it was first taken over.

Famous people, nonentities, generals and

CLOSED

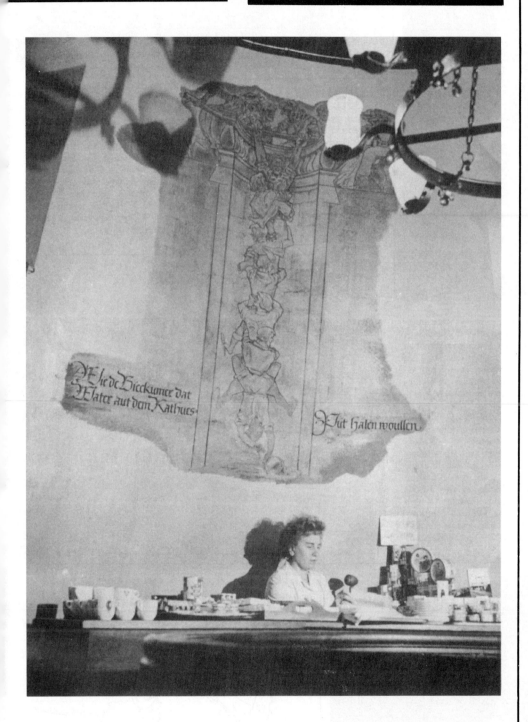

gunners, have all called there, many recording their appreciation in the well-worn pages of the visitors' book.

In the grounds is a tiny building with three beds inside and almost every night these are occupied by soldiers marooned by the weather or too tired to continue.

This month the manager of the Windmill, 74-year-old Mr Henry Dolden, celebrates his seventeenth year at the canteen. "It has been a wonderful time and I hope I will have many more years here," he said. "I must have met enough soldiers to form a fair-sized army—up to 3000 a day stop here and nearly all the generals of Rhine Army have called in."

On one occasion over a cup of tea a general told a little Cockney soldier how lucky he was to be in the Army, ending with: "I think you have got a very good job." "Yes sir," replied the soldier, "and so have you."

Sign in, please

Proudest possession of the Windmill is the well-thumbed visitors' book. Sir Beverley Baxter held the honour of making the opening entry—until "Scouse and Crasher" decided to squeeze their names in first.

Through the months and years the entries record the tired travellers from all over the world who have stopped for a cup of tea. "Hell on Wheels" from Celle was closely followed by a priest (in pursuit or vice-versa?) and a mysterious thumbprint with a message in Arabic.

Two officers on their way to drink vodka with the Soviet Army (happier days then) may not have been so frivolous had they known that the next signature was to be Sir Hugh Stockwell, then commander of the 1st British Corps.

Comedian Arthur English signed soon after "Get Knotted 317" while a more debonair caller records: "A far cry from its namesake in Piccadilly, but just as welcome."

"The Bomb—the best Scammell in BAOR" comes in for some derisory comment as does modest Jock Green who described himself as "the Windmill's most popular visitor and if you don't believe me ask Margaret and Kittie."

Vic Oliver . . . Arthur, late for a chaplain's conference . . . the Hameln Rats . . . Carole Carr Company, 1957 . . . recovery in BAOR will soon be looking up, Lou is back . . . the English motor racing team.

"Two hungry and lonesome Americans looking for advice and food," gratefully entered their appreciation and Gracie Fields finds herself on the same page as the inevitable Kilroy. "Blimey, is this place still standing?" asks one anonymous writer.

Verse comes thick and fast, like "We came, we saw, we conked out. But not to worry, we weren't in a hurry." Two "wild Colonial boys" passed through closely followed by three girls from Texas.

Sincerity is there, too. "See you at the Windmill. No one will ever know what that has meant to tens of thousands of Servicemen and women." Or "after 200 miles just the job—nice tea, food and bed."

"The last Life Guards to visit the Windmill" were a bit premature as the next entry—"No you aren't, mate"—indicates. Mormons from Salt Lake City in America were soon followed by blissful newly-weds who recorded proudly: "Married today—first meal, Mr and Mrs J A White."

One of the more recent entries is intriguing. It appeals plaintively: "I am here, Desireé, but where are you?"

◀The only English pub-type club in Detmold, Germany, has been opened by men serving in 20 Ordnance Field Park, Royal Army Ordnance Corps. Behind that hanging sign hangs a tale. The spare-time pub-builders needed a swinging sign and successfully appealed to a London brewers for help. Major-General B O P Eugster unveiled the sign to open the "Ordnance Arms"—and drank a glass of stout in its honour.

▲This housewarming parade was given by men of 16 Independent Parachute Brigade Group when Field-Marshal Viscount Montgomery of Alamein DSO came to open their new barracks in Aldershot. He christened the Brigade's £3 million home and headquarters, Montgomery Lines, and joins the elite of British generals—Marlborough and Wellington—who have important Aldershot barrack areas named after them.

A pinewood pyre blazes on St George's Day and the 13th Shoreham Platoon of the Army Cadet Force know that Enterprise Neptune is on the wing throughout the land. Their beacon on the summit of Chanctonbury Ring, South Downs was one of 500 burning simultaneously on hilltops in England, Wales and Northern Ireland to warn the nation of invasion from within—by developers who are spoiling Britain's 3000 miles of coast. Neptune is the code name for the National Trust project to raise £2 million for preservation and many Army Cadet Force units co-operated with other youth organisations by lighting the ▼chain of warning beacons.

Despite being two weeks late on▶ parade, the men of 1st Battalion, The Lancashire Regiment, trooped the Colour in memorable style in Swaziland. They were commemorating the 150th anniversary of Waterloo, the Regiment's proudest battle honour. Two weeks before, the last of 22 full rehearsals had just ended when the Battalion was called out to cordon off an outbreak of foot and mouth disease (SOLDIER, April). The whole affair ended happily with the Battalion winning the thanks of the Swazis for controlling an epidemic which threatenened the nation's economy and giving an immaculate display in brilliant sunshine on the Mbabane cricket ground.

WATERLOO

1800 hours. British Troops stand firm.

1966

Change, the greatest constant

Though the Defence Review dominated much of the news about the Forces this year, Overseas operations were also prominent. Indeed, the headlines from the Borneo confrontation, which by this time was on the way to a settlement, included the award of the first VC since the Korean War, to L/Cpl Rambahdur Limbu of the 10th Princess Mary's Own Gurkha Rifles.

Meanwhile in Aden things were becoming very hot indeed. Arab terrorists, both in the Urban areas of Crater and Little Aden as well as up-country in the Radfan, were becoming ever more active - and vicious. Daily casualty rates were increasing among soldiers and terrorists, as well as women and children in the civilian and military populations.

The Defence Review however, was the real news for the year - certainly among those serving, or intending to serve, in Britain's Armed Forces. From it came yet more change as the Government stated its intention to withdraw British influence from as much of its territories East of Suez as possible. In doing so there was to be, yet again, further reductions in the Regular Army. There was also to be complete re-organisation and reduction of the Territorial Forces. All these change were scheduled to be completed by the end of the following year.

The year finished on a happier note however, with the rebuild of Aldershot garrison well on the way to completion. And in BAOR, British tank gunners in the form of the 13/18 Royal Hussars proved themselves to be the top NATO tank gunners when they won the coveted Canadian Army trophy competition.

Built on the lava afterbirth of a volcano, Aden now faces a new onslaught of violence—self-destructive. The Biblical state experiences the bomb-blast and gun-shot of so-called freedom fighters. Egyptian-paid hirelings peddle indiscriminate death on the open streets, showing callous indifference in their choice of victims: Arabs and Britons, women and children have been slain and maimed. The fleeting hours of peace that descend on this malignant isthmus in South Arabia are earned by the patience, courage and determination of the British soldier. A day free of bloodshed counts as his victory

ADEN'S DIRTY WAR

By night, Crater simmers in uneasy peace. Soldiers put their backs to a wall and cover one another.

BEHIND the mesh the carbon snout of the sub-machine gun was chest high and steady. "Step through that door and I shoot, and shoot to kill," said the British Soldier in Aden.

He spoke his stark orders in the sorrowing tones of a man announcing a funeral. He was guarding the tree-shadowed entrance to the Joint Security Centre, a tempting flashpoint in Aden's explosive night-life. A harshly lighted room in this building is the axis of a labyrinthine internal security operation. From here the three battalions of the Aden Brigade have hounded to the brink of disintegration the Aden network of the National Front for the Liberation of Occupied South Yemen.

The future of the British base in Aden awaits a political decision. The role of the Army has been to hold the forum until the talking is done. And by a prodigy of effort the soldiers have succeeded. Three battalions are keeping the peace in 75 square miles of desert, waterfront, gaunt, God-less mountain and ugly townships. The multi-racial 300,000, who defy climate and geography to stay here at all, live in packing case shanties, unsanitary hovel-warrens and in poky flats in jerrybuilt Western blocks.

In the quiet times a soldier gets four nights a week in bed. When a whirlwind riot fills the fetid air with flying rocks he spends tense, edgy hours on the street. He snatches meals and cat-naps on the stone floor of the police barracks. Like every Briton in Aden he is a terrorist target. Not a comforting thought to live with for the two years some non-Infantry soldiers are serving.

No effort has been spared to curb the men who want to railroad the British out in a shower of grenades. Flatly worded entries in the operations log sketch the pattern of NLF move and hard-hitting counter-move by the security forces.

A wanted car crashes through a check-point and roars away, in seconds the squawk box in the operations room blares with the report. A cliff-hanging close, "Am manoeuvring vehicles to chase him," leaves the duty controller sitting tight with fingers crossed. Radio reports give him an

In Aden's chaotic streets even an armed soldier is unobtrusive. Killers melt easily into the bustle.

Below: A searchlight exposes an unlit boat crossing Aden's dhow harbour. Gentle interrogation and investigation of several packages disclosed harmless mirrors decorated with Nasser's picture. The Royal Corps of Transport share harbour patrol duties with the Royal Navy. Below right: Off Slave Island, soldiers go aboard a souvenir boat to make a routine search for arms and ammunition.

idea of the situation. Wits and instinct decide his action. The net has to be thrown fast and cunningly to make a catch. For eight hours at a time the duty officers play a hair-raising game of chess against an opponent who seeks to strike at any undefended target.

The battalions "mind" a slice of territory apiece and generally keep their troubles in the family. The security centre keeps the defence plan cohesive with "all station" orders for curfew or reinforcement (swiftly imposed roadblocks can seal off turbulent Crater and chop Aden into manageable sectors).

Scrawled on a blackboard is the name of a technical officer whose line of duty calls him to deal with what are politely dubbed "explosive devices." Phones which bring news of riot and civil disturbance from the police stations ring too often. One remains silent for weeks at a time although the number is the best known in Aden. In spite of £5000 rewards, calls from informers are extremely rare.

Men are gunned down in crowded streets. People melt away and no one remembers—"I saw no shooting" is the parrot-cry.

Even those who oppose the NLF keep their knowledge of its activities to themselves. Fear plays a large part in their silence. Sana Radio broadcasts Hitlerian tirades daily. Absurd allegations against the British and farcical news bulletins are partially digested by the Adenis because the overall message is one that exerts a certain fascination—the dream of Arab nationalism triumphant.

Kid-glove treatment of the population has won no support for the British cause. Terrorists regard restraint as weakness and take full advantage. Escaping terrorists rush for crowds knowing that the soldiers will not risk a shot, hide in mosques and traverse Aden under the inviolable veil of the Moslem woman.

Cairo plans all subversion and pays blood money to some of the successful "heroes". A full-scale training centre and headquarters with Egyptian soldier instructors is located in Taiz, twin capital of the Yemen.

The security forces were able to shrug off the first attacks—by waterfront thugs who were untrained and irresolute. Customarily they threw grenades with the pins in or lobbed them in places where only Arabs could be hurt.

The Egyptians rethought and sent in some bazookas to their gangs to make rocket attacks on the family blocks in the mile-long Ma'alla Straight. By blocking alleys, patrolling incessantly and using wardens and snipers, the Army has put up its guard over these soft targets.

The first murder operation of the Killer Gang signified the opening of a dark phase. Unmistakably, it was the work of professionals. They were confident, daring, and they used their 9-millimetre pistols as accomplished marksmen. The five Arab Special Branch officers in Aden were killed with ruthless efficiency. A number of the killers are still loose, so naturally few Arabs dare work with the security forces.

Each day men of 1st Bn, Coldstream Guards, make checkpoint searches of 600 cars and 2000 people. Body searches (right) rarely produce a single round of ammunition, yet ten miles north of the state border every Arab carries a rifle. The checkpoints and the six-mile Scrubber Line of barbed wire have cut the smuggling of arms into Aden. At one checkpoint the guardsmen live on a roundabout for seven-day duties. Wanted cars are listed in three categories, but at least 2000 cars in Aden are unregistered and number plates can be changed with chameleon rapidity to confuse the searchers.

Left: A patrol of 1st Bn, The Prince of Wales's Own, operating in Crater. Below: Under the guns of the Infantry, children board wire-screened school buses.

This is the story of two weeks in the two lives of Staff Nurse Frederick Nock of Tooting Bec Hospital, London, alias 23924706 Corporal Frederick Nock of the City of London Battalion, The Royal Fusiliers. Recently Nurse Nock left the ordered calm of a hospital ward and flew 4000 miles to Aden; there, as Corporal Nock, he was involved in quelling riots and investigating a terrorist killing; before two weeks elapsed Corporal Nock shed the trappings of his second life and returned to his hospital as Nurse Nock. He volunteered for his schizophrenic existence when he became one of Britain's 6000 Ever-Readies, the trained force of part-time soldiers permanently available to be called up to reinforce the Regular Army. Men like 24-year-old Fred Nock prove the concept works—one day he is a civilian tending the sick in a London hospital; the next he is a soldier patrolling streets of hate in Aden's Crater with a loaded rifle . . .

PEACE AND WAR

"I started nursing when I was 18. At that time I was working as a mortuary attendant and one day I saw two dead children brought in and I thought to myself that it would be far better to nurse the living than the dead—so I started training. I had been training for about a year when it occurred to me that I could probably get useful experience of nursing work if I joined the TA. I wanted to specialise in dealing with accidents and I thought that in the TA I could be the chap who is there at the time and able to help. I called in at the local drill hall here in Tooting and asked a sergeant how I could join. He just said 'Sign here.' I did and that was that. The funny thing was that I was the first casualty—during my first training session I stuck a bayonet through my wrist!"

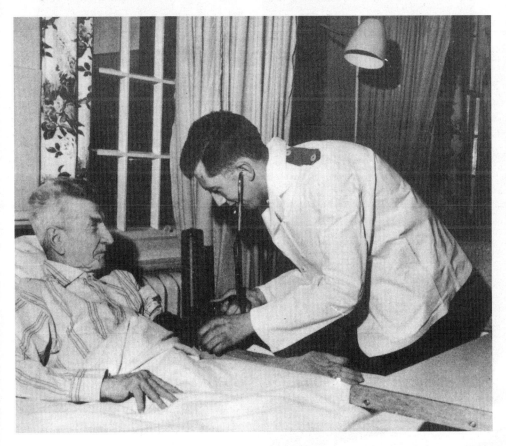

"This is my second engagement with the Ever-Readies. I suppose you could say I joined for the adventure—although the bounty has come in handy and helped go towards the deposit to buy a house for my mother in Tooting. Last year I went to northern Norway with the Ever-Readies and when this chance came to train in Aden for a couple of weeks I jumped at it. I live in the nurses' home at the hospital because it is more convenient for work but I always go round and say goodbye to my Mum before I go off anywhere. I try to keep it as short as possible because she usually sheds a tear—you know what Mums are. She thinks that if I go off to somewhere like Aden I will get blown up or something."

continued over ▶

"The following evening when we were doing a turn of standing by ready to move at a minute's notice, we were called out to a murder. It was a man who had been shot three times and the body was lying face down on the road. It was sickening to see the people round about take it as an everyday happening —a woman was quietly drinking tea nearby and on the other side of the road some men were playing cards and not even bothering to look. We were all put out as sentries to surround the area. It was very dark by then and a bit scaring—once a car slowed down and I thought 'If anyone wants to get rid of me they could do it now and never get caught.' We finally got back to the barracks in the early hours of the morning and I washed down the stretcher on which we had taken the body to the morgue —it was like being back at the hospital. We only had a few hours' sleep that night as we were off at dawn on more foot patrols in Crater. Every time I passed the spot where we found that body I was doubly careful to look all around. *(Picture below.)* There was a bit of a scare when one of the other lads saw a double barrelled shotgun pointing at him through a window—he got it in his sights when a small child appeared behind it—it was just a toy. A couple of days later we had to break up riots by schoolchildren who were shouting 'Nasser is good man.' They were throwing stones at us and although they were only about five to 14 years old, the girls were the worst. The funny thing about incidents like this was that you knew when something was going to happen—the place went very quiet and the shopkeepers all hurriedly put up their shutters."

"We only had one afternoon off and most of us went for a quick swim at the Mermaid—I thought it was a pretty good club and I was surprised at all the facilities—and then we all went shopping in the Steamer Point area. I really enjoyed all the bargaining with the shopkeepers and I bought a small pair of binoculars to use when I am climbing, a watch, two dressing gowns—one for my girl friend and one for me—a necklace for my mother and two wall mats—one for my sister and one for my brother. I was astonished how low the shopkeepers would drop their prices if you kept bargaining."

GURKHA VC

LAST month a little Gurkha flew in to London from Singapore to keep an appointment with the Queen at Buckingham Palace. Lance-Corporal Rambahadur Limbu is here to be invested with Britain's highest award for valour—the Victoria Cross.

The first Victoria Cross recipient since the Korean War, Lance-Corporal Rambahadur won the medal during a hillside battle in Sarawak on 21 November last year after his company of 2nd Battalion, 10th Princess Mary's Own Gurkha Rifles, discovered and attacked a strong enemy force near the Indonesian border.

The enemy was strongly entrenched in platoon strength on top of a sheer-sided hill, approachable only along a knife-edge ridge wide enough for three men to move abreast.

Determined to gain first blood, Rambahadur led his support group in the van of the attack and inched himself forward until, ten yards from the enemy, he was spotted by a sentry who opened fire with a machine-gun, immediately wounding a man to his right.

Rushing forward he reached the enemy trench in seconds and killed the sentry, gaining for the attacking force a first firm foothold on the objective. The enemy was now fully alerted and brought down heavy automatic fire on the attacking force, concentrating on the area of the trench held alone by Rambahadur.

Realising he could not support his platoon from the trench, he courageously left its comparative safety and, completely disregarding the hail of fire aimed at him, got together his fire group and led them to a better position some yards ahead.

He attempted to indicate his intentions to his platoon commander by shouting and hand signals but failed because of the deafening noise of exploding grenades and continuous automatic fire. Not to be thwarted, he again moved out into the open and reported personally, despite the extreme danger of being hit by fire not only from the enemy but from his own comrades.

At this moment both men of his group were seriously wounded. Knowing their only hope of survival was immediate first aid and evacuation from their very exposed

Lance-Corporal Rambahadur Limbu VC, whose wife died in February, embraces his eight-month-old younger son, Chandraprakash. The elder of his two children, Bhaktabahadur, is five years old.

position near the enemy, Rambahadur began the first of three supremely gallant attempts to rescue his comrades.

Using what little ground cover he could find he crawled forward in full view of at least two enemy machine-gun posts which concentrated their fire on him. For three full minutes he crawled forward but, when almost within touching distance of the nearest casualty, he was driven back by the heavy fire covering his line of approach.

After a pause he started to crawl forward again but he realised that only speed would give him the cover which the ground could not. Rushing forward he hurled himself on the ground beside one of the wounded and, calling for support from two light machine-guns which had come up on his right, he picked up the man and carried him to safety out of the line of fire.

Without hesitation he immediately returned to the top of the hill, determined to complete his self-imposed task of saving his men. The increased weight of fire concentrated around the remaining casualty made it clear the enemy was doing all it could to prevent further rescue attempts. Despite this Rambahadur again moved out in the open for his final attempt.

In a series of short rushes—once he was pinned down for some minutes by intense and accurate automatic fire which could be seen striking the ground all round him— he eventually reached the wounded man. Picking him up and unable now to seek cover, he carried him back through the hail of enemy bullets.

The citation says: "It had taken 20 minutes to complete this gallant action and the events leading up to it. For all but a few seconds this young NCO had been moving alone in full view of the enemy and under continuous aimed fire from automatic weapons. That he was able to achieve what he did against such overwhelming odds without being hit is miraculous."

Finally rejoining his section on the left flank of the attack, Lance-Corporal Rambahadur recovered the light machine-gun abandoned by the wounded and with it won his revenge, giving support during the later stages of the prolonged assault and killing four more enemy as they attempted to escape across the border. The hour-long battle, fought throughout at point-blank range with the utmost ferocity by both sides, was finally won.

The citation says that Rambahadur "displayed heroism, self-sacrifice and a devotion to duty and to his men of the very highest order. His actions on this day reached a zenith of determined, premeditated valour which must count amongst the most notable on record and is deserving of the greatest admiration and the highest praise."

The last action to win the Victoria Cross for Private (now Sergeant) Bill Speakman was in November 1951 during the Korean War. Lance-Corporal Rambahadur is the 1344th individual to win the medal since it was instituted in 1856. It was the first VC the 10th Gurkha Rifles have ever won, although among recent awards they have won in jungle battles in Borneo are one OBE, five MCs, one DCM, and three MMs.

Rambahadur comes from a village on the border of Nepal and India near Darjeeling. His family tradition of military service is strong—his father served in the Indian Army and he has at present two cousins and four nephews in the Gurkhas. His second name, Limbu, identifies his tribe and all Limbus, who are recruited only by the 7th and 10th Gurkha Rifles, have a reputation for dourness and hot tempers when roused!

GUNS IN ANGER

Above: Stripped to the waist in the jungle heat, men of 176 (Abu Klea) Battery fire their Pack Howitzer in close support in Sarawak. Below: An observation post party of 70 Light Battery is briefed. They are (left to right) Captain A J Pinion, Gunner I R Dover and L/Bdr D E Naylor.

THERE was no sound but the jungle as a platoon of Gurkhas waited silently in ambush for an Indonesian patrol. The metallic buzz of jungle life dominated everything until a sharp-eared soldier picked out an odd sound and, almost immediately camouflaged Indonesians appeared moving swiftly along a narrow track.

The gunfire was deafening. Brens blazed, Claymore mines belched steel destruction, rifle grenades lobbed lazily through the air and punctuating this cacophony were the screams of the dying.

A Gunner officer, crouching beside the Gurkha commander, got busy and seconds later 105mm shells howled overhead, bursting with thunderous cracks in the tree canopy a hundred yards away and spreading death among the Indonesian troops massed in confusion outside the ambush killing zone.

In three minutes the ambush was over. Twelve Indonesians lay dead and screams rang out down the track where the shells were falling.

And while the Gurkhas moved with practised ease along their withdrawal route, the Gunner forward observation officer continued to bring down shellfire on the remnants of the Indonesian patrol.

This was an incident typical of scores of similar actions experienced by men of 45 Light Regiment, Royal Artillery, who were due to return to England last month after more than two years in the Far East.

It has been an exciting tour for the Regiment. Part of 28 Commonwealth Brigade stationed at Terendak Camp, Malacca, the Gunners spent much of their time spread out in Borneo along the Indonesian border.

170 (Imjin) Battery was the first in action and was followed by 70 Light Battery. Only a few weeks after arriving in the area, B Troop of 70 Battery fired 168 rounds at maximum charge in support of a Gurkha assault on a stores dump in a cliff-top cave. Later B Troop suffered seven slight casualties in a night mortar attack on its hill-top base.

In the ambush which claimed 12 Indonesians, A Troop fired the first defensive fire SOS since the Korean War and killed eight more Indonesians in the subsequent shellfire.

Soon after 176 (Abu Klea) Battery took over the field, the guns of the Regiment were covering a frontage of 173 miles. All the guns were deployed singly in Infantry company locations under the command of a subaltern or warrant officer, who usually spent most of his time on patrol as a forward observation officer.

Battery Sergeant-Major Webster, of 176 Battery, earned a Mention-in-Dispatches while commanding his gun position in an open-sights engagement at a range of 80 yards, and 70 Battery was credited with 23 kills when it helped break up a large enemy infiltration in March last year. 102 Field Battery, Royal Australian Artillery, the Commonwealth battery attached to 45 Regiment, was sent to Borneo in May last year after kicking its heels in frustration for some months after taking part in the repulsion of Indonesian landings on the Malayan mainland.

During its tour in Borneo and Malaya, 45 Light Regiment gave artillery support to 22 Infantry battalions—a proud record to bring home.

BEGINNING OF THE END

The sun sets on a British patrol in Sarawak.

And as these men of 1st Battalion, The Queen's Own Buffs, squelch along the stinking mud flats of a river estuary watching for members of the Clandestine Communist Organisation flushed from the nearby jungle by their comrades, they know that the sun is setting too on a campaign—the three-year-long Confrontation in Borneo.

The Queen's Own Buffs are now out of Malaysia. Soon there will be no British troops in Sarawak—no more hacking through steaming jungles, no more heaving mud, no more ambushes.

It is not yet the end. But for the British troops supporting Malaysian forces it is the beginning of the end.

WEST TO A WILD SUNSET

THE American General threw an encompassing hand towards the British soldiery and the loudspeakers boomed with his Deep Southern voice: "I'd go to combat with these men any day of the week."

Louisiana-born Major-General Autrey J Maroun, jaw like a buttress, rumbustious, scowling, larger than life, is patriarch and commander of the United States Army's 5th Infantry Division (Mechanised). World War Two veteran, regimental commander in Korea—a soldier who scorns the banal "Good show!"—he went as close to eloquence as he ever will in praise of the 178 British troops serving a three-week attachment to his beloved "Red Devil" Division in Fort Carson, Colorado.

As it was only the third time British troops have trained on American soil, enormous interest enveloped the visit by C Company, 1st Battalion, The Cheshire

Regiment, and a troop of 16th/5th The Queen's Royal Lancers. Both armies have fought many battles since the Americans trounced Britain in the War of Independence, so there was a mutual curiosity in finding what made the other soldier tick.

Curiosity, or as officially stated, "familiarisation of British troops with American equipment and procedures," and the practised integration of units from the two armies, were the joint aims of Exercise Wild Sunset. Although handicapped by shortness of training time the British troops left senior US Army officers enthusing over their performance and talking in terms of another Wild Sunset in 1967.

The flight to Peterson Field, Colorado Springs, was another of those Transport Command earth-girdling operations starting in the middle of one night and ending in the throes of the next. The first of two Royal Air Force ferrying Britannias afforded its passengers the pleasure of a night's stopover in Newfoundland. The other plugged straight on to deliver bleary eyed soldiers and their freight after only two short stops for fuel, one at Gander and the

second in the concrete core of the Strategic Air Command. Offutt in Nebraska is the force's headquarters and vast silver B52s—their swept wings lazily drooping as if tired—stood at dispersal near a runway as long as last year.

The pioneers who trekked west in horse-drawn, canvas-covered armoured personnel carriers won the seventh largest and one of the most pictorially exciting states in the Union when they wrested Colorado from the Indians. It is 104 years since the fabled gold rush spawned Denver, the State capital, yet this is still awesomely wild country free from the fetters of hedge and fence.

What begins as a plain on the eastern border with Kansas rises to a 6000-foot plateau and ends with dramatic abruptness at the marching line of the Rockies. Carson camp itself is dwarfed by Cheyenne Mountain—a monster with the lowered head and powerful shoulders of a bison. Mornings dawn majestically with the sun throwing multi-coloured headlights over the yawning plain and bringing a warm smile to Cheyenne's brooding face.

Story by JOHN SAAR
Pictures by ARTHUR BLUNDELL

Top NATO tank gunners

Above: National flags flying behind the 13th/18th Hussars individual top-scoring crew of (from left to right) Cpl M Howlett, Cpl A R Edwards, L/Cpl D Ellin, Tpr R Turton.

Left: A 13th/18th Centurion (right) sits on the firing pad next to the Germans' American M48A and Belgian M47.

Below: The Hussars' captain, 2/Lieut Roderick Cordy-Simpson, receives the trophy from Maj-Gen Sir Walter Walker.

AFTER months of intensive training the 13th/18th Royal Hussars, stationed in Paderborn, Germany, have won for the British Army the annual NATO tank gunnery competition for the Canadian Army Trophy.

Last year The Royal Scots Greys gave the United Kingdom a first victory in the event which had previously been won by Belgium.

This year the United States and France again did not compete and there were teams from Germany (firing the M48A's 90mm gun), Belgium (M48A and M47), Canada and United Kingdom (Centurion with 105mm gun) and the Netherlands (Centurion with 20pr gun).

The competition, first held in 1963, is designed to test the speed and accuracy of tank gunnery. Each nation enters at least nine crews of commander, gunner, loader and driver. Of these, three crews chosen by ballot and two nominated by regiments must fire seven practices, three of them at moving targets, with one crew from each nation firing on each of the competition's five days.

At the end of the first day, on the Hohne Tank Range in Germany, Corporal Michael Howlett's crew (with Corporal Arthur Edwards as gunner, Corporal David Ellin as loader and Trooper Raymond Turton as driver) put the 13th/18th Royal Hussars

well in the lead by 1020 points with a score of 6830. This was 500 points better than the competition's previous highest individual score obtained last year by a crew of The Royal Scots Greys.

The 13th/18th led their nearest rivals, the Belgians, by 1380 points at the end of the second day, the Canadians having dropped from second place, but on the third day the Belgians narrowed the gap to 220 points and, after a splendid day's shooting, took the lead by 600 points on the fourth

day. All depended on the competition's fifth and final day and the 13th/18th Royal Hussars team—Staff-Sergeant John Hatton, Trooper Peter Rutherford (gunner), Trooper John Wild (loader) and Trooper Arnold Casterton (driver—fired first and shot the second best score of the competition, 6500 points.

Final scores were: 1 United Kingdom (27,070), 2 Belgium (26,310), 3 Germany (23,920), 4 Canada (23,810), 5 Netherlands (10,980).

The ET316, pictured here in a firing position (above) and packed up on its trailer behind a Land Rover (below), has attracted many serious inquiries from other Allied military powers.

MISSILES THREE

TWO new missiles have been accepted by the Army. Swingfire is a vehicle-based anti-tank weapon for the Royal Armoured Corps and the ET 316 is an anti-aircraft missile for the Royal Artillery capable of speeds in excess of Mach 2.

Rumours at the Farnborough Air Show and subsequent newspaper reports indicated recently that the Army was about to order another new weapon—Blowpipe, an anti-aircraft "mini" missile designed for the infantry. This is not quite accurate.

Blowpipe has been developed by Short Brothers of Belfast as a private venture to meet an infantry requirement for self-defence against very low-level aircraft. It can be fired from the shoulder, weighs only about 28 pounds and can intercept its target, unlike Redeye, the American equivalent, which can only chase its target, probably after the enemy aircraft has dropped its "eggs."

But there is certainly no order imminent —in fact it has not yet even been decided what type of weapon system should protect infantry on the battlefield against low-level aircraft. The choice is between the conventional "gun" or guided weapons.

There is no doubt of the urgent need for what is officially called a "unit self-defence surface-to-air weapon" and most of the great powers consider it one of the most important of the unsolved problems. Redeye, which homes on the heat of an aircraft's engines or on the hottest part of a

jet engine's tail-pipe, is only a partial solution.

Even if the Army finally accepts a guided weapon as the answer, there would still be many difficulties—not least the problem of aircraft recognition before the weapon could be brought into use.

Swingfire and ET316 are brighter news for the Army. Sometimes described as a successor to Vigilant, Swingfire is more accurately a replacement for the Malkara missile in that it is specifically designed to be mounted on a vehicle, unlike Vigilant which was designed as an infantry weapon and was adapted for use on a vehicle.

A wire-guided missile with jet deflection incorporated for in-flight manoeuvring, it has a good close-range performance and a very long maximum range. Because it needs no traversing gear and fires from a fixed angle of elevation irrespective of range, it is ideally suited to fitting on vehicles and can be adapted for use from helicopters.

Immune to all known electronic countermeasures, it can be fired from behind ground cover. The missile needs no testing in the field and it lives in and is launched from a robust hermetically sealed package which is easily handled and protects the missile during movement in unit transport.

ET316 is a joint service project as the system is destinated for use by both the Royal Artillery and the Royal Air Force Regiment. It is designed for operation against low-flying aircraft beneath the

coverage of existing surface-to-air guided weapons and with missiles speeds in excess of Mach 2 it can engage supersonic and subsonic aircraft from near ground level to an altitude of several thousand metres with a high single-shot lethality.

Like Swingfire, ET316 has been developed by the British Aircraft Corporation's Guided Weapons Division, which produced Thunderbird and Vigilant, now in service in many countries throughout the world.

The system is mounted on a two-wheeled trailer which carries four launching rails and the automatic target detection and acquisition radar. Towing vehicle is a Land Rover, which also carries spare missiles. The fast reaction time of the ET316 will enable it to destroy fast-flying aircraft low enough to be screened by the terrain until fairly close to their target.

Above left: Swingfire pictured a split second after launching. Below: Mock-ups of Blowpipe, the "mini" missile designed for the infantry, appeared on a stand at the Farnborough Air Show.

LET'S GO ORIENTEERING!

Starting gate for the world championships men's individual event. Ahead lie nine gruelling miles.

Competitors set off at two-minute intervals into the forest. Map in hand is Lieut David Griffiths.

Checkpoints in the world championships were camouflaged—this is a normal competition checkpoint.

Eleven countries_ Austria, Bulgaria, Czechoslovakia, Denmark, East Germany, England, Finland, Hungary, Norway, Sweden and Switzerland, competed in the first orienteering world championships held near Helsinki over a difficult course in an area of small lakes and swamps, hills and forests.

The men's individual event was won by the Norwegian, Aage Hadler, in one hour, 36 minutes and two seconds, with a Finn second and a Swede third. The six English placings in the field of 58 were: 42 Alistair Patten (2hr 33min 9sec); 46 Gordon Pirie (2hr 43min 48sec); David Griffiths (2hr 47min 7sec); 49 John Disley (2hr 48min 56sec); 54 Mike Murray (3hr 16min 52sec); 58 Tony Walker (3hr 29min 12sec).

Because of a misunderstanding The English team had to compete in the following day's team event on a non-scoring basis. This was a relay in four legs over a total distance of 22 miles and the first leg man, Chris Brasher, came in only 20 minutes behind the leading time and well within the allowance. Unfortunately the next man, Bob Astles, did not meet the next time limit and the team had to drop out with Toby Norris and Chris James still to run.

Above: Gordon Pirie, as an international figure, was loudly cheered by spectators as he spurted to the finish in the men's individual world championships.

Left: Orienteering dress is colourful and bizarre but must protect without hampering. Most competitors wear some form of leg guards against scratches.

Right: This complex scoreboard at the world championships indicated individual finishing times and margins left to competitors still on the course.

Takeover in the world championships four-man relay. Exceeded margins brought disqualification.

Orienteering can equally be practised at night. Here a competitor halts for a compass bearing.

Watched by Chris Brasher (centre), Lieut David Griffiths checks in at the world championships.

IT is a cross between a car rally without car, a treasure hunt and a cross-country run. It spread from Scandinavia to Scotland five years ago and is now one of Britain's fastest-growing sports.

The answer? Orienteering, the sport which is now taking root in the British Army and which may soon challenge its nearest neighbour, cross-country running.

Cross-country, over a fixed course, offers little to a soldier who is not a reasonable long-distance runner. Orienteering, as the name implies, involves map-reading and navigation between fixed checkpoints and indeed depends so much on accuracy in these military arts that navigational skill alone can defeat the best athlete.

The fact that a competitor can win by using his head—and not just relying on his feet—is one of the reasons why this sport attracts international athletes like John Disley, Bruce Tulloh, Roger Bannister, Martin Hyman, Gordon Pirie and Chris Brasher, and makes enthusiasts of people who have never previously competed in anything.

Orienteering is both individualistic and sociable and above all is almost infinitely variable in its permutations. The overall distance, stretches between checkpoints and the number of checkpoints, can vary as much as the chosen terrain. Checkpoints can be announced at the start—they are, of course, kept secret until just before then—or only the first given and the competitors then passed from one to the next.

Competitions can be on an individual or team basis or both and can be run in daylight or at night. And it is a sport that can be practised on motorcycles, cycles, horseback, skis or in canoes.

Preceded and followed at timed intervals by other competitors, the orienteer sets off with his marked map and compass. He is immediately on his own and has to decide for himself which route he should follow to the first checkpoint—he may see other runners but it would rarely pay him to try and follow them.

He is equally unlikely to be able to make a bee-line for the checkpoint—the organisers will have located it so that some natural obstacle presents itself. A good runner may be outstripping everyone else—and find his superior speed merely taking him the more rapidly in the wrong direction. A steady plodder may be making good time on a well-chosen longer but easier route while a faster man ensnares himself in brambles or dense forest.

Until he reaches the finish—and long after that—a competitor does not know his final placing and so does not give up, as he would perhaps in cross-country because he thinks, or knows, he has no chance.

Orienteering was born in Sweden in 1919 and has become one of that country's top sports with more than 40,000 enthusiasts in 1500 clubs. It is much more popular than either athletics or cross-country running and every week there are competitions in which from 100 to 300 men and women, in an age bracket from 13 to 57, take part.

The sport has become almost equally popular in Denmark, Norway and Finland and has been taken up by other European countries—France, Austria, Switzerland, East Germany, Hungary, Czechoslovakia, Bulgaria and West Germany.

Scotland has practised orienteering since 1961 and an English Association, formed in October 1965, now controls five regional organisations.

Story by
JOHN SAAR

FEET AND KNEES

Left: Kicking up the sand, two riders race for the finishing post.

Right: Gunner David Mortimer on one of the stallions presented to the Club by the Sheik.

BAHRAIN racecourse erupted dust and excitement as three stallions raged down the final straight inches apart. Two Arab riders beat their bare heels in a ruthless tattoo on glistening flanks and the frenzied mounts carried them ahead to a dead-heat finish.

Honour satisfied, both turned to congratulate the third man home, Gunner Dennis Williams, of G Light Parachute Battery (Mercer's Troop), Royal Horse Artillery.

The Ruler's Races are the most spectacular events in the Bahraini social calendar and the field of riders usually includes one or more British paratroopers. Race days glitter with the splendour of an entertainment ordered by a supremely powerful and wealthy Middle East monarch. The Ruler presides with a retinue of attendants and courtiers. Brave riders are rewarded in coin.

The Ruler takes a special interest in the Royal Horse Artillery entrants because they ride horses he gave the Battery to found a now flourishing Saddle Club. In Bahrain,

G Battery supports 1st Battalion, The Parachute Regiment, and through the Saddle Club 60 soldiers in the Battalion Group have been taught to ride.

Bahrain's intensely hot and sticky climate discourages most sports, but by going out at dawn and sunset the riding parties have had tremendous fun racing over the beaches and threading through the date palm plantations.

On this desolate slice of burnt toast in the Persian Gulf, recreational facilities began and ended at Hamala Camp with the swimming pool built by 16th Independent Parachute Brigade Group. Now riding—and on pure-bred Arab stallions at that—provides a welcome distraction from boredom and heat.

At a rupee (1s 6d) an hour—and in temperatures up to 110 degrees Fahrenheit —it must be the cheapest and hottest riding in the world.

When the first Royal Horse Artillery battery arrived in Bahrain, the Ruler asked about the "Horse" in the title. The explanation delighted him and he presented the Battery with four stallions from his

own stables. The Regiment granted £300 for the purchase of tack.

In the early days no charge for the maintenance of saddlery was necessary. Every time one of the six experienced horsemen in the Battalion Group rode in a race, a 300 rupee starting fee clattered into the club's coffers. Starting money is no longer accepted.

The four Royal Horse Artillery mounts and three presented to 5th Royal Inniskilling Dragoon Guards are stabled near Hamala Camp. The part-time groom is Gunner Dennis Williams who began to ride only two months before he came to Bahrain. All the new riders are likely to find English horses tame after their fiery Hamala steeds. Tumbling beginners are told: "Never mind, lad, if you can ride these you can ride anything."

Apprentice riders are apt to be intimidated when they meet their first-ever mounts, neighing like steam whistles, pawing the ground and throwing up their flashing hooves in blatant practice kicks. The drill is to follow the paratroop maxim of "feet and knees together"—keeping

Left: Bareback riders on their Arab stallions arriving for the Ruler's Races. Above: Gunner Dennis Williams, Royal Horse Artillery, thunders down the straight during one of the races.

TOGETHER

Pictures by ARTHUR BLUNDELL

Bareback this time, two RHA Gunners exercise Saddle Club horses on a beach in Bahrain.

the horse in between where possible.

Nearly everyone has been run away with once, and spills are many though injuries have not been serious.

Battery Sergeant-Major Mitchell enhanced his reputation as a hard man when his horse came down at full gallop and rolled on him. He got up—and walked away with a broken collar-bone.

When in stables the stallions are tethered separately to prevent fighting. Through some hard lessons Gunner Williams has learned that caution pays when handling horses like these. One kicked him in the stomach and another bit him on the head. "I got a bit too confident," he said.

The races are an inviting challenge and a tough proposition for the British Serviceman. From November to April the Battalion Group riders battle it out with the rough-riding Arabs over the mile-long course below a ruined hilltop palace. One of the most successful riders is a Royal Air Force parachute jumping instructor, Sergeant Jessy Pye. Another, Private Michael Walls, 1st Battalion, The Parachute Regiment, has been invited to ride horses from the Sheik's stables.

All have some way to go to match the local enthusiasm for horses and racing. The Bahrainis watch "Bonanza" (in Arabic) on television—and ride their donkey carts three abreast in whip-cracking, hell-for-leather pursuits along the main roads.

SOLDIER PICTURES

Copies of SOLDIER photographs can be obtained from:

**Picture Editor
433 Holloway Road
London N7**

They can be supplied in glossy finish, unmounted, at the following prices:

6in × 4in	..	2s 6d each
8in × 6in	..	3s 6d each
10in × 8in	..	5s 6d each
12in × 10in	..	8s 6d each
15in × 12in	..	12s 6d each
20in × 16in	..	17s 6d each
24in × 20in	..	22s 6d each

Orders to Picture Editor with cheque, money order or postal order made payable to "Command Cashier."

NATO elbow-to-elbow

FIRMLY established behind a defined front line, formation headquarters once upon a time enjoyed immunity from attack. World War Two swept all that away—headquarters were overrun, attacked from the air and raided on the ground by parachutists or special forces.

Clerks, batmen, cooks, orderlies—every man in the headquarters—became first and foremost fighting soldiers again.

For men of Headquarters Northern Army Group, who keep their skills fresh at an annual summer camp, there is another problem besides that of forsaking their normal tasks—that of serving in a multi-national unit.

At Arnsberg in Northern Germany, these soldiers, most of them clerks, practised fieldcraft, patrolling and other tasks connected with emergency defence of their headquarters in the field.

Each section of ten men, commanded by a corporal, comprised Belgian, British, Dutch and German soldiers. They used a special system of hand and whistle signals to help overcome language difficulties.

NATO units frequently train alongside each other—this was international co-operation at elbow-to-elbow level.

Above: Section attack with (left to right) a German corporal, Cpl A J McNally and L/Cpl Sid Jones. Left: Cpl McNally inspects the rifles of a German corporal and lance-corporal in his section. Below: Multi-national queue for rations.

ADEN'S
MEN-OF-ALL-WORK

"LIFT it; lower it; build it up or knock it down... You name it, we'll do it!" The longest serving unit in South Arabia lives by an uncompromising cock-a-doodle-do motto and in work and play the soldiers of 518 Company, Royal Pioneer Corps, have backed it to the hilt. Any unit that has called for their services knows them as a tight-knit team of high morale with the drive to carry out any unskilled or semi-skilled job sent their way.

Nor is the work of 518 Company limited to supporting military construction commitments. It is an accepted feature of local Arab labour that frequent religious recessions, innumerable tea breaks and the lethargy engendered by three-figure temperatures will prolong the simplest task. Civilian contractors in and around Aden, who occasionally run into trouble by underestimating on projects, have reason to be grateful to the 518 "heavy mob."

From his office at Normandy Lines, Aden, the officer commanding, Major Barry Webster, has built an organisation any construction firm would be proud to own. He approves method and construction outlines, passes on his orders to Mauritian-born Company Sergeant-Major Ramjannali and confidently leaves detailed supervision to his able corps of non-commissioned officers. When the men return from work he sends them out to the soccer field with even more explicit instructions—to win!

Football League managers get sacked in their hundreds—Staff-Sergeant Barry Price, the 518 team's manager, is there to stay. So far this season the team has won 13 games out of the 15 played and the victims include two much-vaunted battalion teams from The Somerset and Cornwall Light Infantry and The Cameronians.

The Pioneers chat with admirable sang-froid about the times they have come under fire while working on the Dhala' Road. The British Army's major engineering work in the trouble-torn Federation has been pressed through with constant Royal Pioneer Corps support in the teeth of sniper fire from all manner of weapons.

Soldiering in South Arabia has seen the Pioneers engaged to their eyebrows in infantry business. They have taken their turn at security patrols in Aden, dog patrol sweeps in the Radfan, mine-sweeping along desert tracks and mounting guards.

Yet heavy construction is their primary duty and they have no rivals. On routine jobs a Pioneer team will in the course of a single day move 55 tons of materials and lay as many as 750 wall blocks weighing 65 pounds apiece.

A typical job for 518 Company is the erection of a 64-foot Twynham hut. A seven-man team, usually led by a lance-corporal, will lay the concrete base and assemble roof and walls in 12 days.

The Pioneers have a reputation of working as a self-contained unit reliant on nobody but themselves. In work and play they reckon their independence and team spirit will continue to keep them way ahead of the game.

From a report by Army Public Relations, Middle East.

Top: Building walls and muscles—two of Aden's Pioneers play pat-a-cake with this concrete block which weighs in at 65lb.

Above: It's only a kick-around practice, yet the Pioneers play as if the World Cup depends on beating goalkeeper Graham.

Right: Many spanners make 518's kart faster still. From left, Sgt Peters, Major Webster, Pte Kellow and Pte McGrath.

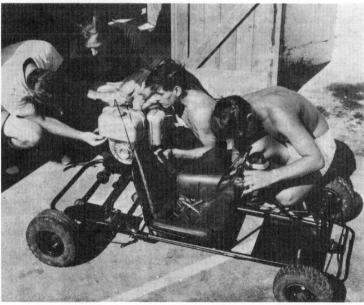

PURELY PERSONAL

THEY GOT THEIR SKATES ON

Fifty miles a day on roller skates —that is the average speed set up by two young Gunners who roller-skated from Leicester to London to collect money for Dr Barnardo's Homes. **Gunner Tony Duffy** and **Gunner David Ashdown,** both of 47 Light Regiment, Royal Artillery, stationed at Barnard Castle, County Durham, dreamed up the stunt as part of their Regiment's recruiting tour. After a few weeks' practice they skated the 150 miles without any difficulty in just three days and on the way collected more than £16 for the children's homes. They are pictured (right) arriving in London.

ALL THE WAY FROM MAURITIUS

Among the recruits on the last passing-out parade at the Wessex Brigade Depot at Lichfield were five men from the Indian Ocean island of Mauritius. They were recruited last year when a company of 1st Battalion, The Gloucestershire Regiment, was flown in to the island to assist with internal security duties. Short-listed from 12 volunteers, the five young men are to serve with the "Glosters" and at their passing out parade (right) the Mayor of Lichfield, who took the salute, had a special word for them. Left to right they are **Alan Reid, Douglas Smith, Orlando Vasquez, Ivan Roberts** and **Louis Castillo.**

OUTBACK BOUND

Corporal Mike Green (below) has landed a plum job—a free tour of Australia. An Army test driver at the Fighting Vehicles Research and Development Establishment in Surrey, he was sent down under to test a new air-conditioned Land-Rover ambulance designed by Army scientists. For six months he will be driving it around the deserts of north Australia to see how it stands up to rough use in rough conditions. With him is **Corporal John Hortop** who is to test a new four-ton truck. During the past three years these two drivers, both in the Royal Electrical and Mechanical Engineers, have clocked up more than 200,000 miles on test tracks alone.

YES, IT'S JOHN !

This scruffy soldier (above) earns far more than the Chief of the Defence Staff. Teenage girls fight to get a look at him. His views on religion recently caused a world-wide rumpus. Recognise him? Yes, it's **John Lennon** of the Beatles (his back view is pictured on page 4). Shorn of his famous locks, Lennon is taking part in a new British film "How I Won the War" being shot near Hanover in Germany. He plays the role of a tough Tommy in World War Two and agreed to have a haircut for the film—a traumatic shock for thousands of his fans.

YOU'RE IN, SON !

Recruiting is **Warrant Officer Deryck Maidment's** job at the Army Careers Information Office, Southampton. Twenty-seven years ago he was recruited into the Army by his wife's uncle. Determined to keep it in the family, he got busy with his sales talk when his son **Robin** left school and the boy was soon signing up. He is pictured (left) being welcomed by **Major R V Cartwright,** Careers Officer.

1967

A fighting withdrawal

In accordance with government policy 1967 was the year that Britain and its Forces bade farewell to the majority of its overseas bases. It was also the year that saw the end of several long-running and bloody conflicts.

The first departure in the early part of the year was from Sarawak, where British troops had been fighting a long three-year campaign through steaming jungles and heaving mud against terrorists supported in the main by President Sukarno's Indonesia. The second took place much later in the year, in the autumn, when the British Garrison and the Governor-General departed from the strife-torn Protectorate of Aden. The conflict in this most barren and inhospitable of places had been long, and toward the end extremely violent and bloody. Many British soldiers had lost their lives during the period as the graves in "Silent Valley" could confirm. There were no tears of sadness here when the last troops pulled out.

The British Army bade another farewell during the year, this time to one of its favorite and longest serving pieces of artillery equipment, the 25 pounder gun. In a well attended and moving ceremony at Paderborn in West Germany the last regiment to be equipped with the gun, the 25th Field Regiment Royal Artillery trooped the gun through the ranks of the regiment.

By the end of the year many of the changes that were contained in the latest Defence Review had been implemented. And with the withdrawal of British Forces from many overseas conflicts, the Army looked forward to peaceful new year with the possibility of no active service for the first time since the end of the second world war.

24 HOURS AT OSCAR FOUR

High above Sheikh Othman an Oscar Four observer watches the rooftop antics of FLOSY and NLF.

In the last violent, unpredictable days of British presence in Aden, SOLDIER visited the observation post codenamed Oscar Four in the heart of Sheikh Othman . . .

Four hours after midnight Sheikh Othman is still uneasily asleep, wrapped in a cloak of hot moist darkness. A three-ton "armoured pig" growls into the police station courtyard and 17 men from B Company—the young soldiers company—of 1st Battalion, The Parachute Regiment, change places with the outgoing guard in a mutter of banter and whispered briefings.

In its first three months in "Shakers" 1 Para recorded over 700 grenade and small-arms attacks on its positions or patrols. The Battalion battle map records them faithfully up to 600 and odd—when the pins, and spaces to plant them, ran out. Around the police station the coloured pins stand clustered shoulder-to-shoulder. Daybreak reveals what those pins mean in real terms and the B Company men take note of a multitude of bullet holes newly arrived since their last 48-hour stint.

Oscar Four stands as squarely as Arab building permits on the main Sheikh Othman crossroads and has come under fire from every point of the compass. The ground floor is almost intact—a tribute to the fence-sitting diplomacy of the policemen who nervously inhabit it. The first storey accommodates off-duty soldiers and has, despite heavily sandbagged windows, been well knocked about. The tower which is manned as an observation post round the clock projects up into the line of fire between rooftops and bears the chips and gouges of accidental hits as well as the specifically anti-British stuff. Life has been safer for the defence of Oscar Four since sappers knocked up an anti-Blindicide screen and a Scout pilot taxed his machine to the legal limit to hoist it aloft.

The interior is lined with $\frac{3}{4}$-inch steel plating. The eye falls on steel and concrete plugs for the loopholes. "We had to get those made when a bloke with a Mauser was popping them through."

The electricity is off. Some slaphappy marksman cut down the wires during a FLOSY versus NLF shoot-up. Someone else picked off the Arab linesman as he climbed up to make repairs. The fridge is useless and without the fans to stir up the turgid air the detective office, now tripling as kitchen, mess hall and dormitory, is murderously hot.

Short-term, these conditions produce discomfort and listlessness. Long-term they produce the ugly outbreaks of prickly heat and monsoon blisters seen on most of the platoon.

The off-duty men wile away the slow hours in smoking, reading and haggling over the price of cold drinks with an eight-year-old Arab. Most of all they talk. They joined The Parachute Regiment together, survived 22 hard weeks of recruit training together and emerged in April this year with a spirit so strong that their Commanding Officer kept them together as B Company. They have done well. They started slowly but learned fast in a hard school to become "second to none" in 1 Para. They talk never endingly about nothing, about everything, in a crude rough chat full of life and humour.

Often these lads who in different circumstances might be studying in the sixth form or working at an apprentice's bench, talk about the battles they have been in. Some of the veterans skilled in small arms are still unacquainted with the razor.

Private Don Geddes is a hoary old second-tour man who must be all of 25. He accepts the sobriquet "Dad" and allegations of decrepitude with easy tolerance, is a popular character.

"Come on Don, there's some rations to come up from downstairs."

"Hang on, I'll just get my rifle."

"You won't need that, it's only downstairs."

"Here we go again. That's what they said last time."

Oscar Four, battered and bruised by bullets, wears its anti-Blindicide mini-skirt with proud defiance.

They call it Miswat Road. It looks peaceful enough but hereabouts tranquillity is a very fleeting thing.

Para 2nd Lieut D L Roberts picks up a terrorist leaflet—only communication link with the gunmen.

This 1 Para radio operator knows trouble may be lurking round any corner in Sheikh Othman.

It's a long way from Sandhurst to Oscar Four but 2nd Lieut Roberts made the trip quickly.

2nd Lieut Roberts calmly disarms a grenade in dangerous condition—a matter of course.

After a spell at Oscar Four, the platoon back in Radfan Camp, the Paras' home in Aden.

Arnhem Day parade rehearsal. Aden is far away from Holland but these men are still Red Devils.

The "last time," a 36 grenade pooped over the wall and wounded Geddes in the hand and leg.

Up in the observation tower the truce, the policy of watch and don't shoot, is accepted with regret. The hours are dragging their feet. Evidence of halcyon days surrounds Oscar Four—walls pitted with GPMG patterns, broken tiles, a minaret eroded to the point of collapse by bullets questing a sniper.

One of three sentries, head well over the sandbags, lowers his binoculars, says defensively "Not so long ago we wouldn't have dared have put our heads up like this." The spectacularly tattered canvas awning which flutters overhead makes his point.

The active phase of the Sheikh Othman campaign wound up in an extraordinarily ferocious inter-factional fight. The contestants fought among the rooftops but indiscriminating mortaring and rocketing killed and wounded dozens of innocents at lower levels. The incredulous defenders of Oscar Four held their fire as bullets from both sides buzzed angrily around them. They watched in blank disbelief as men toppled screaming off rooftops into the streets. Hollywood might have run it as "For a Fistful of Dinars" and been proud.

Now the shooting has stopped and the soldiers in Oscar Four's ivory tower are in the middle of an absurd, typically South Arabian, situation. Armed NLF and FLOSY men openly hold strongpoints in the town and keep observation on one another and the British. All three parties exchange greetings with gay waves. Any relief from the boredom is welcomed and two non-serious car smashes in the street below set the lookout men chortling.

Tension briefly returns while two hastily gathered posses make forays outside the barbed-wire perimeter to collect PORF pamphlets and disarm a grenade in a policeman's home. The machine-gun covers their every move. The patrols hug the walls with rifles at the ready as they move along the crowds of overtly hostile Arabs.

That night a single unexplained shot rings out. It is the excuse for whispered chinwagging when the reliefs come up through the trapdoor and in the hubbub the platoon commander—asleep on a camp bed —is generously trampled on. "All right kids," he says in a surprisingly mild tone, "stop chatting and get on with it."

A cartoon by Pte D McMeekin of 1 Para Intelligence Section. One of his fans is his CO.

"So me Mum says, 'Why don't you do something useful,' she says, 'like joining the Army,' she says, 'instead of hanging about on street corners looking for trouble,' she says . . ."

TOWN OF TENSION AND TERROR

As tension and terror mounted to welcome the visiting United Nations mission, SOLDIER's Arthur Blundell joined the world's Press in Aden to picture the British soldier in the toughest of peace-keeping roles, that of guarding his family and his comrades against an unrecognisable enemy.

The soldier may not appreciate just why he should risk his life in an unpleasant outpost where a people already promised independence approach it with useless and indiscriminate bloodshed. But he can see and understand the writing on the wall—No freedom without blood. And he knows how to meet this kind of threat with the firm no-nonsense stand that has earned him in innumerable situations like this the deserved respect of the world.

With each of four infantry units—1st Battalion, The Lancashire Regiment; 1st Battalion, The Royal Northumberland Fusiliers; 1st Battalion, The South Wales Borderers; and 3rd Battalion, The Royal Anglian Regiment—Arthur Blundell went out on patrol to picture the British soldier in the town of terror. He amplifies these pictures in his own words . . .

"The apparently casual pose of the soldier on the left is misleading. He is in fact extremely alert—his life depends on being so. He is serving in the Royal Anglians' 'Special Branch and it is the Battalion policy to try and make friends with the local population. The success of this policy can be measured by the fact that sick and ailing Arabs approach them for treatmen the moment the Royal Anglians enter one of thei patrol areas. The girl in the Women's Royal Army Corps (below, left) is searching Muslim women for hidden arms at Checkpoint Bravo. The girls have been invaluable in this essential security task. From behind this wall of Bayoomi College (bottom left, along the road to Sheikh Othman, terrorists fought a 50-minute gun battle against the Royal Anglians at Checkpoint Golf, and came off a very definite second best. In this picture of the actual checkpoint (bottom right), Ferrets are keeping a close eye on movement in the area Sheikh Othman, part of which can be seen in the background, has been one of the notorious troubl spots during the campaign of terrorism and the scene of more incidents than in any other sector of the Colony. During my week's tour of Aden I found ample opportunity to record the alertness, tension and strain of long hours on duty revealed in the faces of British soldiers. Below are some examples—a Royal Signals radio operator attache to The South Wales Borderers, a Royal Northumber land Fusilier, a Borderer and a Royal Anglian."

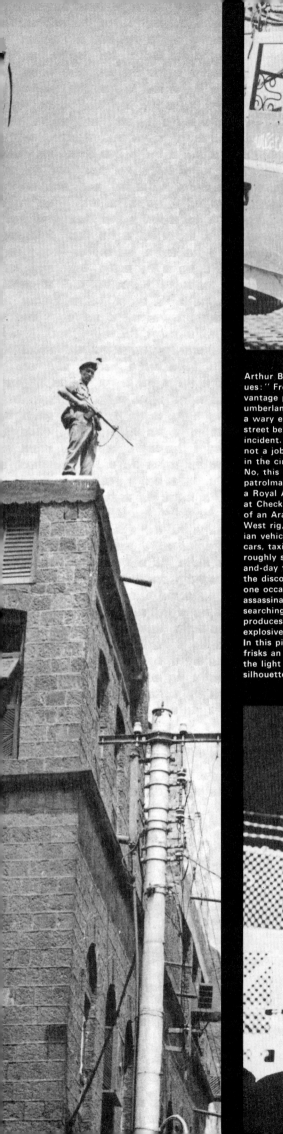

Arthur Blundell continues: " From a precarious vantage point a Northumberland Fusilier keeps a wary eye on the street below, after an incident. This was not a job I envied him in the circumstances. No, this is not an AA patrolman (above) but a Royal Anglian sentry at Checkpoint Bravo searching under the bonnet of an Arab Land-Rover while its driver, in East-West rig, watches. A random selection of civilian vehicles, including buses, lorries, private cars, taxis and camel carts, is stopped and thoroughly searched at the checkpoints. This night-and-day task is routine but can be rewarding in the discovery of illegal arms and ammunition. On one occasion a snap check produced a plan to assassinate a British official. Parallel to vehicle searching is the frisk-and-search technique which produces at times surprising results in arms and explosives concealed in voluminous Arab clothes. In this picture (right) a South Wales Borderer frisks an Arab in the back streets of Ma'alla by the light of a shop doorway. At bottom right is a silhouette of a sentry at Waterloo Cantonment."

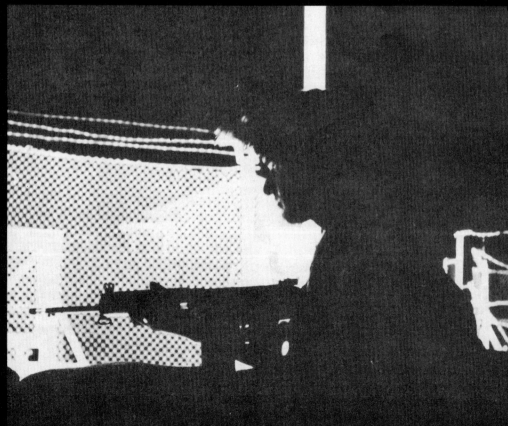

"The lines of washing hung outside the buildings and across this street, in North Country fashion, give it an innocent air, but at any moment a bomb or bullet may change the scene. Right is a Lancashire Regiment's patrol in an off-the-Crescent street leading abruptly to the hillside shanties. The picture below shows Royal Northumberland Fusiliers cordoning off an area in Crater within a minute of shots being fired at a patrol. But this time the terrorists escaped in the labyrinth of warren-like alleys. Below, left, a soldier of The South Wales Borderers is digging in the choking dust and stifling heat of the Kutcha hut area at the back of Ma'alla in the hope of uncovering a Blindicide missile or Energa grenade. Information is only too rarely forthcoming on the whereabouts of these hidden weapons but when it is, then the Army acts quickly. Bottom left is The Lancashire Regiment's paint lorry with a generator-operated hose which sprays red paint over demonstrators. Bottom right, a South Wales Borderers patrol behind Ma'alla. Right, checking identity on a bus."

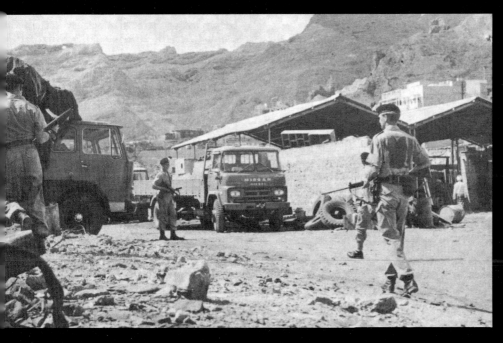

THE END

IT is typical of today's fast-moving world that a word on everyone's lips one minute is banished to a far corner of the mind the next—and moves equally quickly into the history books.

Ask a man in the street what happened on 29 November 1967. In all probability he will reply with a blank stare.

Ask the British Forces what happened on 29 November 1967. They will reply: "We left Aden."

Already the gun battles that stained the streets of Crater, Sheikh Othman, Ma'alla and Steamer Point with British and Arab blood are a thing of the past. The wave of violence that unlike Canute the British Serviceman was able to divert, if not halt, no longer has a British beach to dash against. Aden—both the colony and the South Arabian Federation—has become the independent People's Republic of Southern Yemen.

We have gone for good.

A description of the former Aden Colony reads: "It consists of two extinct volcanic craters forming rocky peninsulas joined by a flat sandy foreshore enclosing the only good harbour along the Arabian coast." A British soldier in Aden last year would have put it differently.

In an atmosphere of savagery, cruelty and bloodshed the British soldier had a job to do. He did it well. It now only remains to record the last chapter of the story of Britain's 128 years in Aden—a story that ended in the last days of November with the withdrawal, mercifully peaceful, of British soldiers and airmen and their comrades of the Royal Marines.

Top left: The piper plays "Barren Rocks of Aden" as Argylls prepare to leave Crater. Bottom left: He wasn't taking any chances! Below: Lieut-Col Colin Mitchell, Argylls' CO, plans his evacuation.

Above: Men of The King's Own Royal Border Regiment pull out of Steamer Point past a line of Arab troops waiting to take over their posts.

Left: Crater—Maj-Gen Philip Tower, GOC Middle East Land Forces, on a tour of area, inspects an armoured vehicle of The Queen's Own Hussars.

Far left: The last post in Aden is a quayside one for these two alert men covering troops of Royal Corps of Transport leaving Steamer Point.

Below: The naval task force. In front is the assault ship HMS Fearless, behind (left) is her sister Intrepid and (right) Commando ship Albion.

RED BERETS ON ROYAL DUTY

Parachutists stream from an Argosy in the massed drop of 540 men of 16th Parachute Brigade, watched by the Queen and Duke of Edinburgh and, between, Brig Farrar-Hockley, Brigade Commander.

HER Majesty the Queen's review of 16th Parachute Brigade was the very opposite of the starchy parade ground norm. Since World War Two the airborne soldiers have travelled the world, living out of mess-tins, as the Army's star trouble-shooters—and they wanted the Queen to see them at work.

They would have liked to have taken her to Palestine, Cyprus, Bahrein, the mountains of Radfan, the jungles of Malaysia or any one of the other danger points where the Brigade has been in action. They made do with Long Valley and Caesar's Camp, Aldershot.

From the same vantage points used by Queen Victoria to survey the Royal Review of 1856, the Queen and the Duke of Edinburgh watched a military happening that in a few kaleidoscopic hours brilliantly unveiled the Brigade's abilities and capabilities.

The opportunity of mustering The Parachute Regiment's three Regular battalions and their supporting elements for the first time ever, came with a hiatus in the Middle East comings and goings which

and transport aircraft, the programme continued with demonstrations of heavy drop, the low-altitude trefoil parachute and the carrying of guns and armoured cars by helicopter.

In a spectacular finale two 3rd Battalion companies made a heliborne assault on Caesar's Camp with Hunters, Vigilants and artillery firing them in.

The Royal Review ended with a scene evocative of bygone days when British troops rallied to their monarch on the field of battle. A sea of maroon ringed the Queen as the Brigade's 2000 soldiers let loose with a full-throated three cheers.

In a telegram to the Brigade Commander, Brigadier Tony Farrar-Hockley, the Queen said: "I send my warmest congratulations to all officers and other ranks who took part in the magnificent demonstration at Aldershot this morning. I was much impressed by the skill and spirit displayed by all concerned and by the admirable inter-Service co-operation which contributed so much to the success of the display."

IT WAS A GOOD GUN

Story by JOHN SAAR

AT solemn intervals the superseded 25-pounders spoke their last word. The empty crashing of blank rounds faded quickly into silence until the next gun in line took up the refrain of salutation and gushed a blue cordite haze over the escort party slow-marching another of the British Army's famous gun-howitzers into obsolescence.

Twenty and more years after its heyday as the standard British field artillery weapon of World War Two, and in Germany where it wrought so much destruction, the 25-pounder was at last passing out of service with the Regular Army. The death was neither sudden nor unexpected. In recent years new guns have been challenging loudly for the 25-pounder's role, but the old friend of half-a-million wartime gunners refused to be hustled from the scene.

Premature reports of the gun's phasing out have been peremptorily and effectively squashed by the roar of 25-pounders engaging operational or practice targets somewhere in the world.

This time there was no mistake, no exaggeration. The funeral was categorical and the last serving 25-pounders were booked for one-way rides to the knacker's yard. The programme to re-equip the field artillery with the Abbot self-propelled gun in Germany and the 105mm pack-howitzer elsewhere is now complete.

With the arrival of the new, it fell to 14 Field Regiment, the last unit to make the changeover, to provide the trappings and ceremonial of a formal farewell to the old.

The parade at West Riding Barracks, Dortmund, coincided with the Regiment's imminent return to the United Kingdom after a five-year tour in Rhine Army. Was the parade for the gun or the Regiment? "The gun *is* the Regiment" said a bombardier, and in a reproachful phrase he summed up the Royal Artillery's feeling for the 25-pounder.

In 1940 the Royal Artillery was archaically and shamefully armed with modified World War One guns. Although deprived of a proper trials sequence by the rush to bring it into service, the 25-pounder instantly earned the thanks, admiration and confidence of the gunners. They gratefully accepted it as the gun the artillery needed to discipline the battlefield and in their courageous hands it played no small part in the winning of the war.

In his end-of-the-war message to the Royal Artillery, Field-Marshal Viscount Montgomery wrote: "The gunners have risen to great heights in this war . . . The contribution of the artillery to final victory in the German war has been immense. I think all the other arms have done very well too. But the artillery has been terrific . . ."

Since the gunners, however brave, would have been helpless without the right guns, the tribute to the men is also praise of the 25-pounders with which they fought.

The 14 Field Regiment guns, last fired in earnest on the Hohne ranges in March,

Dramatic desert setting for "the best all-round field gun in the world." Thousands of them were used to blast Italian, German and Japanese armies.

AUTOMATED ARTILLERY

Story by JOHN SAAR / Pictures by ARTHUR BLUNDELL

BARRING an issue of walking, talking battlefield Daleks to the infantry, the Royal Artillery are way out in front with robot warfare. Computers have made a giant impact on commerce and industry; now the Gunners have conscripted 76 synthesised brains for active service.

The computers are the major element in an artillery control system called FACE due to go into service at the end of next year. FACE elasticates to Field Artillery Computer Equipment and is the joint product of Elliott-Automation Limited and, via the Ministry of Defence, the School of Artillery and the Royal Armament Research and Development Establishment.

Ahead of any other European army, Britain will employ computers in the combat area. As a real breakthrough in artillery control, FACE is a small revolution and it will put the Royal Artillery on the crest of the technological wave. Halcyon days for the Gunners, and ominous news for enemies likely to come under the automated fire. Within seconds of ingesting target information the computer puts up the bearing and elevation on a figure-board that flickers with action like a rioting pin-table.

Mounted in Land-Rovers or armoured personnel carriers, FACE will be available to every battery. The tin slave's prodigious mathematical capabilities will take the drudgery of calculation out of gunnery. The result is automation as she was intended; the men are easier to train and their work less tiring; shooting is faster, more accurate and less vulnerable to human error.

Active British interest in computers dates from the appraisal and rejection of an American system in 1959. Elliott's pondered and produced a prototype for evaluation.

The computer used was from the previous generation of this fast developing industry. Large and cumbersome, it fitted with difficulty into a trailer to lay a diffident claim to mobility, yet it readily proved the concept sound.

FACE incorporates the 920B mobile computer originally designed for another military purpose and since adapted for use in research and industry. After exhaustive environmental tests in hot and cold rooms and jolting cross-country marathons in Land-Rovers, the makers declare the system's reliability "rugged" and say that on average it will function for 300 hours between failures. The computer itself has a predicted span of more than 1000 hours between failures.

As the controlling unit for a battery of six guns, FACE will supplant the gunners who laboriously work to the formulae of gunnery science with logarithm book and slide-rule.

Good gunnery depends on the correct solution of complex and inter-related sums. The exact position of each gun must be calculated by the survey team and a meteorological group also working behind the guns supplies data on weather likely to affect the shell in flight. The battery command post blends this mass of information and modifies the result with ammunition temperature, gun barrel wear and radioed corrections.

Add in changes of target, the necessity of recording events, imagine a battery in action round the clock and the prognosis is strain, fatigue, a slowing down and, eventually, mistakes.

The survey team guards against error by comparison of answers from two men working separately on the same problem.

Above: The Tournament's nerve centre with radio contact with all parts of the arena. Right: In the roof, men control a parachute which is part of the exciting RAF display.

IT'S THE SERVICES SHOW!

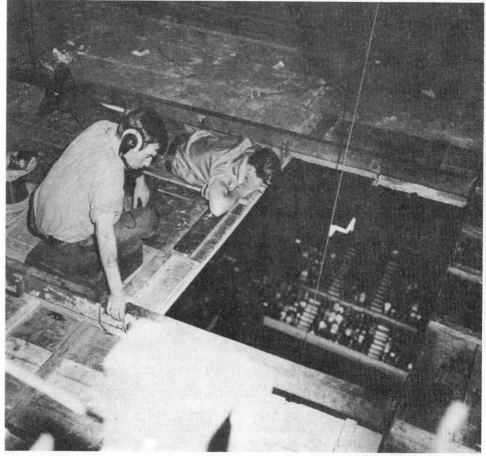

Above: A pilot is ejected from his aircraft—part of the realistic RAF display. Bottom left: The ever-popular Royal Navy field gun competition. Below: Musical ride of the King's Troop.

A S this year's Royal Tournament thrills thousands the men whose meticulous planning ensures that the show runs like a giant piece of clockwork will be already thinking of next year's event.

Yes, it takes a year to produce the 17 days of glittering spectacle. And many spectators prepare for the next Tournament by booking for it during the current one, often asking for the same seats.

Behind the Tournament is a policy-making three-Service committee. Vice-chairman and responsible for detailed planning and running is Colonel B L Gunnel who says:

"Object of the Tournament is two-fold— to raise money for Services charities and to popularise the Services in the eyes of the public. The programme is designed so that it is a combination of the traditional and more modern aspects of the Services."

Each Royal Tournament costs more than £100,000 to stage.

At the moment participation is restricted to British and Commonwealth troops. So when planning begins this is the framework within which the committee works. But there are three displays that are "musts"— the Royal Navy field gun competition, the Royal Horse Artillery musical drive and the massed bands feature.

Then at least one display is allocated to Commonwealth troops. About six gaps are left to fill. Usually one goes to the Royal Navy, one to the Royal Marines and two each to the Army and Royal Air Force. All Services are then asked to put forward display suggestions.

Colonel Gunnel declares: "The primary object is to entertain the public rather than demonstrate new Service techniques. For instance, last year the Royal Navy put on a display of anti-submarine warfare designed to entertain as well as educate people in the technique."

A committee meeting is held in November to agree the form the Tournament will take. Then it is decided what men and equipment will be needed.

In April, Colonel Gunnel visits the units concerned to see them rehearsing. He says: "This rehearsal business is a delicate problem. If the chaps start training too early there is a danger that they will become bored, but if they begin late they can easily get into a muddle during the display. Half the art is having the men and women taking part in good temper and humour."

Earls Court is taken over by the Tournament organisers a week and a day before the show starts. Usually it is nothing but a shell. During the following four days the arena and seats are erected, the floor put in and the prefabricated camp built.

Then the administration moves in and on the Sunday before the Tournament the publicity march through Battersea Park takes place. During the next two days there are detailed rehearsals.

The displays teams come to Earls Court trained and rehearsed and usually it is just a matter of fitting them in with management, lighting and commentating. On the Tuesday a dress rehearsal is held and on the following day is the private view—a purely charitable affair which usually attracts the best house.

The Army's home at home

Pictures by LESLIE WIGGS

COULD it be that the mock battles staged to divert the citizens of ancient Rome are coming back as a public entertainment?

Bulleted blank and simulated casualties are a long way from mass bloodshed at the Colosseum, but the crowds at the Aldershot Army Display were large enough and interested enough to cast doubt on the national claim that "we win the wars, but we don't really like playing soldiers."

From such regional shows the Army is winning tremendous public goodwill and a reputation for promoting well-organised spectaculars with an enticing flavour of audience participation.

Static exhibits and arena displays blending pageantry and thrills covered the enormous range of work and hobbies open to serving soldiers. There were things to interest all age groups and both sexes, sunshine spiked the soft drinks and, in a time-honoured phrase verified by these pictures, a good time was had by all.

The boys wanted to fire the Bofors 40/70. The girls preferred to treat it as a merry-go-round.

Brawny APTC bodies haul away while a youngster plays human fly on their wooden climbing wall.

Coolest job of the day belonged to the soldier riding the stretcher on this Para Brigade Scout.

The Army cast its net wide and caught any number of promising small fry.

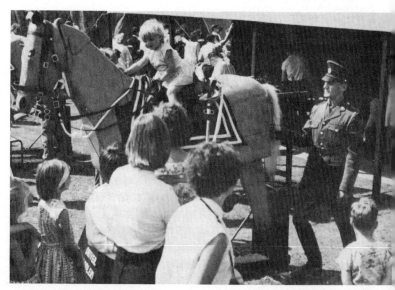

Bronco-busting toddler of the mounted infancy tackles an RCT steeplechaser.

1968

All quiet at the Barrack gate

1968 was dominated largely by the Army's involvement in the domestic affairs of the United Kingdom. The year began with an outbreak of Foot & Mouth disease, which quickly swept the country and involved the use of troops to help seal contaminated areas and control further infection.
No sooner was this problem brought under control than troops were sent to Glasgow to aid the civil powers after a freak hurricane had caused much damage to buildings and brought many of the services in the city to a standstill.

Despite these mundane tasks there was some overseas action during the year when troops were deployed to Mauritius to quell civil disturbances there in the run-up to independence. A similar task was required a little alter in Bermuda. Amalgamations and disbandments of ancient regiments however, kept many soldiers busy at home. The creation of "large" infantry regiments began during the middle of the year when all of the four existing Light Infantry regiments amalgamated to form "The Light Infantry"
Others were not so fortunate. In a very moving ceremony near the spot in the lowlands of Scotland where they had been raised in the 17th century, the 1st Battalion The Cameronians (the 26th of Foot, the Scottish Rifles) disbanded and marched off into history.

The best news of the year came almost at the very end, from the Olympic games in Mexico, where among others, S/Sgt Ben Jones of the King's Troop RHA had gained a gold medal in the equestrian discipline of three-day eventing. On a more sombre note – but no less remarkable, 1968 was the first year of the century that the British Army had not suffered a fatal casualty on active service.

The President's son and the Scandinavian countess—when troubled Cyprus seemed once more on the brink of an explosion one was the welcomer and one the welcomed in . . .

THE ARMY'S SANCTUARY

AS tension between Turkey and Greece mounted and Cyprus became an international flashpoint, 1400 people of many nationalities flocked from North Cyprus, where it was feared the Turks might land, to the British Sovereign Base Area at Dhekelia.

The way the Army welcomed them won international praise. Sir Norman E Costar, British High Commissioner, in a letter to the Commander British Forces Near East, Air-Marshal Sir Edward Gordon Jones, said: "I am sure that I speak for the whole British community when I say that the job done by the Servicemen was quite outstanding in every way. From all sides I have received laudatory comments, and the representatives of the United Nations and the foreign countries you received have called to ask me to add their thanks."

The evacuation of Nicosia and Kyrenia areas, recommended by Sir Norman and taken up by friendly foreign embassies, was carried out under a carefully-rehearsed plan used for the first time.

Every British unit in the island can share in the praise showered on the Army by refugees surprised and impressed by their barrack-room accommodation, food and sympathetic treatment at Dhekelia.

As hundreds of vehicles followed the signposts to the garrison and poured into the British-protected area, their worried occupants were received at the Church of England Soldiers', Sailors' and Airmen's Club by Royal Army Educational Corps officers assisted by High Commission officials and the base customs officers.

Evacuation of the risky north was suggested over the British Forces Broadcasting Services network, and as the numbers reaching Dhekelia grew the base's Key Cinema was taken over as a reporting centre. Sandhurst cadets, field training on the island, acted as refugee processors. One of them, unknown to those being processed, was Panji Kaunda, son of the President of

Zambia. The Church of England Club staff welcomed the arrivals with food and—of course!—cups of tea.

And Royal Corps of Transport drivers transported the refugees to barrack accommodation at five centres. Then it was a matter of looking after the sanctuary-seekers.

Men of the Army Catering Corps had to provide something like 4000 extra meals a day plus a continuous service of baby foods and milk—and even water for hot-water bottles!

The tension lasted for the last seven days of November—and then the tributes to the British protection and hospitality rolled in. Thanks came from the Israeli Ambassador, the commander of the United Nations force in Cyprus, a Danish countess caught up in the crisis . . .

The Cyprus affair of last November might have caused the world a few uneasy days—but it boosted the prestige of the British soldier in no uncertain way.

Top left: Turkish tanks and crews prepare for a possible invasion. Above: A precautionary checkpoint at Dhekelia manned by the Royal Horse Guards.

1

2

3

1 Capt Ann MacGregor, Women's Royal Army Corps, and an armful.

2 Harding Barracks, Dhekelia: Some of the evacuees queue for a meal.

3 Maj-Gen D L Lloyd Owen, GOC Near East Land Forces (left) chats to the Garrison Commander, Lieut-Col Petty, and WO II A Holmes.

4 Domestic routine goes on—an evacuee mother preparing baby food.

5 Maj Norman Thacker RAEC settles a query by a Sandhurst cadet at the Evacuation Reception Centre.

6 ACC cooks prepare for the influx of many nationalities at Dhekelia.

4

5

6

Mauritius was unsettled as the big day approached. But British troops helped to make it . . .

INDEPENDENCE WITHOUT TEARS

Independence dawned quietly, preceded by mob violence quelled with the help of the Shropshires.

THE red, blue, yellow and green flag soared to the masthead. The Union Jack was hauled down. And Mauritius was independent after 150 years of British rule.

It happened peacefully on a day in March. But there was underlying tension. An outbreak of violence in January had sent B Company of 1st Battalion, The King's Shropshire Light Infantry, rushing the 4000 miles from Singapore (see SOLDIER, March)—and as independence came the Shropshires were still keeping inter-community strife in check.

The trouble had resulted in killings—had stopped Princess Alexandra from attending independence celebrations. The British troops were taking no chances.

The guard that took part in the flag-raising ceremony on Champs de Mars racecourse at the capital, Port Louis, was on patrol just before the parade—and back on operations immediately afterwards.

A Far East Land Forces spokesman said of the Shropshires (B Company was later replaced by C Company): "There is no doubt that their hard work, good humour and impartiality helped enormously to keep the situation under control as Independence Day, 12 March, approached."

Now SOLDIER tells in pictures the story of the part the Shropshires played in independence celebrations—and their work in the stormy days leading up to this momentous event in the island's history.

Above: Men of this 33-strong KSLI guard at the flag-raising were on patrol before the ceremony and then immediately after it.

Opposite page: A higlight of independence Day celebrations was a "Dance of the choppers" staged by the Battalion Air platoon.

Right: The Independence Day display by the KSLI band and bugles brought applause and then cheers as it ended with "Tigers Rag"

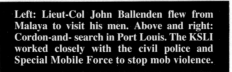

Left: Lieut-Col John Ballenden flew from Malaya to visit his men. Above and right: Cordon-and- search in Port Louis. The KSLI worked closely with the civil police and Special Mobile Force to stop mob violence.

British military presence east of Suez is constantly under discussion, but little is heard of our garrison . . .

NORTH OF PANAMA

AT a certain night club in Belize, coastal capital of British Honduras, the rum is good—but the catfish are magnificent. Whiskered, large and evil-looking, they lurk in their closely-packed thousands in the smelly river a few feet below the bar.

When a scrap of food or even a cigarette end is thrown from the balcony the black fishy mass, illuminated by carefully sited lamps, explodes. You shudder and swallow a little more rum.

The frenetic catfish of British Honduras are certainly remarkable and not least for

their "aquabatics" in a country that is a millpond in an area of much turbulence—a country that is approaching independence.

It is in this emerging nation of 115,000 people, already internally self-governing, that Britain has her last garrison in the Americas. How long it remains there depends on the independence agreements and exactly when independence will be is anybody's guess—but it could be anytime.

Recently B Company of 1st Battalion, The Green Howards, made the long journey from Colchester to British Honduras—or Belize as the whole country probably

will be called after independence—to replace 2 Company of 1st Battalion, Coldstream Guards, who returned to Chelsea with deep tans and two pet parrots. The Guards had spent six months at Airport Camp, strategically sited next to Belize International Airport and ten miles northwest of the capital.

The Army's prime role here is to protect the country from any threat from its neighbour Guatemala, which has long claimed the colony.

The British soldiers act as a deterrent; they aim to show the flag quietly and by

Above: British Army reconnaissance Land-Rover in the remote west of British Honduras. The huts were built by the American Peace Corps.

Roads like this (above) spell slow journeys and frequent repairs to vehicles. Right: Coldstream Guardsmen demonstrate how buildings at Airport Camp are made fast when a hurricane approaches.

Coldstreamers at home and away. Right: A duty vehicle is checked at the Camp—and (above) a patrol moves through jungle near San Antonio in the Toledo District of south British Honduras.

Left: Colonel F W Cook (wearing beret), commanding the British Honduras Garrison, and Lieutenant-Colonel M Atherton of The Green Howards.

mere presence rather than armed strength.

In 1963 the dispute led to ending of diplomatic relations between Britain and Guatemala, and for the last two years a United States lawyer has been mediating. Although independence—British Honduras wants it within the Commonwealth—is not conditional on a satisfactory settlement with Guatemala, a constitutional conference in London is unlikely before the mediator's findings are made public.

The Army is there also to help in any internal security difficulty. This happened last in 1966 when soldiers were out in the streets of Belize helping police to restore order. It was not a serious disturbance and was for this country out of character. The trouble that marked the independence of Guyana—not far away on the north coast of South America—and, more recently, that of Mauritius, is thought unlikely in happy-go-lucky British Honduras.

The colony's people—a colourful mixture of Creoles, American Maya Indians, Caribs and persons of East Indian and Spanish descent—draw most comfort from the fact that British troops are among them to help in a situation that is summed up in one terrible word—HURRICANE.

On 31 October 1961 Hurricane Hattie swept in from the Caribbean Sea at 200 miles per hour to pay a visit of incredible violence to the colony. With her came a tidal wave. Belize City was shattered, devastated.

Soldiers from Aldershot area maintain disinfectant-soaked pad at Cookham Bridge, Berks.

In Oswestry area: Well-protected men of 17 Training

THE INVISIBLE ENEMY

AS the creeping horror of foot-and-mouth disease brought animal slaughter on a vast scale to the lush pastures of Britain's countryside—and heartbreak to its farmers—the Army was heavily involved in a task that injected fresh vitality into the prosaic phrase "aid to the civil power."

It was grim work. As they toiled amid the funeral pyres that were once lusty cattle and sheep, the soldiers understandably lost their appetites for meat and were fed an alternative fish and chicken. Some suffered a rash from disinfectant. But their efforts—still continuing as SOLDIER went to press and the number of slaughtered animals neared 300,000—won praise from many people in many places ranging from the Ministry of Agriculture to a farm over which the smoke still hung . . .

While the Army was busy fighting the outbreak—as Christmas approached, 700 men were engaged—the disease was hitting back. Because of the risk of spreading the epidemic, Army movement all over the country was restricted and training areas were closed or used sparingly.

The disease had some curious effects on Army life. Helicopters dipped their skids in disinfectant baths before landing; an armourer of the Royal Electrical and Mechanical Engineers serviced humane killers for the Ministry of Agriculture; young soldiers passed out of brigade training depots and boys' units in Western Command without their parents watching because of a ban on outside spectators at ceremonial parades. . . .

Western Command was where the Army fought and was hit hardest, for it was in the area covered by Western Command that the disease raged most fiercely.

In North-West District, men of 14 Light Regiment, Royal Artillery, 5th Inniskilling Dragoon Guards, Lancastrian Brigade Depot, 17 Training Regiment, Royal Artil-

Regiment, RA, spraying disinfectant on a farm.

Large amount of fuel needed delayed carcass burning. Here RAVC personnel disinfect waiting bodies.

lery, and 1st Battalion, The Lancashire Regiment—moved in from Catterick—were involved, mostly in disinfecting farms when outbreaks occurred and in some cases slaughtering and disposing of bodies.

In West Midland District, men from the Light Infantry and Mercian brigade depots, 1 Engineer Stores Depot, 2nd Battalion, The Royal Anglian Regiment (from Felixstowe in Eastern Command), 1st Battalion, The Worcestershire Regiment (from Bulford in Southern Command), and 22nd Special Air Service Regiment, joined in the fight.

Veterinary officers and non-commissioned officers from the Royal Army Veterinary Corps Depot at Melton Mowbray were on hand to give expert help. They included an officer normally employed with The King's Troop, Royal Horse Artillery.

In Shropshire 100 Royal Air Force men in groups of ten joined the fight. Almost all training areas and open ranges in Western Command were closed, including Castlemartin and Sennybridge. Sports fixtures were cancelled and men were not allowed leave until seven days after they had been doing foot-and-mouth work.

What was it like down on the farm during those grim days during which many a proud herd was slaughtered in the interests of the majority? A sergeant of 17 Training Regiment, Royal Artillery, in charge of a "foot-and-mouth squad," says:

"There were 20 mature cattle in the main cowshed, 20 young cattle in two other stalls and 350 sheep in a makeshift pen in the yard. The vet had confirmed the disease the day before and shot three badly-infected cattle. . . . Gunners Barton and Dowling were detailed to tie sacking over the heads of these animals to prevent virus being spread over the yard when the cattle were hauled out by tractor one by one to a burial pit in an adjoining field.

"The pit, 30 yards long, five yards wide and 18 feet deep, had been dug by a large mechanical shovel. We had also a small bulldozer for pushing the dead animals into the pit and filling it on completion. The gunners were shown how to connect and disconnect the chains from the animals' feet for dragging. The animals' stomachs were slit to prevent bloating which would tend to push up the soil after filling in.

"We began spraying the dead animals' sheds but on the arrival of the slaughterers the real work started. While part of the squad continued spraying the others began their 'chain gang' work. First to die were the mature cattle followed by the young ones and sheep. . . .

"The gunners were involved in holding the sheep while they were dispatched and loading them on to the trailer and the bulldozer bucket. When all the animals were dead it was 1730 hours and dark. . . ."

There were lighter moments. The Sergeants' Mess of 2nd Battalion, The Royal Anglian Regiment, took along its fruit machine to keep members amused during intervals in the grisly work.

Northern Command was severely affected by the outbreak. Most training came to a grinding halt with the closure of training areas and movement restrictions. In Southern Command, Dartmoor was completely closed to soldiers and training on Salisbury Plain was strictly controlled. Tanks stayed on the Plain at night, covered with canvas sheets, instead of using the roads. Fifteen London bridges and various sections of road were covered by straw soaked in disinfectant in an effort to halt the disease.

And so the fight against the invisible enemy went on. If the soldiers grumbled sometimes—and who, after hearing what they had to do, can blame them?—they could content themselves with the thought that for many years to come farmers would remember not only the sorrow of their loss but the humour, cheerfulness and the physical help of the soldiers who came to their aid.

The Services' contribution to restricting the foot-and-mouth epidemic has not gone unnoticed:

Mr Fred Peart, Minister of Agriculture: "We are engaged in a struggle against the most serious epidemic of foot-and-mouth disease this century. I am most grateful for the magnificent job that the Armed Services are doing in helping us combat the spread of the disease. The work is often hard and distasteful but it has to be done if we are to overcome this terrible scourge. I am sure that with everyone's help we shall succeed."

Mr G T Williams, President of the National Farmers' Union: "After last year's outbreak of foot-and-mouth disease in Northumberland the National Farmers' Union asked that the Army should be brought in to assist in any further serious epidemic.

"At that time no one imagined that such a catastrophic outbreak would again so swiftly strike Britain's farms. But strike it did—and within a week, as soon as it was perceived that an emergency had indeed arisen, the Army was on the scene.

"No one who has witnessed the efforts made by the various units involved can have anything but unstinted admiration. The Army has, in fact, gone to battle.

"The training and discipline of all concerned have been of untold worth in the front line of defence against this dreadful scourge, and have been an invaluable reinforcement to the efforts of veterinarians and the police and the farming community itself.

"It has not gone unnoticed in the afflicted areas that quite a large proportion of the troops involved are very young men, in all likelihood unblooded in battle. The manner in which they have got 'stuck in' to a number of very unpleasant jobs has been widely commented upon, and I would like to add my personal tribute to all that has been done."

Mr Graham Wooley, a Cheshire farmer: "Like most of the Cheshire farmers who have had soldier labour I was most impressed with and grateful for the efficient and disciplined way the soldiers tackled the unpleasant work."

OPERATION MOP UP

WHEN a 120-mile-an-hour hurricane tore across Scotland recently it caused more damage than the Blitz. Glasgow—the worst hit with nine dead and 700 homeless—was declared a disaster area.

The Army's offer of help was gratefully accepted by the shattered city. An "Ops Room" for Operation Mop Up was established at HQ 13 Signal Group (Volunteers) in the centre of the city. The operation was masterminded by Brigadier G Hoerder and Brigade Major K Lloyd.

Convoys of lorries, driven by men of the Royal Corps of Transport, arrived through the night with thousands of tarpaulin roof covers from Government stores as far away as Huntingdon.

More than 300 troops were brought in to help: 38 Engineer Regiment from Ripon; 1st Battalion, Scots Guards, and 1st Battalion, The Cameronians, from Edinburgh; and The Royal Highland Fusiliers in Inverness.

They moved furniture out of damaged houses into stores (mostly disused TA centres), helped police to cordon off dangerous areas with guards and road blocks, cleared trees from the highways and parks, and carried out demolitions and roof repairs.

The whole operation lasted two weeks. At weekends, men of local Territorial & Army Volunteer Reserve units such as 71 (Scottish) Engineer Regiment (Volunteers), Glasgow University Officer Training Corps, 15 Parachute Battalion and the Lowland Regiment, Royal Artillery, turned out to help.

Said Major Lloyd: "This is probably the biggest operation of its kind ever run by the Army in Scotland."

Back to steam on the LMR

Lieut Castell, who drove 92203 on the last leg, from Liss to Longmoor, with 92203's new owner.

RAILWAY enthusiasts flocked to Longmoor Military Railway to give a great welcome to two ex-British Railways steam locomotives as they arrived from Crewe with their new owner, artist David Shepherd.

The locos, 2-10-0 9F 92203 and 4-6-0 MT 75029, made the journey under their own steam, after a change of heart by British Railways, and after 16 hours on the footplate of 92203, Mr Shepherd arrived grimy but very happy. Originally Southern Region had decreed that the two engines would have to be towed ignominiously by diesel over the Southern's all-electric tracks, but relented to allow the engines to bring steam back to the Region for the first time since the completion of electrification in July last year.

Mr Shepherd's two locomotives join three other "steamers" of the Association of Railway Preservation Societies which have been given temporary accommodation by the Royal Corps of Transport at Longmoor —the Longmoor Military Railway is itself a member of the Association.

Among the enthusiasts who packed a special train from Longmoor to Liss and back, hauled by 92203, was the Transport Officer-in-Chief, Major-General E H G Lonsdale.

Foot(plate)note: David Shepherd's friend and rival artist, Terence Cuneo, who is as well known for his railway paintings as Shepherd for his African wildlife scenes, was not at Longmoor for the big reception but hoped to make his first visit there shortly. Both artists have undertaken many commissions for the Services in recent years.

Above: 92203 approaching Longmoor after a round trip to Liss with railway enthusiasts. Top: David Shepherd's other loco, 75029, at Longmoor Station.

MEXICO MEDALLISTS

Above: Success smile. S/Sgt Jones with his gold medal. Below: The Duke of Edinburgh congratulates the triumphant British equestrian quartet.

Left: Almost a naval salute for the National Anthem. Captain A Jardine with yachting bronze.

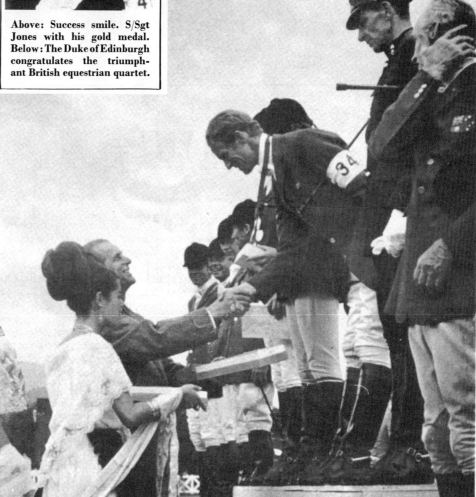

S TAFF-SERGEANT Ben Jones, Royal Horse Artillery, rode to victory in the Valley of the Brave. The Valley, 80 miles from Mexico City, was the scene of the three-day equestrian event in the Olympic Games.

Immaculate in dress uniform, Staff Jones rode a flawless round in the final show-jumping section to clinch the team gold medal. Two of his three team-mates had earlier collected 25 penalty marks between them, so everything rested on him.

After he had completed the 12 jumps faultlessly, the British contingent broke the silence of the Mexican afternoon siesta with cheers and cries of "Jolly good show! Well done, old boy."

Staff Jones said afterwards: "The Poacher did not give me a moment's worry. He tried to take the bit and make his own pace, but I soothed him down and told him to take it easy. He must have known what I was saying because he relaxed and I had a wonderful ride."

The gruelling course—two horses were killed on it in one event—was compared to the Burma Road by a newspaper correspondent. When Staff Jones set out on the steeplechase, the track was under water and the fences invisible in the mist.

The Poacher, who is partial to ale and stout, began to get "hooked" on the oxygen he was given after strenuous work-outs at the high altitude. Said the staff-sergeant with a smile: "I don't mind having a boozer with me but when I get a hippie thrown in, then it is too much."

The gold medal was won three days after his 36th birthday. He has been in the Army since 1952 and has just over five years more to serve. He is married with twin children and stationed at the Royal Army Veterinary Corps Depot at Melton Mowbray. His equestrian career began in 1960 and took in the Badminton horse trials, Irish and French internationals, European championships in Moscow and the Tokyo Olympics.

The Army won another medal, a bronze, for yachting. Captain Adrian Jardine, T & AVR helicopter pilot, was a member of the three-man crew of Yeoman XVI which came third in the 5.5-metre class.

They beat a German yacht by only two feet in a hard fought race. Captain Jardine explained the tactics: "We decided when we rounded the last mark in seventh position that it was time to do something different. We broke away to starboard out to sea. We moved across and went by all their sterns, and it looked quite good. Amazingly, no one tacked to cover us even when we were laying to the finishing line. It was tremendous and it paid off."

His twin brother, Major Stuart Jardine, of the Royal Engineers, was tenth in the Star class.

Maj Monty Mortimer, RCT, manager of the British modern pentathlon team.

Sgt Jeremy Robert Fox, of REME, who came ninth in the modern pentathlon.

L/Cpl Barry Lillywhite, RCT, who was thirty-first in the modern pentathlon.

Capt Michael Howe, Para, reserve for the pentathlon but did not compete.

S/Sgt Instructor Ronald Bright, APTC, coach for modern pentathlon team.

Gnr John McGonigle gave a spirited performance in flyweight but outpointed.

Lieut Rodney Craig, RCT. His team eliminated in the fencing (sabre) quarter-final.

Sgt-Instructor W Tancred, APTC, was below his best in discus. Non-qualifier.

There's a soldier at the bottom of my garden

Story by **JOHN WRIGHT**/*Pictures by* **LESLIE WIGGS**

MANOR Park is very much the same as hundreds of other housing estates in the prosperous commuter-belt south of London, and the man who lives at Number 12, Sycamore Court, is similar to thousands of other men hereabouts...

A large, comfortable-looking individual, he lives in his pleasant two-bedroomed house with his wife and teenage daughter and commutes 18 miles a day to work. If he meets his neighbour at Number 29 they are quite likely to talk about a petition to improve the refuse collection or road dangers faced by their children on the way to school.

All around live ordinary men with ordinary jobs, ordinary wives and ordinary children. Yet the tenants of Numbers 12 and 29 are soldiers. Manor Park, Uckfield, Sussex, may be similar to other estates in the vast conurbation of the south-east but there is *one* difference. Here the Army has moved in.

Of the estate's more than 1000 houses, 332 are being occupied by Army families living cheek by jowl with civilians, sharing with them the problems, the crises and the delights of moving into a new house.

To help solve, accommodation problems created by the rundown of overseas bases the Army has bought, or is buying, about 5000 homes in 30 locations all over the country. Most are new houses on new estates built with civilian homeseekers in mind. Uckfield is the largest single purchase.

The British civilian has a habit of talking in glowing terms of his country's brave soldiers when they are several thousand miles away defending the country's interests at great personal risk.

But he is apt to be not quite as warm-hearted when the same soldiers move in next door.

With soldiers returning to this country in ever-increasing numbers, this attitude must change. Perhaps it is changing already. At Uckfield, civilians and soldiers undoubtedly have mutual reservations about each other but the invasion of Army families has not on the face of it made Manor Park different from any other housing estate. As the soldiers say, "Why should it?"

Top: These houses at Uckfield are graceful, on an open-planned estate—and they belong to soldiers. Above: His neighbours go to work in grey suits but Sergeant Archer goes in service dress. Left: Sergeant Archer and his family at home.

That man at Number 12, Sergeant Archie Archer, says: "I prefer this to living in married quarters. It is not like being in the Army." His house is in a quiet leafy backwater a few hundred yards from Number 29, Corporal Derek Bennett's three-bedroomed house where he lives with his wife and little girls. "Lovely to get away from the barracks," he says. "And living among civilians is a good thing—prepares you for when you leave the Army."

IT'S SEVEN PER CENT MORE !

AS a result of the two-yearly review of Service pay, increases of seven per cent came into effect on 1 April this year.

The previous three biennial reviews, under the Grigg formula, took into account changes in the Civil Service administrative and executive classes in adjusting officers' pay, and in arriving at other ranks' pay reflected changes in the average earnings and wages in manufacturing and certain other industries.

After the 1966 increases were referred, for the first time, to the National Board for Prices and Incomes—and approved in full —the Ministry of Defence set up a Pay Steering Committee to examine levels of pay and the method of review. It was also ruled that Services pay should become a standing reference to the Prices and Income Board.

Since current Government policy restricts increases to 3½ per cent a year, the maximum permissible increase in Services

| The next eight pages give the detailed increases in pay, increments and additional pay. The scales of retired pay, pensions and gratuities were not available when SOLDIER went to press but will be published in a future issue when they have been approved. |
| These eight pages can easily be removed from the magazine for future reference by unfastening and refastening the two wire staples which bind this copy. |

pay was seven per cent, which the Board considered justified.

Out-of-quarters marriage allowance in the United Kingdom has been increased by 3s a day from 1 April.

Separation allowances have also been increased from 4s to 5s a day at the lower rate and 8s to 10s a day at the higher rate.

Officers of the Royal Army Educational Corps, who previously had their own scale, are now to be paid at the normal rates.

While it was strongly recommended that doctors and dentists should have a larger increase because their position had deteriorated, relative to their civilian counterparts, since their pay scales were established in 1962, this was rejected—doctors and dentists receive the same increase as other officers.

Changes in additional pay include flying pay, arctic or tropical experiments and volunteers for experiments at the Chemical Defence Experimental Establishment, Porton.

None of the changes in pay apply to locally recruited officers and soldiers overseas.

SOLDIERS' PAY

NON-TRADESMEN

Rank	Committed to serve for:				
	Less than 6 years	6 years but less than 9 years	9 years or more	15 years having completed 9 years	21 years having completed 15 years
	Scale A	Scale B	Scale C	Scale D	Scale E
	Daily	Daily	Daily	Daily	Daily
	s d	s d	s d	s d	s d
Private Grade IV	18 9	22 6	28 3		
Private Grade III	21 9	25 6	31 3	33 6	33 6
Private Grade II	24 0	27 9	33 6	35 9	35 9
Private Grade I	25 6	29 3	35 0	37 3	37 3
Lance-corporal Grade III	25 6	29 3	35 0	37 3	37 3
Lance-corporal Grade II	27 3	31 0	36 9	39 0	39 0
Lance-corporal Grade I	28 9	32 6	38 3	40 6	40 6
Corporal Grade II	31 0	34 9	40 6	42 6	45 0
Corporal Grade I	32 6	36 3	42 0	44 9	47 3
Sergeant	39 6	43 3	49 0	53 9	56 6
Staff-sergeant	45 3	49 0	54 9	59 6	62 9
Warrant officer Class II	48 0	51 9	57 6	62 3	65 6
Warrant officer Class I	51 9	55 6	61 3	66 0	69 3

GROUP A TRADESMEN

Rank	Committed to serve for:				
	Less than 6 years	6 years but less than 9 years	9 years or more	15 years having completed 9 years	21 years having completed 15 years
	Scale A	Scale B	Scale C	Scale D	Scale E
	Daily	Daily	Daily	Daily	Daily
	s d	s d	s d	s d	s d
Private Class III	22 9	26 6	32 3	34 6	34 6
Private Class II	25 0	28 9	34 6	36 9	36 9
Private Class I	26 6	30 3	36 0	38 3	38 3
Lance-corporal Class III	26 6	30 3	36 0	38 3	38 3
Lance-corporal Class II	28 3	32 0	37 9	40 0	40 0
Lance-corporal Class I	29 9	33 6	39 3	41 6	41 6
Corporal Class II	32 0	35 9	41 6	43 9	47 0
Corporal Class I	34 0	37 9	43 6	45 9	49 0
Sergeant	42 3	46 0	51 9	56 0	59 3
Staff-sergeant	48 0	51 9	57 6	62 3	65 6
Warrant officer Class II	50 9	54 6	60 3	65 0	68 3
Warrant officer Class I	54 6	58 3	64 0	68 9	72 0

Sergeants and above whose trade classification is lower than Class I and corporals whose grade classification is lower than Class II shall be paid 1s 6d or 1s 0d a day respectively less than rates shown above.

GROUP B TRADESMEN

Rank	Committed to serve for:				
	Less than 6 years	6 years but less than 9 years	9 years or more	15 years having completed 9 years	21 years having completed 15 years
	Scale A	Scale B	Scale C	Scale D	Scale E
	Daily	Daily	Daily	Daily	Daily
	s d	s d	s d	s d	s d
Private Class III	21 9	25 6	31 3	33 6	33 6
Private Class II	24 0	27 9	33 6	35 9	35 9
Private Class I	25 6	29 3	35 0	37 3	37 3
Lance-corporal Class III	25 6	29 3	35 0	37 3	37 3
Lance-corporal Class II	27 3	31 0	36 9	39 0	39 0
Lance-corporal Class I	28 9	32 6	38 3	40 6	40 6
Corporal Class II	31 0	34 9	40 6	42 6	45 0
Corporal Class I	32 6	36 3	42 0	44 9	47 3
Sergeant	39 6	43 3	49 0	53 9	56 6
Staff-sergeant	45 3	49 0	54 9	59 6	62 9
Warrant officer Class II	48 0	51 9	57 6	62 3	65 6
Warrant officer Class I	51 9	55 6	61 3	66 0	69 3

TECHNICIANS

Rank	Committed to serve for:				
	Less than 6 years	6 years but less than 9 years	9 years or more	15 years having completed 9 years	21 years having completed 15 years
	Scale A	Scale B	Scale C	Scale D	Scale E
	Daily	Daily	Daily	Daily	Daily
	s d	s d	s d	s d	s d
Private	29 3	33 0	38 9	41 6	41 6
Lance-corporal	32 6	36 3	42 0	44 9	44 9
Corporal	37 9	41 6	47 3	50 6	52 9
Sergeant	48 3	52 0	58 0	62 3	65 6
Staff-sergeant	55 9	59 6	65 6	70 3	73 6
Warrant officer Class II	58 6	62 3	68 0	73 0	76 3
Warrant officer Class I	62 3	66 0	72 0	76 9	80 0

Sergeants and above whose trade classification is other than the highest in their trade shall be paid 1s 6d a day less than rates shown above.

"Many were in tears"

ADEN. Hot, dusty, dangerous Aden. For 128 years the British soldier guarded this inhospitable tip of Southern Arabia. And often he died here.

He died in countless skirmishes with anonymous killers among the jagged peaks of the Radfan Mountains and on the vague border. He died as squalid urban terrorists tried in vain to panic him. He died most frequently in an era when the majority of his fellow countrymen were enjoying unprecedented luxury—which included watching his death on television!

Recently he was remembered. The scene was Aldershot's Royal Garrison Church of All Saints. The occasion, a service in tribute to the Dead of Aden. In particular, the soldiers killed in the last three stormy years of British presence, but also all those others who died during an occupation that began in January 1839.

The Chaplain-General, the Venerable Archdeacon J R Youens, dedicated a book of remembrance containing the names of more than 500 officers and men who lie buried in Aden military cemeteries.

Eight hundred people attended the service. They included 300 relatives of those who died between 1964 and November last year when we left Aden. Reported one newspaper: "Many were in tears."

Also there were an officer, a senior non-commissioned officer and a soldier from each of the 39 regiments and corps that served in Aden in those three years.

The service was conducted by the senior chaplain of the Royal Garrison Church, the Reverend M G T Farnworth, and the prayer for the departed was led by the senior chaplain to the Forces (Roman Catholic) in South-East District, the Reverend A K Cluderay.

Lord Trevelyan, Aden's last High Commissioner, read the lesson; also there was Sir Richard Turnbull, the previous High Commissioner. Mr Gerry Reynolds, Minister of Defence for Administration, and Mr James Boyden, Under-Secretary of State for the Army, were also there—as were many high-ranking Service officers, civic dignitaries and ordinary people filled with a desire to pay their respects.

The choir of the Royal Garrison Church and the Band of 2nd Battalion, The Parachute Regiment, took part; trumpeters of the King's Troop, Royal Horse Artillery, sounded the Last Post and Reveille; and pipers of 1st Battalion, The Argyll and Sutherland Highlanders, played the Lament.

Later, as the string orchestra of the Irish Guards played, the congregation drank tea in a nearby gymnasium and thought of the men whom Britain left behind when she pulled out of Aden—and of their lonely sand-swept graves.

June 1967—funeral of 24 British soldiers killed in a particularly ferocious incident in Aden. Remembered at Aldershot.

Above: As they file into the Royal Garrison Church they think of their comrades who did not return to England. Below: The book recording the price Britain paid for 128 years in Aden.

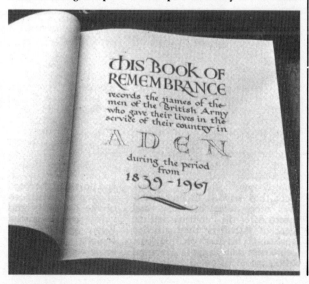

Half a mile from where the Regiment was raised 279 years ago to the day, 8,000 Scotsmen mourned the passing of The Cameronians (Scottish Rifles) as with impeccable dignity Scotland's only rifle regiment disbanded

"SIR, WE'LL HAVE TO GO NOW"

Story by Peter N Wood / Pictures by Trevor Jones

The conventicle is ended, the Regiment no more. Second Lieutenant David Corkerton and Lieutenant Rory Grant keep vigil over the Battalion flag.

IT was a Tuesday afternoon in the heart of Lanarkshire, but to the quiet beauty of Douglasdale came in their thousands the villagers and schoolchildren, the Regiment's wives and families, the "old and bold" and the serving Cameronians.

They came to pay their tribute and to share in the proud wake for a Regiment which, never yielding in war, had fallen victim to the demands of peace—and honourably chose death rather than surrender to amalgamation.

At their disbandment The Cameronians (Scottish Rifles) expected 2500, even perhaps 5000 people. There were 8000 there to join the 1st Battalion in its final conventicle at Castle Dangerous, to share in the singing, to "Crimond," of the 23rd Psalm, to hear the last speeches, to watch in moving silence the lowering of the Battalion flag and to leave behind, in symbolic finality, the solitary figures of two officers standing vigil over the flag as it lay draped over the Communion Table...

It was indeed a sad occasion but the sadness of extinction was tinged with the resilience of men keenly aware of their Regiment's 300 proud years, men who knew that they and their Battalion were at a peak of morale higher than even that of the recent hard days in a torn Aden...

An infectious resilience, too, which drew the more closely together the 250 Cameronians on parade with the thousands of others to whom the Regiment meant so much. A resilience reflected in impeccable marching and drill movements which even in so solemn a context the spectators, like Tuscans, could not forbear to applaud...

The Communion Table, made by Italian prisoners-of-war at Lanark in 1946, is on a knoll behind which the hills roll gently away from the valley floor. On the table stand the Cleland Sword and the Cross

presented to the Kirk of the 1st Battalion by past and present members . . .

Behind the table are two sentries of the picquet traditionally posted at the holding of any conventicle, a practice stemming from Covenanter days when clandestine religious meetings required a sharp and ready eye for approaching enemies. Two more sentries keep watch on a hill, another pair guard the flank near the ruins of Castle Dangerous.

Across the grass and up the slight slope towards the Cross the 1st Battalion marches on parade to form up as converging sides of a triangle. The Commanding Officer stands by the flagpole, facing his men. The clergy walk to the Communion Table and the Battalion comes to attention to hear Lieutenant-General Sir George Collingwood, Colonel of the Regiment, read a message from the Queen:

"This is a sad occasion but the Regiment can look back with great pride, as I do, on a distinguished history of nearly 300 years' service to this country. As your Sovereign I wish to pay tribute to the splendid achievement of a fine Scottish regiment and wish you all every good fortune in the future."

Then General Count Thord Bonde, Aide-de-Camp-General to King Gustav of Sweden, delivers a message from the King, Colonel-in-Chief of the Regiment.

Three cheers for the Queen, three cheers for the Colonel-in-Chief, then Lieutenant Jeremy Cox, the picquet officer, salutes the senior minister:

"Sir, the picquets are posted. There is no enemy in sight. The service may proceed."

The National Anthem . . . Prayers by the Reverend T J T Nicol, Chaplain to the Forces . . . The lesson, read by Lord Clydesmuir, Lord Lieutenant of Lanarkshire and formerly commanding 6th/7th Battalion . . . The 121st Psalm . . .

And now a stirring address by the Reverend Donald MacDonald, a Cameronian padre of World War One:

"This is a grievous day for you and all of us here, and for all Scotland . . . It has never been the habit of The Cameronians to whimper . . . To most of us here and to many not here this Regiment will never die . . . It will live in our hearts . . . It is not you who are being proved unworthy or unwilling . . . You move out of the Army List because of changes in our defence system, economic duress and political expediency . . . As you march out you are marching into history, and from your proud place there no man can remove your name."

Quietly, triumphantly, the 23rd Psalm. Now Lieutenant-General Sir George Collingwood, charging the Colonel Commandant of The Scottish Division with safe custody of the Battalion flag:

"We shall deliver this flag to you for safe custody on behalf of the regiments in The Scottish Division, to keep among you as a token of our Regimental spirit which through our long history has inspired all our devotion, all our valour and all our sacrifices in the service of the Sovereign and of the country . . . That spirit will of course live on in our Territorial Volunteers and Cadet units and our associations and clubs . . .

"We Cameronians cannot regard this disbandment as final because we have sufficient conceit of ourselves to believe that in time of stress our country could ill afford to dispense with the services of such a well tried and renowned fighting unit . . . If and when it becomes necessary to expand the Armed Forces we would ask that you or your successor should urge the highest military authorities and the Secretary of State for Scotland as a first step, to remuster our Regular battalion."

In reply, the Colonel-Commandant of The Scottish Division, Major-General F C C Graham:

"On this sad day we from sister regiments stand beside you with the deepest sympathy. We believe like you that the Cameronian spirit cannot die . . . We accept your trust and pledge ourselves to do all we can to keep your memory alive not only in all ranks of the Scottish infantry but in all Scotland . . .

"We intend to keep this day annually as Cameronian Day. On that day your flag will fly at HQ Scottish Division at Edinburgh Castle, and at the depots . . .

"We hope that one day we shall see you remustered . . . I salute your illustrious regiment."

The Commanding Officer, Lieutenant-Colonel Leslie Dow, reads from Ecclesiasticus, Chapter 44:

"Let us now praise famous men, and our fathers that begat us . . .

Colonel Dow is to report to the General Officer Commanding Scotland, Lieutenant-General Sir Derek Lang, for permission "to disband the 1st Battalion." The Colonel says simply:

"Sir, we'll have to go now."

The Battalion presents arms. Lance-Corporal Jock Morrison sounds the Last Post while the flag is lowered. Pipe-Major Roddy Gillies plays "The Flowers of the Forest" as the senior subaltern, Lieutenant Rory Grant, and the junior subaltern, Second Lieutenant David Corkerton, bear the flag to the Communion Table.

A silent prayer and silent benediction by the Reverend Donald MacDonald end the conventicle and close the pages of history. The men march smartly off parade, the crowd drifts away . . .

Flanking the Communion Table the two officers, heads bowed, stand in lonely vigil over the flag of what was once 1st Battalion, The Cameronians (Scottish Rifles).

Left: General Sir Richard O'Connor, one of the 11 Cameronian generals at the ceremony. **Above:** The "old and bold" march in to the conventicle site. Young Cameronian soldiers who had recently been drafted were there too to pay their tribute.

The Cameronians disbanded in the Douglas estate of Sir Alec Douglas Home who was represented at the conventicle by his daughter, Miss Caroline Douglas Home.

Castle Dangerous, made famous by Sir Walter Scott's novel of that name, was built in the 13th century or earlier but later completely destroyed. Only the tower now remains of the rebuilt castle.

"REBORN WITH INCREASED SPLENDOUR"

WITH poignancy and panache they faded into history. In Cyprus the Colours of The Durham Light Infantry were lowered to the sounding of the Last Post; in Malaysia the band and bugles of The King's Shropshire Light Infantry beat Retreat at sunset; in Berlin The King's Own Yorkshire Light Infantry re-enacted their battle honours as a pageant; at Truro the Colours of The Somerset and Cornwall Light Infantry were slow-marched up the nave of the cathedral and laid to rest near the altar.

But like the motto of The King's Shropshire Light Infantry—*Aucto splendore resurgo*—they are "reborn with increased splendour." They have become one great regiment called The Light Infantry. The 1st Battalion, The Somerset and Cornwall Light Infantry, is renamed 1st Battalion, The Light Infantry; 1st battalions of The King's Own Yorkshire Light Infantry, The King's Shropshire Light Infantry and The Durham Light Infantry become respectively the 2nd, 3rd and 4th battalions.

The 4th Battalion of the new regiment is being axed in April 1969. But by this time it will have lost all identity with The Durham Light Infantry and be completely integrated into the new regiment (all officers and men coming on a common roll).

The history of the light infantry spans two centuries. It was developed by General Sir John Moore. Soldiers had previously fought in tightly packed ranks rallying round the Colours but the light infantry had open formations moving to bugle calls and whistles. They had no Colours, carried only light packs and observed discipline based on respect rather than fear. They were expert marksmen, self-reliant, and alert in thought and action, as reflected in their marching pace of 140 to the minute. Their rôle was to skirmish ahead, harassing the enemy and giving the main body time to prepare an attack (up to then skirmishing had been done only haphazardly by light companies).

The light infantry distinguished themselves in many battles, but notably at Salamanca on 22 July 1812. In the words of a French observer: "Wellington defeated 40,000 men in 40 minutes." It was a major victory which was the turning point in the Peninsular War. Salamanca, in which all four regiments fought, will be the new regimental day.

Although each of the new battalions loses its former individual identity, many of the customs and traditions are being retained—red backing to the cap badge (the Light Company of the 46th South Devonshire Regiment, later the 2nd Duke of Cornwall's Light Infantry, inflicted such heavy casualties at Brandywine in the American War of Independence that the Yankees swore revenge. So their comrades would not suffer, the Company dyed its cap feathers red); sergeants' and warrant officers' sash worn over the left shoulder, knotted on the right side, as in The Somerset and Cornwall Light Infantry (authorised in 1865 in view of the length of time the practice had existed); the silver whistle and Inkerman chain (a relic of former dress) of sergeants and warrant officers of The Durham Light Infantry; no Loyal Toast in the officers' mess (a right conferred on the 85th, later the 2nd King's Shropshire Light Infantry, by George IV after officers of the Regiment had dealt with rioters who insulted him in the theatre at Brighton; also a privilege of The Durham Light Infantry originating from a campaign against the Caribs in the West Indies).

New Colours, incorporating some of the battle honours of the former regiments, have been designed and will be presented in 1969 or 1970.

The regimental march will be "The Light Infantry" (used previously). "The Keel Row," of the King's Own Yorkshire Light Infantry and The Durham Light Infantry, will become the regimental double-march past.

The Queen Mother is Colonel-in-Chief of The Light Infantry and Princess Alexandra the Deputy Colonel-in-Chief. The Queen Mother was Colonel-in-Chief of The King's Own Yorkshire Light Infantry and Princess Alexandra of The Durham Light Infantry.

Shrewsbury

It was a mixture of the old and the new at Sir John Moore Barracks, Headquarters of the former Light Infantry Brigade. At the same time as the change-over ceremony, a platoon of recruits passed out at the end of basic training.

The parade was taken by the Adjutant-General, General Sir Geoffrey Musson, who was Colonel of The King's Shropshire Light Infantry and is now Colonel of The Light Infantry.

Afterwards, he opened the new light infantry museum in the barracks. The day's programme of marching and displays was brought to an end by a sounding the retreat ceremony by the junior soldiers' band.

Left: March past in quick time led by Lieut-Col P Johnson, commanding the depot. Badges top (left to right): SCLI, KOYLI, KSLI and the DLI.

Gravesend and Truro

The Colours of The Somerset and Cornwall Light Infantry were trooped for the last time through the streets of Gravesend (their present station) and Truro. The Battalion marched through the streets of Truro with Colours flying, band playing and bugles sounding—thereby exercising its privilege of the Freedom of the City.

After being slow-marched up the nave of Truro Cathedral, the Colours were presented to Field-Marshal Lord Harding who handed them to the Dean. They were laid to rest near the altar.

Field-Marshal Harding took the salute at the vesting day parade in Gravesend two days later.

Top: The regimental band leads the SCLI through Truro to the cathedral where (left) Field-Marshal Lord Harding hands the colours to the Dean.

Front Cover

SOLDIER's front cover shows a Sioux helicopter of the air platoon of 1st Battalion, The Queen's Regiment, in a practice casualty evacuation in Bahrein. The helicopter is "parked" and its rotors are not revolving—otherwise the soldiers would not be wearing steel helmets and carrying rifles. Picture by Sergeant K Lloyd, a platoon sergeant in 1st Queen's and a keen photographer.

Berlin

A floodlit pageant, depicting incidents in the history of the light infantry, performed by men of The King's Own Yorkshire Light Infantry at their present camp, Kladow Barracks. The pageant, although treated light-heartedly, demonstrated the vital and world-wide rôle of the light infantry. Beginning with early methods of recruiting, it featured the ceding of Gibraltar, storming of Badajoz and slaughter at Culloden, leading up to actions in the two world wars and the present disposition of the various battalions. At the end of the 90-minute programme, the floodlights were symbolically faded out.

Left: Part of the Berlin pageant—Ensign Dyas's party storming the fortifications at Badajoz.

GETTING TO KNOW YOU

Story by John Wright

A RETIRED brigadier wrote to the *Daily Telegraph*: "Your illustration of the new Recruit Selection Centre at Corsham, Wiltshire, takes some beating.

"An obsequious field officer bends over the shoulders of a lounging potential recruit whose pointed boots rest on the nearest table. If that is the new approach to Army recruiting, thank God we have a Navy. Yours sorrowfully . . ."

Times, Brigadier, have changed. That "lounging potential recruit" represents the Army's—and the country's—greatest asset: manpower. Winklepickers or not, employers are competing fiercely for his services. He chose the Army—and at Corsham the Army is trying its best to make sure he fits into its machinery like a well-oiled bolt.

Good men are in short supply and the Army is budgeting for men just as economically and sensibly as it has in the past budgeted for money.

Join the professionals, the recruiting advertisements say. And the new Recruit

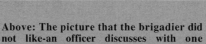

their jobs, on which their morale and efficiency depends.

A system of centralised selection was evolved. Harrogate and Corsham are the result. If the pilot schemes are successful it is intended to spread centralised selection of adult and junior entrants countrywide.

Under the present recruiting system—which will continue in other areas for the time being—a recruit goes straight to a training depot of a specific unit from a local Army Careers Information Office.

Corsham provides an important halfway house between the Army Careers Information Offices and the training depots. Those recruits who wish to join a specific unit are enlisted into it before going to the centre; those who simply wish to join "the Army" go to Corsham in the General Service Corps. The aim of the centre is to ascertain whether the committed men are suited to the unit of their choice and what unit the undecided men should go into. An important element of the scheme is the recruit's views on his future. And if things do not work out to his

Above: The picture that the brigadier did not like—an officer discusses with one recruit the important matter of unit choice.

Right: A battery of recruits being tested.

Left: Two recruits discuss their future.

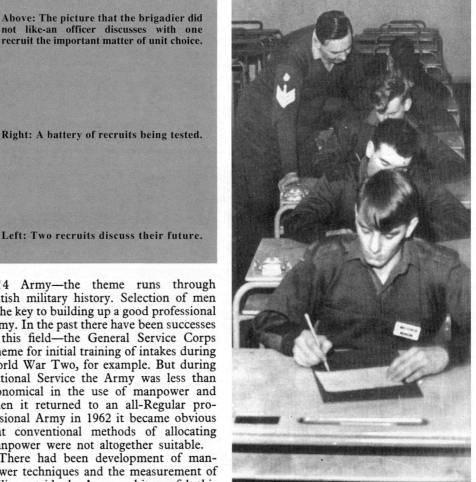

Selection Centre at Corsham is the sort of place where this professionalism begins. Its aim is not to beguile potential recruits —in fact, the men are already in the Army when they go there—but to assess their abilities and greatly increase their chances of going into the right job in the right regiment or corps.

The Corsham pilot scheme is allied to the Youth Selection Centre at Harrogate—described in the August 1968 SOLDIER—and is for the moment confined to one command, Southern. The Harrogate centre is for selecting junior soldiers in Northern Command, Corsham is for adult entrants.

The concept of a professional Army is nothing new. The New Model Army of Cromwell, Sir John Moore's Army, the

1914 Army—the theme runs through British military history. Selection of men is the key to building up a good professional Army. In the past there have been successes in this field—the General Service Corps scheme for initial training of intakes during World War Two, for example. But during National Service the Army was less than economical in the use of manpower and when it returned to an all-Regular professional Army in 1962 it became obvious that conventional methods of allocating manpower were not altogether suitable.

There had been development of manpower techniques and the measurement of ability outside the Army and it was felt this could be the key to reducing wastage and increasing the satisfaction of soldiers with

The new scheme attracted much publicity. Left: TV cameras at work. Above: On the march.

and the Army's satisfaction he can leave the Army after his week at the centre.

The centre, capable of dealing with 60 recruits a week, receives an intake on a Monday and kits the men out in a paramilitary garb. Said Major Alan Willdridge, The Royal Anglian Regiment, the senior personnel selection officer: "They are treated as soldiers from the word 'Go'—marched around, given a haircut, told to stand to attention; but we don't give them any military training except on the .22 range and in the gymnasium. We find they love all this. They join the Army expecting to be soldiers."

The next day they are given their job-briefing—told in the clearest possible way the nature of various jobs in the Army and the training and prospects involved, so that each individual can make an informed choice. The briefing is a vital part of the scheme and is as dynamic and effective as possible. Then a medical check establishes from what employment, if any, the recruits are debarred.

In groups the recruits then undergo a battery of psychometric tests to assess general intelligence, learning potential and mechanical, numerical and verbal aptitudes. One of the aims of the Corsham pilot scheme is to develop testing procedures. A programme of experimental tests was drawn up by the psychological staff of the Army Personnel Research Establishment.

Each recruit is interviewed twice by a personnel selection officer. Aim of the first interview is to assess and make an unbiased judgement of the man's interests, preferences and motivation. The officer records a rating of each man's chances of success in each of three choices of employment—and, if necessary, records two more employments and the man's prospects.

The recruit is then allocated to an appropriate regiment or corps at a special weekly allocation conference. The recruit's choice plays an important part in the decision. The aim of the conference is to bear in mind the needs of the Army and see that as far as possible the supply of men matches the demand both in quantity and quality.

During the second interview the recruit is offered a career in a specific regiment or corps and a choice of employment in two specified employment groups. In difficult cases, where the proposal is against the man's wishes, the personnel selection officer discusses the problem with the man and gives him the choice of accepting the allocation or being discharged.

After they have been allocated, the recruits are sent to the appropriate training depots. In the first two months of the scheme 259 men went to Corsham—236 later went to corps or regiments and 23 were rejected.

Ultimately every recruit in the country will go to this or another centre. The scheme was neatly summed up by Lieutenant-Colonel John Ware, chief personnel selection officer of the Army: "You come and look at us while we look at you."

PURELY PERSONAL

Bugler Brown's record blow

When 19 buglers of 1st Battalion, The Durham Light Infantry, began blowing at Colchester in the annual competition to select the commanding officer's bugler, Lance-Corporal Bob Brown, pictured above, was a firm favourite—for he has held the title for the last five years. And when his two-minute rendering of the Long Reveille clinched victory he had set a new regimental record. Lance-Corporal Brown must be able to play from memory any of the 50 regimental bugle calls in daily use. His silver bugle, worth £130, is engraved with the Battalion's battle honours. He became a bugler when serving in the Army Cadet Force.

Bearded BEM

Colour-Sergeant Bill Street's work as pioneer sergeant of 1st Battalion, The Royal Welch Fusiliers, has not only entitled him to wear a beard—it has also won him the British Empire Medal. And he is pictured above receiving it from Major-General Tom Acton, GOC South-West District, at a parade at Honiton, Devon. The award recognised "prodigious work carried out with outstanding willingness and enthusiasm" during 15 years as pioneer sergeant, including two stints in Cyprus.

Prince on parade

One of the cadets who passed out at the recent Sovereign's Parade at Sandhurst was Bohamed Bolkiah, Crown Prince of Brunei, pictured left. He was appointed an ensign in the Irish Guards. He became Crown Prince when his brother succeeded their father on the latter's abdication as Sultan of Brunei. The Crown Prince's brother was also a Sandhurst cadet but had to return home when the Sultan abdicated.

Commission for West Indian

Second-Lieutenant Donald Browne, recently commissioned, is believed to be the new Reserve Army's first coloured officer. Mr Browne, a schoolteacher from the West Indies, joined the Territorial Army as a gunner in 1958 and reached the rank of sergeant in 1965. When the Reserve Army was reorganised last year he was posted to The Greater London Regiment (Territorials). He is pictured above with three of his unit's senior soldiers.

Ringing the changes

The Newman twins, Vernon (left) and Victor, of 1st Battalion, The Gloucestershire Regiment, who were simultaneously promoted to lance-corporal, are pictured below sewing on their "tapes" in the room in the corporals' mess that they now share in Berlin. It was Victor's idea to join the Army and he persuaded Vernon; both enlisted in April 1965. They are in the same company and have served together in Cyprus, Swaziland and at home. They are constantly being mistaken for each other and once a platoon commander told Vernon, the elder by 15 minutes, to wear a ring to aid identification. But soon Victor is to marry—then he will be the one with the ring.

1969

An old problem brings a new challenge

With the sort of prophetic accuracy normally associated with those who study astrology, a brigade of British troops began the year by deploying to Northern Ireland to take part in large FTX. By the end of 1969, many others would be deployed there for very different reasons.

In the meantime however, the bulk of the Army, both Regular and Territorial, at home and overseas, busied itself with the continuing business of reorganisation and rationalisation as yet more famous regiments joined together or disappeared from the order of battle. A pleasant interlude with fairly serious overtones occurred in the middle of the year when a company of paratroops was deployed to Anguila to prevent an attempted coup on this idyllic Caribbean island. In the event the emergency proved to be easily resolved and the paras were subsequently replaced by Metropolitan Policemen.

As the year progressed, events in the troubled province of Northern Ireland, where a campaign of Civil Rights marches and demonstrations had been waged during the year, began to take a more serious turn. After a particularly serious episode of rioting and civil disorder over several weeks during the summer, the RUC were exhausted. In August, troops were ordered onto the streets of Britain for the first time since the General Strike of 1926.

As the decade that has been dubbed the "Swinging Sixties" ended the British Army faced an uncertain future. The emergency in Northern Ireland continued to cause concern and required the deployment of ever more troops. This problem, combined with the swingeing cuts in manpower imposed by Government, would have a telling effect upon recruiting and morale during the early years of the new decade.

First days on Anguilla

IT was 116F in the Anguillan sun. Political controversy reached boiling point. The paras were sent in to cool things down.

From frost-bound Aldershot they came —125 men of 2nd Battalion, The Parachute Regiment. By Royal Air Force Hercules and VC 10 to Antigua, then by Royal Navy frigates across the clear turquoise Caribbean.

In a dockside warehouse at Antigua their commanding officer, Lieutenant-Colonel Richard Dawnay, briefed the paras: "We are going to Anguilla. Our mission is to restore law and order in the island. Minimum force will be used to achieve this aim."

Troops would open fire only in immediate self-defence or if really effective fire were brought to bear on them. They would be installing the commissioner, Mr Tony Lee, and with them would be a detachment of Metropolitan Police. Reports had indicated a strong possibility that the paras would meet a certain amount of resistance so they had to be fully prepared. They would land on Anguilla under cover of darkness, just before first light.

In overall command of the operation was Commodore M N Lucey, Senior Naval Officer West Indies; Colonel Dawnay was to command the land forces.

With the paras of D Company group embarked in the frigates Minerva and Rothsay were a sapper detachment from 9 Independent Parachute Squadron and a 20-strong platoon of Royal Marines. The ships hove to a mile off shore, Rothsay to the north off Crocus Bay and Minerva south off Road Bay. A single light glowed in the gloom, marking the landing jetty.

Shortly before first light the paras and marines sped towards the shore in outboard-motored Gemini assault craft. All was silent as the troops landed and set off at a brisk pace to the airfield near the centre of Anguilla.

Above: Army "ambassador" wins over the Anguillans. Below: Unloading an RAF VC 10 in Antigua.

Above: Armed soldiers became a feature of life.

Above: It all comes out in the wash. Their work done, the Paras find time to wash their "smalls."

Above: A sympathetic ear and some kind words.

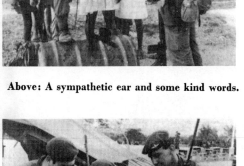

Above: Some Press reaction to the Paras action.

Right: The Sappers work on a water purification plant. A rifle and machine gun lay close at hand.

So ended the Army's first two days on Anguilla.

The work went on. Patrols found a cache of dynamite sticks hidden in a wall, and blew them up. They ripped up floorboards and dug up gravel drives in a search for a hidden hoard of American carbines.

There were protests. A crowd of Anguillans shouted to some paratroopers: "Give us our freedom." Came the reply: "Give us some rum"—and four bottles were promptly produced.

But for the most part it was a battle of icecream and cool tempers. The soldiers joined the locals in football and bathing on the palm-fringed beaches. A party for 78 delighted children aboard the frigate Minerva earned it the nickname "The good ship Lollipop." Sweets and icecream were handed out by the paras, policemen and sailors.

WATCHFUL, WARY, WAITING

The calming influence of the British soldier was obvious once again when units were brought in to safeguard life and property in Belfast and Londonderry after the fierce communal disturbances in August. Earlier, as recorded in the August SOLDIER, the troops had been called upon to guard vulnerable points in Northern Ireland such as remote reservoirs, pipelines and electricity power stations.

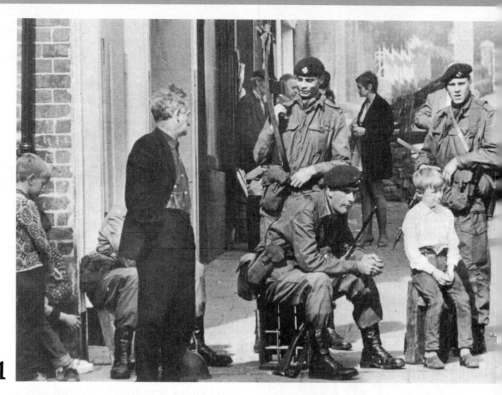

1

2

1 Security for the residents. Soldiers chat with people in Crumlin Road area, Belfast.

2 Alertness and preparedness were impressive but there was no animosity in Londonderry.

3 Devastation in Falls Street area, Belfast, that led to the troops being asked for.

3

5

6

4 A bad trouble area in the Belfast riots but there is safety with the soldiers around.

5 Commanding the troops in Northern Ireland, Lieutenant-General Sir Ian Freeland.

6 The Army lends a hand to get the streets tidy again. Sappers provide a bulldozer.

Across the sea to Ireland

Top: A chopper from Fearless picks up invasion troops on the deck of Sir Tristram. Above: Ferrets of 3rd Royal Tank Regiment splash ashore complete with waterproofing "mini-skirts." Left: A medium wheeled tractor laying assault tracking.

THE quiet lanes and bleak mountains of County Down in Northern Ireland echoed to the sounds of war—the harsh thrumming of helicopters flying troops into assault areas, the rattle of machine-gun fire and the deep roar of powerful vehicle engines . . .

Swap, the largest exercise in Northern Ireland in peacetime, involved more than 6000 Servicemen. Its aim—to practise joint Service techniques, including amphibious, in a limited war setting.

The exercise was delayed for three days because the commando-carrying HMS Fearless, which played a large part in the operations, had been used at Gibraltar by the Prime Minister and Mr Ian Smith for their dramatic meeting over Rhodesia.

As thick fog closed in over the Irish Sea in the early hours of a Monday morning the main tactical phase began with a landing by 45 Royal Marine Commando.

To add realism the setting envisaged a Federation of North Atlantic islands— Saxonia (parts of England and Wales), Manlia (Isle of Man) and Downia (County Down). Manlia and Downia had broken away from the Federation and the Saxonian forces aimed to land in Downia and seize control.

The Saxonian force comprised 24th Infantry Brigade of The Strategic Reserve's 3rd Division, commanded by Brigadier H D G Butler, supported by the Royal Navy, 45 Royal Marine Commando and the Royal Air Force.

Representing breakaway Downia were 39th Infantry Brigade, commanded by Brigadier J M Strawson, and elements of The North Irish Militia.

Supporting Fearless in the landings were two of the Army's logistics ships, Sir Tristram and Sir Percival.

Although hampered by fog the landings went well and soon Bishops Court airfield, just inland from the coast, was in the hands of the invaders. The amphibious operation was controlled from the operations room of Fearless.

And as soon as a firm footing ashore was established Brigadier Butler moved from Fearless to the mainland to take control of the battle.

His forces moved steadily inland against tough Downian opposition and it soon became apparent that the defenders would have to be removed from the commanding heights of Slieve Croob.

The persistent fog made things difficult for the Saxonian forces as often it was not possible to make full use of the Royal Navy's Wessex helicopters and troops had to move forward on foot or in the available wheeled transport.

The battle raged over a wide area—from the beach head at Ballyhornan to Slieve Croob and then south into the wild, romantic heights of the Mountains of Mourne.

Then the seven-day war ended and the sea birds settled again in the sheltered bays and inlets. The grey shape of Fearless and the white hulls of Sir Tristram and Sir Percival no longer loomed through the offshore mist—and only the tracks of heavy plant vehicles at the landing beach remained to bear witness to this invasion of Northern Ireland.

Above: Brigadier Butler of 24 Infantry Brigade checks plans for the advance with Lieut-Col H G Dormer, 47 Light Regiment, RA (centre), and the Brigade Major, Major J R A Macmillan (left).

Top: Men of 2nd Battalion, The Royal Regiment of Fusiliers, move inland through a quiet village in County Down. Above: A gunner of 4 (Sphinx) Light Battery and a "native" of Downia.

MULES and hovercraft, the Army's earliest and latest transporters of stores, both played important parts in the three Services' exercise Trident Star held over five days in Hong Kong. It was the biggest in the colony for many years.

To test amphibious warfare techniques two battalions were landed by night on separate beaches on Lantao, the largest and most mountainous island in the Hong Kong group, and the troops then linked up to seek out terrorists.

The 1st Battalion, The Duke of Wellington's Regiment, spent 36 hours aboard HMS Intrepid, the Royal Navy's newest assault ship, before landing on Lantao and 4th Battalion, The Royal Regiment of Fusiliers, went ashore in landing craft and in a hovercraft of 200 Hovercraft Squadron, Royal Corps of Transport.

The Royal Artillery's 25 Light Regiment infiltrated men ashore before the landings to set up observation posts to pinpoint targets for their guns located on the Castle Peak ranges in the New Territories and on islands around Lantao.

Mules of 414 Pack Transport Company, RCT, played a sure-footed role and proved themselves the best means of moving heavy equipment around the difficult terrain in guerilla-type operations. The troops spent two days and nights hunting down the enemy, represented by Gurkhas stationed in Hong Kong.

HMS Intrepid was used as Joint Force Headquarters by the exercise controllers, Brigadier M E M MacWilliam, Deputy Commander Land Forces Hong Kong, and Commodore T W Stocker, Commodore Amphibious Forces, and their staffs. The Royal Navy also provided two minesweepers to clear a path for Intrepid and assist the landing of the assault boats.

The Royal Air Force flew Hunter jet sorties to give ground attack cover—and helicopters to provide unexpected mobility for the terrorists.

From a report by Joint Services Public Relations, Hong Kong.

HOOF *and* CUSHION

Old and new modes of transport supplied by the Royal Corps of Transport. The hovercraft lifted troops to a landing beach on Lantao island. The mules (embarking on landing craft, left) carried the heavier equipment over mountainous terrain.

Right. No pleasant cruise ahead for The Duke of Wellington's Regiment. The assault craft is taking them to HMS Intrepid before the start of Exercise Trident Star. Top right, An assault craft moves in to load stores into Intrepid.

INTRODUCING FOX

A NEW combat reconnaissance vehicle—aptly named the Fox—is to come into service with the British Army in the early 1970s.

At present it is under development at the Fighting Vehicles Research and Development Establishment. It has been made by Daimler of Coventry in conjunction with the Ministry of Defence and FVRDE.

Fox is a successor to the Ferret scout car but is capable of undertaking some roles which previously required larger and heavier vehicles. The Ferret, and the Saladin and Saracen, will however "continue well into the late '70s." Fox is one of a new family of aluminium alloy combat vehicles, which includes the tracked Scorpion.

Apart from armed reconnaissance, Fox can be adapted for liaison use with the infantry, artillery, sappers and other arms. For its main role it is equipped with a 30mm cannon, a 7.62mm general-purpose machine-gun, smoke dischargers, three 9mm sub-machine-guns, hand grenades and comprehensive sighting and vision instruments. It is very manoeuvrable and, with a high power/weight ratio, has excellent cross-country characteristics. It can negotiate three feet of water without preparations and is supplied with flotation equipment for swimming under its own power.

The power unit is a militarised version of the 4.2 litre Jaguar engine. It develops 195 brake horse power at 5000 revolutions per minute. Being in commerical production, spares are readily available. The engine can be withdrawn as a complete unit for ease of maintenance.

Fox is designed to operate in temperatures from 50 to minus 40 degrees centigrade. It is airportable. Three can be carried in a Hercules aircraft and, using a lightweight platform and special parachute equipment, two per aircraft can be paradropped.

Protection: The hull and turret are of aluminium alloy which protects the three-man crew against medium and heavy machine-gun fire, from ground burst or air burst shell splinters, and minimises injury from anti-tank mines.

Armament: The Rarden 30mm cannon will destroy any known or foreseen light armoured fighting vehicle from a range of more than 1000 metres and, loaded with improved ammunition now being developed, is expected to be able to penetrate heavy armour. It has an elevation from plus 40 to minus 14 degrees. With such high elevation it can even deal effectively with low-speed aircraft.

Amphibious operation: The flotation screen, which can be fitted by the crew in 69 seconds, is high enough for entry and exit on 35-degree banks. There is a built-in bilge pump of 45 gallons a minute capacity. Propulsion and steering are by means of the road wheels and a water speed of 3½ miles an hour can be attained.

Crew: Driver, gunner/operator and commander/loader. All controls and ancillary equipment are arranged to allow for reach of one man, if necessary.

Optional equipment: Choice of radios, ZB 298 radar, a Sperry navigator, warning systems for nuclear and bacteriological warfare with respirator pressurisation units for each crewman, infra-red sight, periscopes and spotlight.

Fox has a Daimler pre-selective epicyclic five-speed gearbox and a transfer box providing five forward and five reverse speeds on all wheels.

New multi-purpose helicopter

THE Westland WG 13 high performance helicopter, planned for delivery to Army Aviation in 1974, is a multi-purpose aircraft capable of carrying 12 fully armed and equipped troops, plus the pilot.

Westland Helicopters expect it to be in worldwide demand both by military forces and civilian operators. The British Army is to use the WG 13 as a general-purpose machine that can be armed with guided missiles. Internal and external fixed fittings will enable a wide range of weapons to be carried.

The WG 13 will operate at an all-up weight of 8000 lbs with a maximum speed of 160 knots and a range of more than 500 miles on its 1600 lbs of fuel carried in five tanks. The range can be dramatically increased by the installation in the cabin of an overload tank with a capacity of 1650 lbs.

This helicopter is designed to climb vertically at 1200 feet per minute and obliquely at 2500 feet per minute. It is to be powered by two Rolls-Royce free turbine engines mounted side by side immediately behind the main rotor and which have been specifically designed to meet the requirements of this versatile high-performance craft.

The large capacity cabin allows many variations of seating including the carriage of three stretcher cases with up to three seated casualties. The stretchers will be arranged at an angle to permit easy loading and the provision of medical attention in flight.

The WG 13 can also be used for carrying freight—2738 lbs inside or 3000 lbs underslung. A large sliding door each side of the cabin will provide easy access and exit and the floor is to be fitted with rings to tie down cargo.

A special mini-hoist has been designed to fit on the side of the craft to enable the removal of engines, rotor head and gearbox in the field, while specially designed fore and aft jacks can be attached to the frame to allow renewal of a complete undercarriage assembly under field conditions.

The WG 13 is also being produced for the Royal Navy and the Royal Air Force. The French Navy has ordered a number for an attack role.

An artist's impression of the Army's new WG 13 helicopter. The Royal Navy will use a variant for anti-submarine operations; the RAF for training.

SANDES BUILT ON ROCK

Story by Hugh Howton

CHRISTIANITY — through the juke box, comfortable armchairs, cream buns, tea and sympathy. Such is the mission of the Sandes Soldiers' and Airmen's Homes which celebrate their centenary this year.

Elise Sandes, founder of the homes, was an unlikely person to care for the rough-and-ready soldiery of 100 years ago. She was delicate and shy, the daughter of a Southern Ireland landlord who lived in Oak Villa, Tralee, an imposing mansion with a long drive and ornamental iron railings.

With her mother's approval she invited drummer boys home. Some of them could not read or write. So she and her teenage friend Marie Fry read them stories from the Bible and taught them to sing hymns.

It was crusading in the teeth of Victorian prejudice. Once she visited a barrack room and asked a drunken soldier: "Will you come to see me tonight?" She was greeted with ribald laughter. But that soldier did go to see her and confessed that because of drink he had been reduced through the ranks three times and ruined. The Bible message gave him hope and Elise gained a convert.

While in Cork—a grimy city of reeking pubs and sleazy dance halls—Miss Sandes was told by a soldier: "There is nowhere the men can go in the evenings if they want to stay straight." It was here that she established the first permanent Sandes home in 1877.

She provided a home from home for the lonely soldiers unable to return to England on a 48-hour pass. A kettle was always on the hob, there was community singing round a piano and the reading room was stacked with good books. Soldiers awaiting boats home—they were not allowed barrack accommodation while on leave—were put up overnight. Miss Sandes stood on the quayside at Queenstown waving goodbye to men destined for the Zulu and Afghan Wars. Many were never to return.

By 1914 she was running 30 homes, yet still found time for correspondence. One soldier wrote to her: "The little Bible (received from Sandes Homes) has a bullet hole right through it. I think it was the means of saving my life as it was carried in my breast pocket when I was hit."

During her lifetime she saw more than 40 homes established from Ireland to France, India and South Africa. And when she died in 1934 the Army paid its highest tribute—a funeral with full military honours.

She and Miss Eva MaGuire, who took over as honorary superintendent of the homes until her death in 1967, are among the very few civilians so honoured.

Today there are seven Sandes homes—in Belfast, Ballykinlar and Holywood in Northern Ireland; The Curragh in Eire; Catterick, Singapore and Guildford. All home comforts are provided such as easy chairs, television, quiet rooms and libraries, and meals are available in the canteens. Catterick even has a swimming pool. At Catterick, Belfast and Singapore there is hostel accommodation for men and their families.

The home at Guildford—in the Women's Royal Army Corps Centre—is a new venture in that it caters exclusively for the Women's Services. The girls at Guildford can not only buy snacks and chocolates, but mascara, nail varnish and false eyelashes. And they can invite their boy friends for the evening.

The staff are all Protestant Christians. None is ordained, few have had any formal

Right: VIP visit. The Duke of Edinburgh chats to workers at the Sandes Singapore home in 1965. It will be closed with the Far East withdrawal.

Top of page: Faded Victorian photograph—Miss Elise Sandes who was the founder of the Homes.

SANDES *continued*

heological training but all have done hurch work such as running a Sunday chool or youth club. Gone is the image of he elderly spinster aunt in bonnet, boa nd bustle. Most of the homes are now run y husbands and wives living on the remises with their families.

"I suppose they look on us as a mother nd father," said Mr Leslie Saunders, who uns the new home at Guildford with his vife Eva. Mr and Mrs Saunders, who have hree young daughters, recently moved here from Holywood. "The soldiers can op round to see us whenever they want, neet the family and have a cup of tea and a hat."

Charity begins at home. Sandes workers ave looked after babies when the mothers vere ill; fixed up a bed late at night for a oldier when the home was really full; risited sick soldiers in hospital and run arties for children when their fathers were way on exercise and mothers out shopping. Sometimes Sandes samaritans have ticklish asks—like sewing a badge on a busby. 'The only way to do it was to pull the needle through with the teeth in a most unladylike manner, which resulted in a mouthful of black fur." recalls Mrs Wendy Hume of Catterick in a recent edition of the homes' magazine, Forward. Then, she continued, there was the time a young soldier confessed to her that he had been involved in a fight in his barrack room: "I could not stand him saying things like that about my Saviour, so I hit him."

Although they have great respect for the Royal Army Chaplains' Department, the Saunders think padres have a communication problem. Many private soldiers are hesitant in approaching a padre who wears officer's uniform. "We are a little bit apart from the Army and can give a sympathetic ear," pointed out Mrs Saunders. "The soldiers can come and see us and talk over their problems in a relaxed home atmosphere," she went on.

Right: With drumbeat and twanging guitars, The Followers sock it to them at Guildford. Below: The quiet click of snooker balls at Catterick.

Above: Eva MaGuire was high on visiting lists of generals coming to Northern Ireland. With Lieut-Gen Sir Ian Harris, Ballykinlar, 1966. . .

ow bservant re you?

hese two pictures look ike but they differ in n details. Look at iem carefully. If you annot spot the differences e page 35.

THE NEW PAY STRUCTURE

RECOMMENDATIONS BY NATIONAL BOARD FOR PRICES AND INCOMES

AN interim pay rise of about four per cent backdated to 1 April 1969 and the issue of marriage allowance and other benefits to married officers under 25 years of age and married soldiers under 21 are some of the immediate benefits from the third report on the pay of the Armed Forces issued by the National Board for Prices and Incomes.

A recommendation for the future, even more revolutionary, is that for the first time the Serviceman will receive a gross salary out of which he will pay for his food, lodging and clothing, except uniform. This will place him on the same footing as civilian members of the British community and give him—and potential recruits—a chance to understand the full financial reimbursements of Service life.

The changeover from basic pay and allowances with free food and lodgings to a comprehensive salary has necessitated a large-scale operation to produce a new pay structure. A team is already evaluating jobs and if the practical difficulties can be overcome—not least of which is the huge size of the task—the new pay should be in issue from 1 April next year. The NBPI plans to report again in February 1970 with recommended rates in detail.

The board questioned the system which pays a married man more than a single man for doing the same job. Whatever may have been the justification in the past, says the board, "we can see none for it in the Armed Forces of today." So the proposal is to increase the single man's pay to that of the married and to produce one comprehensive basic rate for each rank and trade.

The consequent "military salary" will be subject to tax in the normal way; any non-taxable elements included (such as ration allowance, at present not taxed) will be increased to allow for this. The "military salary," says the board, must also include an X factor representing those "elements unique to military life which may withstand any measurement but which nonetheless need to be taken into account in the determination of pay."

They include the fact that the Serviceman is wholly committed, is subject to a code of discipline which reaches far beyond that obtaining in any form of civilian employment, is liable to be exposed to danger on active service, is required as part of his normal peacetime routine to endure bad or uncomfortable conditions in the field and on board ship and also that his life is subject to constant upheaval and uncertainty.

The board says: "While it is possible to define the components of the X factor a large element of judgement must inevitably enter into the measurement of them in financial terms. Moreover, the amount of pay necessary to compensate for the X factor may need to be varied from time to time." The board is to make a "provisional judgement on what the amount should be" in its February 1970 report.

It also proposes that there should be a major review of Service pay every six years, with intermediate reviews every two years or more frequently if the board or the Ministry of Defence think it necessary. The Government has accepted all the short-term recommendations and accepted in principle the longer-term ones.

Details from the report:

SHORT-TERM MEASURES

The percentage increase payable from 1 April 1969 is to be treated as a global sum of about £14,000,000 so that the Ministry of Defence may make marginal adjustments between groups and handle it in the way "considered most appropriate by them and most in keeping with the tenor of our longer-term recommendations."

It will increase the weekly pay of a non-tradesman private (recruit) by 8s 9d to £10 6s 6d and of a warrant officer class I technician, aged 36 and committed for 21 years, by £1 4s 6d to £30 14s 3d. The annual salary of officers, four years in the rank, will improve as follows: Captain by £55 to £1469, major by £82 to £2126, lieutenant-colonel by £110 to £2738 and colonel by £137 to £3522.

From 1 July 1969 the age bar to marriage allowance and other married benefits is removed. This improves the rate for the non-tradesman private (recruit) by £2 12s 6d weekly to a total of £18 19s 3d and of the A trade class III private, committed for nine years, to £20 7s 2d. Married men under 21 were previously restricted to the lower rate of marriage allowance but now become eligible for the higher.

Married officers under 25, not previously entitled to marriage allowance at all, are now to receive £123 annually if living in married quarters and £233 if living out.

Also from 1 July, personnel in receipt of marriage allowance are now to have ration allowance continuously when away from their families on duty, in addition to being fed at public expense.

In addition, these officers and soldiers are now able to qualify for other allowances and benefits from which they were previously debarred, such as separation allowance, disturbance allowance, removal expenses, married rates of overseas allowances and family passages to overseas stations.

From 31 August 1969 education allowance is to be grossed for tax purposes when the serving parent is in the United Kingdom. When two or more children are eligible the allowance is to be aggregated and set against the total cost of educating them.

New scales of pay recommended for Army doctors and dentists would give them an average salary of £4000 a year for those not allocated quarters, and the board recommends that in the long term their pay should be determined in comparison with the career earnings of National Health Service general practitioners. They should receive the X factor element and pay the same for quarters as other Servicemen.

MILITARY SALARY CONCEPT

Accepting that the Serviceman's pay should be based on a comprehensive "military salary" irrespective of marital status, the Prices and Incomes Board suggests that charges for soldiers' married quarters should be assessed in the same way as local authorities assess rents of council houses and that rates for officers' married quarters should be related to the costs of an owner-occupier buying a house on a mortgage. Single officers and men would pay less for accommodation, as they probably would in civil life. There should be a reduced charge for sub-standard single accommodation.

Single Servicemen living in barracks should be charged for their rations by a standard deduction from pay and in certain circumstances the charges should be remitted.

The board recommends that the allowances for personal clothing and for laundry should be abolished, that Servicemen should pay the first 10s per week of the cost of home-to-duty travel and that free batman service in married quarters should cease except in some cases of officers holding command appointments.

LONGER-TERM MEASURES

Accepting that the jobs done by Servicewomen are in most cases the same as those performed by men, the board proposes that their work should be evaluated by the same methods as those used for men and that they should be given equal pay for "those components of the work which are shown to be equal."

It is suggested that a system of lump sum payments should be substituted for the present one of increasing the pay of soldiers who extend their service. The board believes the number of free travel warrants should be increased and that all rail warrants should be convertible into a mileage allowance at the Serviceman's option.

Separation allowance should be revised to remove defects and disturbance allowance rates should be set at levels to compensate for the normal cost of removals, even allowing for variations between households.

Services cinemas have now amalgamated. In 1968, the last of its 22 years' existence, the Army Kinema Corporation played to an audience of more than six million. And in some directions **IT**

OUTRANKED J ARTHUR

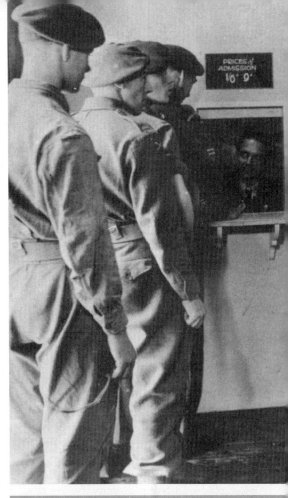

Above: In the days of battledress and hobnailed boots, expensive seats were 1s 6d. National Servicemen on 25s a week paid 9d.

IT began in nissen huts with Abbott and Costello and starlets with peek-a-boo hair-styles and platform shoes. Last year the Army Kinema Corporation had a turnover of nearly £2 million. But now it is no more.

The AKC, with the Royal Air Force Cinema Corporation, has had to keep in step with the march of time. The Ministry of Defence ordered integration. And so on 1 January 1969 they amalgamated to form the Services Kinema Corporation.

But Service cinemagoers will not notice any change, SOLDIER was told by Major-General Sir John Hildreth, managing director of the new corporation and a former director of ordnance services. There would however be a saving of about £80,000 a year.

" How do you tell a general he's sitting on your choc-ice?"

Administered from Dover Street, London W1, former headquarters of the AKC, the new SKC is controlled by a council of senior Army, Navy and Air Force officers and civilians under the presidency of the Adjutant-General. Only ships at sea are outside their scope. The Royal Naval Film Corporation, which handed over its shore cinemas to the AKC two years ago, will continue to be responsible for them.

The new SKC runs 155 cinemas, two ten-pin bowling alleys, a television rental service and a film library for small units, maintains the Services' projectors and visual aid equipment, and is responsible for making Army training films. Like its predecessors, it is a non-profit-making organisation with the legal status of a charity. Nevertheless last year the AKC had a trading surplus of £97,000 and the Royal Air Force Cinema Corporation £12,000. This has all to be ploughed back.

Some has gone towards equipping the air-conditioned cinema just opened at Muharraq, Bahrein—the first under the new SKC. The 416 seats alone each cost £6 10s.

Although there are still a few draughty ex-ENSA halls and the odd Romney hut, the rule today is plush velvet or leather seating and cinemascope screens.

In some ways the Army Kinema Corporation even outranked J Arthur Rank. Its service was worldwide, prices were cheaper and programmes more varied. The AKC seats from 2s 3d to 4s 6d compared with 5s to 7s 6d in a commercial cinema. The average AKC cinema had nine programme changes a fortnight—five new films for two nights each and four old films for one night each. New films were shown overseas only one month after the London release. But in Britain there are stringent trade restrictions. New films cannot be shown by the SKC for six months after the London release and within two miles of a commercial cinema.

Eyes down for bingo in many badly patronised commercial cinemas has made business there look up. But the AKC found little need for it and bingo was played in only three of its cinemas in Britain. Television rental has been a much better proposition. About 11,000 sets were hired out in Britain and Germany in 1968, an increase of 3000 on the previous year. The ceiling is thought to be 20,000. Profits from this service have gone to such charities as the Army Widows' Fund and the Single Soldiers' Dependents' Fund.

Ten-pin bowling alleys have been built at Aden, Brize Norton and Singapore but interest in the sport is waning and this service will not be expanded. The corporation's technicians are kept busy servicing visual aid equipment—still and ciné projectors and closed circuit television etc—belonging to the Ministry of Defence. It is done at cost price. Another service provided for the Ministry of Defence is training films. Although the shooting is done by a commercial firm, the AKC has acted as producer, director and editor.

These films last about half an hour and include such subjects as airborne operations, tank driving and how to fire a gun.

Film libraries are maintained in every command. Units which are out of reach of a cinema—for example the Royal Engineers squadron building an airfield in the Virgin Islands—can hire 16mm entertainment films.

Above: Ultra-modern exterior of the Kent combined cinema and bowl in Singapore. In the tropics cinemas are air-conditioned.

Below: Plush interior of the Globe, Rheindahlen. There is no smoking here. All the smokers go to the nearby Astra.

UPWARD AND ONWARD

Story by George Hogan

ARMY aviation, which has been energetically developing while performing an increasingly important role since the Army Air Corps was formed in 1957, is now undergoing a process of reorganisation that establishes it firmly as a major arm of the Service.

The changes, to be effective generally by the end of next March, include the creation of a Directorate of Army Aviation with Major-General "Dare" Wilson as the first director, in place of the present awkward-sounding and somewhat misleadingly named Land/Air Warfare directorate.

Left: Open day 1969 at the Army Aviation Centre, Middle Wallop, with 75 Army aircraft flying past. Only about half the helicopters are in the picture. The aircraft include Chipmunks, Beavers, Scouts and Sioux, the extremely safe and manoeuvrable Chipmunks being used to train new pilots.

This reorganised directorate is being housed at Middle Wallop, Hampshire, where the headquarters of the Army Air Corps has been based with the School of Army Aviation since 1957 and where before that Army pilots had long been trained at the Light Aircraft School.

The unit of Army aviation is to be the squadron, based on the infantry and armoured brigade, except that Royal Armoured Corps armoured car and reconnaissance regiments are to retain their own integrated air squadrons.

Centralisation at brigade level discontinues the air platoons and air troops that had become part of infantry, engineer, gunner and signal units of battalion strength. It ensures better control and flexibility, especially in maintenance and availability. It also means better cost effectiveness through the more economical use of supporting Royal Electrical and Mechanical Engineers staff and repairs machinery and the need to provide fewer stocks of spare parts.

The new order of battle provides a squadron for each theatre headquarters and for each corps. Divisions are each allocated an aviation regiment which includes a squadron at divisional headquarters and with each brigade. Each is fully supported by a REME light aid detachment.

The reorganisation takes into permanent use some famous Royal Air Force squadron numbers that have long been intimately associated with Army flying. An example is 656 Air OP Squadron RAF, formed in 1942 for air observation post duties with Army gunner officers as pilots of Auster aircraft, gunners as drivers and signallers, and RAF personnel as adjutant, equipment officer and servicing crew.

It's The Blues and Royals

AFTER 308 years of vigorous, independent and distinguished life two famous British cavalry regiments—the Royal Horse Guards (The Blues) and The Royal Dragoons (1st Dragoons)—have joined forces and a new regiment of Household Cavalry has come into being.

The main parade marking the amalgamation took place at Detmold, Germany, while token parades were held at Wellington Barracks in London, Bovington Camp, Dorset, and Pirbright Camp, Surrey.

As Colonel of the new regiment—The Blues and Royals (Royal Horse Guards and 1st Dragoons)—Field-Marshal Sir Gerald Templer took the salute at a march past on a windswept Detmold parade ground. With him was the Deputy Colonel, General Sir Desmond Fitzpatrick, C-in-C Rhine Army.

The new regiment, equipped with Chieftain battle tanks and stationed at Hobart Barracks, Detmold, is the first Household Cavalry regiment to be equipped with tanks.

About 80 old comrades of The Royal Dragoons attended an earlier weekend of special activities at Detmold to mark the end of their regiment as a separate entity.

The Royals were founded in 1661 as The Tangier Horse and on their return to England 22 years later were regimented as the 1st Royal Regiment of Dragoons. Their first colonel was Lord Churchill, later Duke of Marlborough, and among former colonels-in-chief were Kaiser Wilhelm II, King George V and King George VI.

One of their most famous battle honours was won at Waterloo with the capture of the Standard of the French 105th Infantry Regiment. The Royals have taken part in most of the major campaigns of the British Army.

Charles II raised the Royal Horse Guards in 1661. Their first colonel was the 20th Earl of Oxford and because of their distinctive blue tunics they became known as the "Oxford Blues"—later abbreviated to "The Blues." For their gallantry at Waterloo The Blues were elevated to the Household Cavalry and granted honours and privileges formerly restricted to The Life Guards alone.

The new regiment has been accorded the honour of a privileged regiment of the City of London and is being given the Freedom of the Royal Borough of Windsor. Commanding the new regiment is Lieutenant-Colonel R M H Vickers, formerly commanding The Royal Dragoons.

Above: At the amalgamation parade at Detmold of The Blues and The Royal Dragoons, the new regiment marches past Fd-Marshal Sir Gerald Templer. Right: A token parade at Wellington Barracks, London, by The Blues, to mark the amalgamation.

left, right and centre

Miss Saladin is the title given by C Squadron, 3rd Carabiniers, at Chester to their new pin-up girl, "Recruit 362336 Gunter VC." The number has relation to her shapely measurements and as she was born on VE Day (8 May 1945) she was named Victoria. Usually known as Carol, she will be helping recruiting drives in Cheshire and North Wales until the squadron leaves for Münster, Germany, in August.

The Royal Artillery brought out their big guns for the Queen when she visited their headquarters at Woolwich. Her Majesty, who is Captain-General of the Royal Regiment, saw the 31-ton M 107 self-propelled gun and 23-ton M 109 self-propelled howitzer as well as other weapons in the gunners' arsenal such as Honest John and Thunderbird 2 missiles, an 8-inch howitzer, and the Rapier anti-aircraft system. During the inspection the Queen was accompanied by the Director Royal Artillery, Major-General H C Tuzo. After taking the salute at a drive-past, she had lunch in the officers' mess.

Left: The Duke of Edinburgh, Colonel-in-Chief of The Queen's Royal Irish Hussars, drove a Chieftain and fired its 120-mm gun when he visited the Regiment at Bovington Camp, Dorset. He scored a direct hit at 800 yards but was unable to fire at an old Conqueror tank at 1200 yards because of a persistent sea mist. During the mud-spattering three-mile journey he handled the Chieftain well. Tank commander Sergeant Bill McLernon said: "The going was rough but Prince Philip was splendid."

The new museum of The Parachute Regiment and Airborne Forces was opened at Browning Barracks, Aldershot, by Field-Marshal Viscount Montgomery who was Colonel Commandant of the Regiment from 1944 to 1956. After inspecting a guard of honour of the 2nd Battalion and unveiling a plaque, Monty toured the museum and recalled many episodes of World War Two among the models, uniforms, weapons, insignia and equipment.

The brilliant green and yellow "uniforms" of eight girl recruiters attracted the public when they were stationed at strategic points in central London for a day. The object was to highlight the reorganised Territorial Army Volunteer Reserve and, although the weather was cold, they certainly did their duty.

Photographers at war